In Memory of
JEREMIAH F. O'SULLIVAN
Master Teacher and Scholar
Beloved Gentleman
Dean of American Cistercian Studies

CISTERCIAN STUDIES SERIES: NUMBER TWENTY-FOUR

Studies in Medieval Cistercian History II

edited by
John R. Sommerfeldt

CISTERCIAN PUBLICATIONS
Kalamazoo, Michigan
1976

Cistercian Studies Series   ISBN 0-87907-800-6
This volume   ISBN 0-87907-824-3

Published in cooperation with
and with support from
The Medieval Institute
Western Michigan University
Kalamazoo, Michigan

CONTENTS

ABBREVIATIONS

A. GENERAL

CF	*Cistercian Fathers,* Spencer, Massachusetts, then Washington, D.C.: Cistercian Publications, 1970—.
CS	*Cistercian Studies,* Spencer, Massachusetts, then Washington, D.C.: Cistercian Publications, 1969—.
CSEL	*Corpus scriptorum ecclesiasticorum latinorum,* Vienna, 1866—.
MGH, SS	*Monumenta Germaniae historica, Scriptores* Hannover: Impensis Bibliopolii Hahniani, 32 vols., 1826-1934.
MGH, Script. rer. Germ.	*Monumenta Germaniae historica, Scriptores, rerum Germanicarum,* Hannover: Impensis Bibliopolii Hahniani, 1840.
PG	J. P. Migne (ed.), *Patrologia Graeca,* Paris, 161 vols., 1857-1876. The volume number precedes the colon; the column number follows it.
PL	J. P. Migne (ed.), *Patrologia Latina,* Paris, 222 vols., 1841-1864. The volume number precedes the colon; the column number follows it.
RS	*Rolls Series: Rerum Britannicarum medii aevi scriptores,* London: Public Record Office, 99 vols., 1858-1896.

Statuta	Josephus-Maria Canivez (ed.), *Statuta capitulorum capitulorum generalium ordinis Cisterciensis ab anno 1116 ad annum 1786,* Louvain: Bureau de la Revue d'Histoire Écclésiastique, 8 vols., 1933-1941. The volume is indicated by the Roman numeral, the page by the Arabic numeral. The material in the parenthesis indicates the date, then the number of the statute.

B. WORKS OF BERNARD OF CLAIRVAUX

(following the form of *Opera*)

Opera	Bernard of Clairvaux, *Opera,* edd. Jean Leclercq *et al.;* Rome: Editiones Cistercienses, 1957—. The volume number precedes the colon; the page number follows it.
Abael	*De erroribus Abaelardi.*
Adv	*Sermones in adventu Domini.*
Apo	*Apologia ad Guillelmum abbatum.*
Asc	*Sermones in ascensione Domini.*
Asspt	*Sermones in assumptione B.V.M.*
Ben	*Sermones in natali s. Benedicti.*
Circ	*Sermones in circumcisione Domini.*
Conv	*Sermones de conversione ad clericos.*
Csi	*De consideratione.*
Ded	*Sermones in dedicatione ecclesiae.*
Div	*Sermones de diversis.*
Ep	*Epistola(e).*
Humb	*Sermo in obitu Humberti.*
Miss	*Homiliae super "Missus est" in laude Virginis Matris.*
Mor	*De moribus et officiis episcoporum.*
OS	*Sermones in festivitate omnium sanctorum.*
Par	*Parabolae.*
Pl	*Sermones in conversione Pauli.*
PP	*Sermones in sollemnitate apostolorum Petri et Pauli.*

Pre	*De precepto et dispensatione.*
QH	*Sermones super psalmum "Qui habitat."*
Quad	*Sermones in Quadragesima.*
SC	*Sermones super Cantica canticorum.*
Sept	*Sermones in Septuagesima.*
Tpl	*Liber ad milites Templi (De laude novae militiae).*
V And	*Sermones in vigilia s. Andreae.*

C. WORKS OF WILLIAM OF ST. THIERRY

(adapted by the Association for Cistercian Studies, 1972)

Adv Abl	*Disputatio adversus Petrum Abaelardum.*
Aenig	*Aenigma fidei.*
Cant	*Expositio super Cantica canticorum.*
Contemp	*De contemplando Deo.*
Ep frat	*Epistola ad fratres de Monte Dei.*
Exp Rm	*Exposito in epistolam Pauli ad Romanos.*
In lacu	*Soliloquium "In lacu miseriae."*
Med	*Meditativae orationis.*
Nat am	*De natura et dignitate amoris.*
Phy an	*Physica animae.*
Resp Matt	*Responsio ad cardinalem Mattaeum.*
Sacr altar	*De sacramento altaris.*
Spec fid	*Speculum fidei.*
Vita Bern	*Sancti Bernardi vita prima.*

INTRODUCTION

IN SEPTEMBER OF 1970 some fifty scholars from universities and colleges throughout the United States and Canada, along with editors of various Cistercian and monastic reviews, were invited to St Joseph's Abbey in Spencer, Massachusetts, to take part in a meeting sponsored by Cistercian Publications. The primary purpose was to foster studies of Cistercian life and thought.[1]

The meeting was most fruitful. The participants reported on the work in which they were engaged and on the areas of interest of those scholars unable to be present. Many shared interests opened up the possibilities of collaboration on several projects. The presentation of several papers resulted in extended and profitable discussion. Throughout the three-day meeting the group profited by the immense erudition and refreshing wit of Jean Leclercq, surely the foremost scholar in Cistercian studies in the world. The considerations also attained an air of authenticity otherwise impossible from the presence of the dean of American Cistercian scholars, Jeremiah F. O'Sullivan, who contributed his wit and erudition to the gathering. The participants went away refreshed and grateful to Abbot Thomas Keating, Father Basil Pennington (who convened the meeting), and to the community at Spencer.

1. A report on this meeting by Basil Pennington appeared in *Cîteaux,* 21 (1970), 307-315.

That was not to be the end of the matter. The ever-growing group of American, and European, students of matters Cistercian met again—in October 1972 at the Cistercian Monastery near Dallas.[2] The pleasant climate and warm hospitality of Abbot Anselm Nagy, Fathers Louis Lekai and Bede Lackner, and the learned community helped bring forth more good papers and profitable discussion. We resolved to form an Association for Cistercian Studies and to continue to meet regularly at Cistercian abbeys.[3]

Another result of Father Basil Pennington's initial call to gather at Spencer was the decision to hold a Cistercian Studies Conference in conjunction with the Conference on Medieval Studies sponsored each spring by the Medieval Institute of Western Michigan University. Accordingly, the first Cistercian Studies Conference met May 16 to 19, 1971, at Kalamazoo, Michigan. Two sessions were held at which eleven fine papers were presented.[4]

The Cistercian Studies Conference came again to Kalamazoo April 30 to May 3, 1972, once more meeting concurrently with the Conference on Medieval Studies.[5] Jean Leclercq was the principal speaker, sharing his monastic enthusiam with that larger group as well as with the Cistercian scholars.[6] This time there were six sessions devoted to Cistercian topics with seventeen papers presented and discussed.

The papers in this volume, with one exception,[7] were presented at the Second Cistercian Studies Conference. They

2. A report of this meeting appeared in *Cîteaux* , 24 (1973), 53-61, and included a table of the Cistercian authors' abbreviations agreed on at the meeting.

3. Those who wish to join this informal group may contact Professor John R. Sommerfeldt, Executive Director, Institute of Cistercian Studies, Western Michigan University, Kalamazoo, Michigan 49008.

4. M. Basil Pennington reported on this gathering in *Cîteaux* , 22 (1971), 181-84.

5. Basil Pennington has described this Conference thoroughly and well in *Cîteaux,* 23 (1972), 209-217.

6. Father Leclercq's paper, "Modern Psychology and the Interpretation of Monastic Texts," has appeared in *Speculum* 48 (1973) 476-90.

7. Father Leclercq's paper in this volume was given—in a shorter form—the week before the Conference at the University of Chicago at the invitation of Professor Bernard McGinn.

represent the broad range of interests among students of the Cistercian phenomenon. There are textual studies and literary studies, studies of theology and of economic institutions, liturgical and administrative studies, studies of the impact of Cistercians on society and on education. Moreover, even within the disciplines represented, especially the history of theology, the approaches vary radically. This collection is truly a mixed bag. It is so deliberately, for I am convinced that in Cistercian studies, as in medieval studies in general, an accurate picture of the object of our research can only be gained by insights drawn from all disciplines. The growth and decline of the Cistercians—or, better put, the changing Cistercian phenomenon—will be misunderstood if viewed only from a single perspective. Historians of thought, of institutions, of the arts, and of language must share with each other the fruits of their scholarship if a balanced understanding is to be gained. I hope this volume will help achieve that goal.

J. R. S.

SAINT BERNARD'S ATTITUDE TOWARD WAR

JEAN LECLERCQ

Abbaye St.-Maurice, Clervaux

THE ATTITUDE WHICH SHOULD BE ADOPTED toward war is a very real problem today. Thus, when we consider it in relation to a witness from the past, we run the risk of projecting our own prejudices into remote historical periods. This danger should be recognized from the start so that we can avoid it and remain as objective as possible. Since Bernard on three separate occasions expressed his approval of armed combat, the temptation has been to regard him as merely the representative of a long Christian tradition of violence. But the problem is far from being that simple. He took action as a layman, then as a monk, finally and chiefly as an abbot, for more than forty years, from 1111 to 1153. In passing judgment on him, we do not have the right to isolate a few texts and specific actions, as if all the rest never existed. In order to understand him, we must apply ourselves to an investigation of his motives. He always made allowance for complex and varied circumstances, in the midst of which he had to cope with his own inner aspirations as well as events outside himself. These could often appear contradictory.

I. BERNARD AND PEACE

We can say that all his life Bernard was a "peacemaker."[1] Nevertheless, during his later years he promoted two wars of

---

[1] Mt 5:1. Some of the texts in which St Bernard commented on the Beatitudes are edited in *Opera*, III, 64, 85; V. 332; 6/2: 60; and mentioned in H. Rochais, "Enquête sur les Sermons divers et les Sentences de S. Bernard," *Analecta Sacri Ordinis Cistercienses*, 18 (1962), 47, 125.

a special nature. Why? How? To what extent? What were his motives and justifications? To understand this, we must first recall his general and normal attitude and then consider the exceptional conflicts which occasioned his support of war. It will not be a question of his political role, but of his spiritual and doctrinal attitude toward war and peace, violence and non-violence.

1. *Violence in Society*

It is difficult for us to conceive the extent of violence in the society of the twelfth century. And since this same society was also completely imbued with religion, violence and religion tended to be at each other's service. It is not necessary here to offer abundant illustrations of these contentions. By way of example, the violence of individuals appears in a long series of brawls and murders which have been noted in the history of the Cistercian Order.[2] But individuals form a part of social groups and they reflect the violence of the whole. Thus, in the twelfth century, Stephen of Obazine and his entire entourage were considered extremely violent, even if we are justified in assuming that the anonymous biographer has projected much of his own aggressiveness into the account.[3] As for the fact that violence and devotion were continually intermingled, the accounts recorded in the *Miracles of St. Benedict* at the Abbey of Fleury give evidence of this. The true miracle is that the violent monks who sprang from this society still contributed something toward its pacification.[4]

At this time, as in nearly all eras, psychological violence,

2. A Dimier, "Violences, rixes et homicides chez les Cisterciens," *Revue des sciences religieuses*, 46 (1972), 38-57.
3. *Vie de S. Etienne d'Obazine* (ed. and trans. M. Aubrun; Clermont-Ferrand, 1970). I have drawn attention to the part which the biographer could have played in this account in a report entitled "Modern Psychology and the Interpretation of Monastic Texts," *Speculum*, 48 (1973) 476-90. In the footnotes for this present article the titles which are not preceded by an author's name are those works in which I have given more extensive treatment to subjects which can only be mentioned here.
4. "Violence and the Devotion to St. Benedict," *The Downside Review*, 38 (1970), 344-60.

based on ambition and most brutally manifested in armed violence, was aggravated by the battles being waged on an economic level. There was general under-development which resulted from the fact that harvests were at the mercy of atmospheric conditions. This explains the importance attributed to climatic factors: tornados, droughts, floods, comets, etc.[5] Everyone envied his neighbors' possessions, and therefore these had to be defended. It has been demonstrated that, in proportion to the commercial development which evolved in the twelfth century and thereafter, avarice, which consists in perpetual acquisition beyond one's needs, took precedence over pride in the list of vices.[6] If St. Bernard still accorded the greatest importance to humility above all other virtues and opposing all vices, it was because, with regard to the spiritual man, and especially for monks, he was mainly concerned to overcome evil at its source. Another reason was that, since he lived in the country, he found himself less involved with commercial activities than those who lived in the cities. However, his abbey was located in a zone where great property-owners confronted each other. He could not be unaware of their rivalries, though he sought to remain aloof even when, probably without his knowledge, donations made to his monastery occasionally served the interest of one or the other among them.[7] Finally, besides the violence of brute force and that exercised in the realm of economics, there was another kind stimulated by doctrinal controversy: the vulgarity of a man like Beranger of Poitiers when he attacked St. Bernard in order to defend Abelard demonstrates just how far passion could go in this area. Compared to him, Abelard and Bernard were as lambs.[8]

5. "Monastic Historiography from Leo IX to Callixtus II," *Studia Monastica*, 12 (1970), 73.

6. Lester K. Little, "Pride Goes before Avarice: Social Change and the Vices in Latin Christendom," *The American Historical Review*, 76 (1971), 16-49.

7. "St. Bernard and the Contemplative Community," *Cistercian Studies,* 7 (1972), 107.

8. "Le thème de la jonglerie chez S. Bernard et ses contemporains," *Revue d'histoire de la spiritualité*, 48 (1972), 386-99. In the Proceedings of the colloque international Pierre Abélard-Pierre le Vénerable, Cluny, 2-3 July 1972.

One form of violence was that of armed combat. The society of the twelfth century had a hierarchical structure which was not set up according to classes of individuals with divergent economic interests, but according to what were known as orders, among which the common tasks were portioned out. There were three orders, and one of these was composed of the soldiers or knights. The other two grouped together, on the one hand, the men who prayed, the clerics, and, on the other hand, those who worked.[9] It was possible to transfer from the military and the working orders to the one devoted to prayer. Nevertheless, apart from cases where an exceptional vocation led one to leave the category that one was born into, the orders were distinct. Usually there was no conflict among them. The soldiers were even supposed to fight on behalf of the other two groups; for them armed combat was a part of normal existence. To reject the profession of arms was dangerous; it was equivalent to depriving oneself of a means of defense, which was often necessary. It amounted to placing oneself on the margins of society, somewhat like what is happening today in certain countries to conscientious objectors. And, because of the public humiliation implied in this rejection, it involved, in some sense, a banishment from what could be called "proper society," that which appears "respectable" in the eyes of most contemporaries. Bernard belonged to this type of family. William of Saint Thierry tells us that Bernard's father, Tescelin le Sor, although not of the higher nobility, "was by heredity a legitimate member of the military order" (*vir antiquae et legitimae militiae*). This latter expression clearly reveals the legitimate nature of the military profession. William of Saint Thierry affirmed that Tescelin considered his profession to be in conformity with the will of the Lord

---

9. See Y. Congar, "Les laïcs et l'ecclésiologie des *ordines* chez les théologiens des XIe et XIIe siècles," *I laici nella "societas christiana" dei secoli XI e XII* (Milan, 1968), pp. 94-104; P. Rousset, "Les laïcs dans la croisade, *ibid.*, pp. 430-31. For knighthood, its evolution, and its part in the crusades, see Lynn White, jr., *Medieval Technology and Social Change* (Oxford, 1962), index.

because he did not abuse his power but acted within the bounds of the law. He also saw it as a way of serving, by means of arms, those who were his superiors in the feudal hierarchy.[10]

In this milieu, even the gesture of becoming a cleric was considered a disgrace for an adult who could do otherwise— although it was considered normal for the youngest of the family who had been destined for this since childhood. For an elder son such as Abelard, it required a courageous decision to renounce "the fame of military glory, to abdicate the service of Mars for that of Minerva, to exchange the weapons and trophies of martial conflict for the armor of philosophy."[11] Guibert of Nogent, the youngest of a family of the lesser nobility and an orphan, considered it a very special grace from God to have been called to become something other than his fellowmen, who were "as ignorant of God as beasts, or cruel in their use of arms and guilty of crime."[12] His father, if he had lived, would undoubtedly have turned him aside from intellectual pursuits;[13] and even his mother, having once noticed the wounds caused by the brutal whipping of his teacher, suggested that, when he was old enough,

10. William of Saint Thierry, Vita Bern, I, l, PL 185:227. On the social condition of Bernard's family, See J. Richard, "Le milieu familial," *Bernard de Clairvaux* (Paris, 1953), pp. 3-15. Originally, "the nobility, as recently noted (E. Varlop, *De Vlaamse adel voor 1300*, I, 32-35 and 92-108), was not equivalent with knighthood; it was not *per se* a military caste; but noblemen, who were bound as vassals, would necessarily contract military obligations. How many were there in the eleventh century who were not involved in warfare? When a nobleman took up his pen—which only happened if he became a cleric! —his tone nearly always revealed a passion for armed service...." N. Huyghebaert, "Un moine hagiographe: Drogon de Bergues," *Sacris erudiri*, 20 (1971), 212. Some believe that this latter observation also applies to St. Bernard, seen as a "*chevalier manqué.*" Nobility is characterized as follows, *ibid.*, p. 213, in reference to a specific text: "*nam sanguinis serie ducta a patribus pollebat, et substantia quam plurimum abundabat.*" This is precisely the definition of nobility!

11. Abelard, *Epistola 1 ad amicum seu Historia calamitatum*, PL 178:115. The manner in which Canon Fulbert would later punish Heloise's lover is another indication of the violence of the times.

12. Guibert of Nogent, *De vita sua sive Monodia*, I, 2, PL 156:841. On the social condition of Guibert's family, John F. Benton, *Self and Society in Medieval France: The Memoirs of Abbot Guibert of Nogent* (New York, 1970), pp. 11-12.

13. *De vita sua*, I, 4, PL 196:843.

he should be offered the arms and equipment necessary to become a knight, if he so chose.[14] And we could cite other examples of the courage required for a born nobleman to "scorn the military." The story of Guibert of Nogent leads us to believe that it was sometimes easier to learn how to fight than to make progress in the intellectual field. In one case similar to his own—and we know it was not unique[15]—more serious blows were received in school than during war games played while waiting for the time of genuine combat. Furthermore, this latter was considered as an honest activity, even "holy" or "sacred," within the limits and according to conditions which we must now recall.

2. *A Doctrine of Restricted Violence*

We will not attempt here to retrace the complex evolution by which Christians made the transition from the moral program proposed in the New Testament to a theory of the "just war." It was a slow evolution which only came to fruition in the thirteenth century with Thomas Aquinas.[16] It will suffice to mention that two thinkers made a greater contribution to this movement than all the others. The first was St. Augustine, who managed to rise above his own strong personal aversion and come to accept the idea that the Church could summon a defensive war to protect the faith of all Christians against heresies and schisms such as Donatism and other

14. *Ibid.*, I, 6, PL 156:841. H. Platelle, "La violence et ses remèdes en Flandres au XIe siècle," *Sacris erudiri*, 20 (1971), 161-67, has shown, texts in hand, that the "conversion" to the monastic life, such as it is related in some of the hagiographical texts of the eleventh and twelfth centuries, would seem to imply a "brutal and categoric condemnation of the *militia*."

15. See E. Lesne, *Histoire de la propriété ecclésiastique en France*, V, *Les écoles et l'enseignement de la fin du VIIIe siècle à la fin du XIIe* (Lille, 1940), pp. 538-47: *La discipline scolaire*.

16. Among the more recent statements on the history of the Christian conception of war, we may cite an article by R. A. McCormick in *New Catholic Encyclopedia*, 14, col. 802; an earlier study on this subject is R. Regout, *La doctrine de la guerre juste de S. Augustin à nos jours d'après les théologiens et les canonistes catholiques* (Paris, 1935), and a collective work entitled *Le droit de juste guerre: Tradition théologique, adaptations contemporaines* (Paris, 1938).

similar threats. However, such use of force belonged to the secular powers. During the following centuries there was a this regard; but simply according to the pressures of an infi- this reagard; but simply according to the pressures of an infi- nite variety of circumstances and the particular tempera- ments of churchmen, the emphasis was more or less given to a peace accompanied by injustice and violence, or to a war which invariably occasioned others.

In this area as in many others, the period of the Gregorian Reform was decisive. As a result of the Church's seculariza- tion after the dissolution of the Carolingian Empire, many bishops had become fighting men, while many of the bad or mediocre popes, especially during the tenth century, had simply become the pawns of violent opposing factions in Rome and the surrounding territory. By the eleventh centu- ry, the idea of a "holy war" had found its way into Christian- ity. This definitely did not constitute an innovation in the history of religions: in ancient civilizations, the sacred charac- ter of tribal or national wars was recognized; and, in Islam, a war of conquest had been considered a means of spreading the true faith. Likewise the reconquest of Spain, which had suffered Moslem invasion, appeared as service rendered to the Christian faith. Knighthood—the *ordo* of the *milites*—here found its supreme justification. But toward the middle of the eleventh century, Leo IX, the first of the great reformer popes, extended this conception of religious war to cover the repression of the inhabitants of Tusculum who had rebelled against the reform, and then the campaign undertaken against the Normans in southern Italy. Alexander II and Gregory VII would later act on similar principles.[17] In this area, the popes took the initiative.

This manner of extending the domain of legitimate violence aroused the opposition of a number of Christian thinkers, even some who served the cause of reform such as St Peter Damian. He had the courage to stand up against the religious

17. See F. Kempf, "The Papacy, the Holy Wars and the First Crusade," in *The Handbook of Church History* (edd. H. Jedin and J. Dolan; London 1969), p. 441.

politics of Leo IX when the latter was being venerated every-
where as a saint.[18] Another opponent was Guibert, the archbishop of Ravenna. He had been declared anti-pope, under
the name of Clement III, by Henry IV, and commissioned to
take the place of Gregory VII. No doubt this sovereign's
intentions were not entirely disinterested. It always happens
at such times that pacifists and war-mongers accuse each
other of being unfaithful to some passage from the Gospel. In
particular, the precept to "turn the other cheek" was taken
quite literally. The task of presenting a general view of the
problem would fall to a man of great talent, a canonist and
an author of spiritual works, Anselm of Baggio. He was the
nephew of Alexander II who named him bishop of Lucca.
Gregory VII summoned him to Rome and it was there,
between the years 1083 and 1086, that he spoke of the
Church's power to wage war: in Book XIII of his collection
of canonical texts, written at the explicit request of Gregory
VII; in his *Book against Guibert*;[19] and, paradoxically, in a
work entitled *On Charity*.[20] His innovation consisted in at-
tributing the use of armed force to the Church itself, without
need of recourse to the secular power. The rest of his doctrine tends to maintain a difficult balance between violence
and charity, and even claims that violence can be an exercise
of charity. This is readily ascertained from some of the sub-
titles of Book XIII:

> 1. It was not an act of cruelty for Moses to massacre men
> at the Lord's command. 2. Vengeance should be ex-
> ercised not through hatred but through love. 3. Wars
> should be conducted with goodwill. 4. Soldiers can also
> be just men, and the fact of fighting an enemy should be
> a work of necessity and not of desire. 5. He who goes
> into combat should pray....10. Vengeance must be
> tempered....12. Wicked men should be corrected and

18. *S. Pierre Damien, ermite et homme d'Eglise* (Rome, 1960), p. 84.
19. PL 149:415-76.
20. Ed. E. Pasztor, "Motivi dell'ecclesiologia di Anselmo di Lucca," *Bollettino dell'Istituto Storico Italiano per il Medio Evo e Archivio Muratoriano*, 77 (1965), 45-109.

not killed. . . .18. If something bad happens as a result of striving toward the good, it is not a sin. . . .

The rest reveals the same alternation between acceptable violence and the goal of charity up to the twenty-ninth and last chapter which is entitled: "Prayer should contribute to victory, and war should not be sought through a desire to spill blood."[21]

Thus, from beginning to end of this statement, as in the others where he expressed himself less systematically, Anselm of Lucca, while justifying armed violence when it was useful or inevitable, imposed restrictions which were determined by the goal sought, the means employed, and the intentions which should be consistent with the Gospel. The goal could be the correction of heretics or schismatics separated from the Roman Church or perhaps "the defense of orphan and widow by means of arms."[22] The intention should be to "cure" malefactors,[23] or to protect those who wished to lead a good life by repressing those who harried them.[24] In practice, there was danger involved here. Whence springs Anselm's insistence on the need to conciliate war and peace, as he says in a phrase where he associates these two apparently contradictory realities: *Esto ergo bellando pacificus.*[25]

The antinomy between them could never be resolved except on the level of intentions. Violence and non-violence had never been considered as absolute options, as purely exterior realities such as the use of force or the absence of war, neither in the New Testament nor in tradition:

. . .The distinction between non-violence and violence must necessarily be based on the inner attitude, of love or

21. The edition by F. Thaner, *Anselmi Lucensis collectio canonum* (Innsbruck, 1915), is incomplete and does not contain Book XIII. But the list of the chapters of this book has been given by R. Montanari, *La "Collectio canonum" di S. Anselmo di Lucca e la riforma Gregoriana* (Mantua, 1941), pp. 72-73. An earlier and less accurate edition is to be found in PL 149:533-34.
22. *Contra Guibertum*, 1, PL 149:454A.
23. *Ibid.*, 453B.
24. *De caritate* (ed. Pasztor), p. 104.
25. *Contra Guibertum* 1, PL 149:451.

non-love, and it is not external behavior which permits the ultimate judgment.[26]

In this respect, Anselm of Lucca proposed the first doctrinal synthesis which, though undoubtedly incomplete, would affect all subsequent evolution. A quarter of a century later, St Bernard and the Church of his time would feel his influence.[27]

3. A "Peace Corps" in the Twelfth Century

The society at this time existed in a state of perpetual violence which the Church attempted to limit by recognizing only certain forms. How did Bernard react in this situation? As he did in all other areas: as a monk. His guiding principle was always the superiority of the religious vocation over the call to arms. He would state this clearly in his praise of the Templars: as long as it is in line with the conditions recognized by tradition, "the use of the sword is permitted to those who have been given this function by God, and who have not made profession of something better."[28] To what did this second alternative refer? Bernard replied in word and action. Speaking of the Premonstratensians, he applied a term which reflects a similar one found in the works of Anselm of Lucca: *bellando pacificus*. He called them "peaceful warriors," *bellatores pacifici*, and referred to the symbolism of spiritual armor used by St Paul. The only violence which he and the Apostle advocated without restriction is that opposed to the powers of evil: these religious are "gentle toward men and violent toward demons."[29]

26. V. Vergriete, review of J. M. Muller, *L'évangile de la non-violence* (Paris, 1968), in *La vie spirituelle*, 124 (1971), 371.

27. Concerning the influence of the *Liber canonum* of Anselm of Lucca on later canonical tradition see J. T. Gilchrist, in *New Catholic Encyclopedia*, I, col. 585. St. Bernard could have been familiar with Anselm's work either directly or from those texts collected in Book III of the *Liber canonum* which had been used in the *Decree* and the *Panormia* of Yvo of Chartres and would later become part of the Decree of Gratian: a list of these texts is given by A. Friedberg, *Decretum magistri Gratiani* (Leipzig, 1922), pp. liii, lix, and lxii.

28. Tpl, 5, *Opera*, 3:218.

29. Ep 355, PL 182:558.

It was chiefly in regard to Cistercian life that Bernard had occasion to proclaim the superiority of this totally spiritual violence. And he did it in two ways: by finding recruits for Clairvaux and then showing them the meaning and worth of their vocation. Even before entering Cîteaux he had begun to devote himself to this apostolate on behalf of monastic life among his own family. According to William of Saint Thierry, in early autumn of the year 1111, he had gone in search of his brothers who were engaged in an activity which was typical of the period and the milieu: they were laying siege to the citadel of Grancey. Bernard's uncle was also there, as well as the entire army of the duke of Burgundy. From this camp, chosen as his first field of activity, he took a whole group of soldiers away from their profession, "relatives, comrades, and friends" of all ages: from his uncle Gaundry de Touillon, "a man renowned among the knights of his time," to his young brother Bartholomew "who was not yet a knight," without forgetting Andrew who had recently been dubbed, and Gerard, "a gallant soldier in wartime exploits."[30] Thus Bernard went from castle to castle removing the fighting men from their milieu with such persuasion that "mothers hid their sons, wives tried to hold back their husbands, and friends diverted their friends."[31]

Later on, in the same fashion, Bernard "converted" many other *milites*, either individually—such as Arnoud of Majorca in Flanders[32]—or in groups, such as "that cohort of noble knights" who had detoured through Clairvaux in order to see the abbot. What William of Saint Thierry wrote about them says much about their usual occupations: "Nearly all of them were young and devoted to the secular army; they traveled about in search of those abominable contests called tournaments." They even refused to leave off fighting during Lent. They resisted Bernard's exhortations, but not his personal

30. Vita Bern, I, 10-11, PL 185:232-33. A list of the knights who were brought in to Clairvaux by Bernard is given in *Bernard de Clairvaux*, pp. 36-37.

31. Vita Bern, I, 15, PL 185:235.

32. Conrad of Eberbach, *Exordium magnum Cisterciense*, III, 19 (ed. B. Griesser; Rome, 1961), pp. 194-95.

charm—he offered them beer that he had blessed—nor the grace which he obtained for them. That same day, "having been converted, they placed themselves at the service of the spiritual army."[33]

This latter expression shows that entrance into monastic life was not simply an evasion of the normal conditions of existence within the milieu; it substituted another mode of activity which had value and which was superior. This explains Bernard's use of the traditional phrase, the *militia Christi*.[34] No doubt this also explains his preference for comparisons and parables inspired by the symbolism of a citadel and the work of laying siege.[35] Finally, it casts light on his insistence that monks should be forbidden to go on the Crusade; even this religious manner of fighting for Christ, which was not reserved to the knights, was inferior to their vocation to devote themselves to the spiritual battle.[36] There are two roads which lead to the heavenly Jerusalem: one is the holy war which envisions the deliverance of the earthly Jerusalem, and the other is monastic peace. If the former is adopted, it must be done with the least possible violence; and, if the latter, there should be concern for no other violence than that of the interior combat.[37] Also, monks should conduct themselves in their own milieu, and elsewhere by their influence, as professionals in non-violence. For example, when the abbot of Molesmes suffered damages at the hands

33. Vita Bern, I, 55, PL 185:257.

34. Ep 1, 13, PL 182:78; Ep 292, 1, PL 182: 497; Ep 441, PL 182: 638.

35. Ded, III, *Opera,* 5:379-82; studied from this point of view in "Essais sur l'esthétique de S. Bernard," *Studi medievali,* 9 (1968), 726-27. The same symbolism is used in some of the *Sentences* and *Parables* found in *Opera,* 6:2; see also *Recueil d'études sur S. Bernard* (Rome, 1969), III, 168-69.

36. This fact has been emphasized, with supporting texts, by B. Flood, "St. Bernard's View of the Crusade," *The Australian Catholic Record,* 47 (1970), 135-37. James A. Brundage, "A Transformed Angel (X 3.31.18): The Problem of the Crusading Monk," *Studies in Medieval Cistercian History Presented to Jeremiah F. O'Sullivan* (CS 13; Spencer, Massachusetts, 1971), pp. 55-62, has shown, without dwelling particularily on St Bernard, that, from Anselm's time on—and especially in Gratian—there had been an increasingly greater restriction on the participation of monks in the Crusades.

37. Concerning this "devotion to Jerusalem," see *The Love of Learning and the Desire for God* (trans. Catharina Misrahi; New York, 1962), pp. 58-61.

of laymen assigned to the service of his monastery, Bernard recommended that pardon should prevail over justice and, in this regard, he quoted the evangelical precept to "turn the other cheek."[38]

This is a whole aspect of Bernard's ordinary activity which is sometimes eclipsed by the part he played in the Crusade. He made an immense contribution to the expansion of his Order which, at the time of his death, would number approximately 350 abbeys, some of these inhabited by hundreds of religious. Thus he originated a kind of vast and efficacious "Peace Corps." Instead of remaining in the category of fighting men, many passed into the other two orders, while uniting them in an unwonted manner: they prayed *and* they worked. According to the particular territory, they would clear the land, improve it, irrigate and till the soil, plant forests, dig ponds, and thus contribute in many ways to the integral development—material, cultural, and spiritual—of the environment.

By drawing crowds of young men toward these communities of non-violence, charity, and goodwill, by recruiting this peaceable army of thousands of Cistercian monks, and by promoting the other monastic and canonical orders, Bernard appeared as the greatest non-violent leader of his time. How much he knew of the virtue of patience! In a war-oriented world, full of continual problems, where each man was obliged to take up arms to defend himself and his family, he managed to multiply the houses of peace where men from every social rank, and especially young knights, were brought together in a common refusal to bear arms. Within a society which was still "savage" in many respects, he created another society, completely non-violent, whose functions included hospitality: receiving the stranger who was recognized as a brother.[39] Bernard knew that this way of life was more in tune with the Gospel, and he usually acted in conformity with this conviction.

---

38. Ep 80, PL 182:201-202.

39. Concerning the role of hospitality, see "St. Bernard and the Contemplative Community," pp. 77-78.

II. ST BERNARD AND THE WARS

1. *The Actual Problem*

With regard to St Bernard and his times, it is difficult to speak of "war" in general, as if it were a kind of abstract notion and raised a speculative problem. Under one form or another, the state of war in many areas was a perpetual one, or very nearly so. But it stimulated conflicts which were always concrete, particular, either restricted to a local zone or extended throughout a region or a kingdom, and in one instance, as we shall see, even the whole of western Christendom and the Near East. According to what Bernard said and did in each situation, we can distinguish two main categories of war: those waged among Christians, and those between Christians and non-Christians. He intervened in both. Why? Was it by virtue of his role as a man of God who knew that he indeed had authority if not power? Was it as a monk? Every war brings up the question of moral exigencies and, at this particular time, these bore a religious character. Therefore, even a man who was not a professional politician—and perhaps he more than anyone, especially since his life bore witness to a quest for God—could and should take a stand in the face of so much fighting.

The question for him was not whether to be "for" or "against" war: wars were a general reality and it did not rest with him to make them disappear altogether. Moreover, it was commonly acknowledged that they were sometimes justified. His role was rather to encourage his contemporaries, and especially those who were politically responsible, to examine their consciences on two points: their motives for waging war and their methods. Bernard tried to have as few wars as possible and, when they did occur, he advocated the least possible violence. He displayed this line of conduct with regard to both types of war, which must be treated separately.

2. *War among Christians*

There were wars being waged on all levels of social life. First of all, private wars in the form of duels or tournaments. The Church tried to urge Christians to abstain, at least during liturgical times of penance; but we have seen how a group of young knights "in search of tournaments" resisted even Bernard when he reminded them of this law.[40] He tried to prevent this practice of dueling even after Easter; he asked Suger, who was the abbot of Saint-Denis and an important man in the kingdom—*maximus princeps in regno*—to intervene in such a case in which two adversaries were due to confront each other: the king's brother and the son of the count of Champagne. What were his motives here? There was the risk of blood being spilled to no purpose, and, in the king's absence, the peace of the entire country could have been seriously threatened. Three factors were thus to be taken into account: the lives of the persons involved, the tranquillity of the kingdom, and service to the Church, whose faithful clients and ministers always suffered repercussions from these fratricidal conflicts.[41] And we could cite other rebukes from Bernard on the same subject.[42]

Then there were the feudal wars which were not simply games that often degenerated into homicide, but set against each other rival lords and all those bound to them in military service. Bernard was also opposed to these for two reasons: because they were usually motivated by egoism and ambi-

---

40. See above, note 33.

41. Ep 37, 6, **PL** 182:581, and the scholarly footnote of Mabillon, *ibid.*, n. 188.

42. Some of the texts have been translated by P. Lorson, "S. Bernard devant la guerre et la paix," *Nouvelle revue théologique*, 75 (1953), 794-96. Some have likewise been collected and analyzed by E. Platania, "La guerra nel pensiero di S. Bernardo, c. 4: L'azione e il pensiero politico di S. Bernardo di Chiaravalle," in *Istituto universitario pareggiato di magistero "Maria SS. Assunta," Roma, Annuario per l'anno accademico 1947-1948* (Vatican City, 1949), pp. 127-40; A. dal Covolo, *Il problema dell'utilizzazione della spada: la guerra, c. 3: L'idea di guerra santa in S. Bernardo di Clairvaux* (Diss. Catholic University of the Sacred Heart, Milan, 1969-1970), pp. 65-123.

tion, and because their victims were always the poor people whose villages were devastated by the armies. Bernard proposed that these conflicts should be regulated by way of negotiation and agreement—*conventio*. He wrote thus in a letter to the Duke Conrad of Zähringen, who was preparing to attack the count of Geneva, Amadeus III.[43] And the abbot of Clairvaux, who had refused to allow any monks to embark on the Crusade, even went so far as to offer to send several of them to obtain an agreement, a *concordia*.[44] Likewise he begged another counselor of Louis VII to use his influence in urging the king to avoid a violent war with all of its consequences.[45] To the king himself, he denounced war as a work of the devil because it entailed injustices and murder: those who suffer the most from it are not those who make the decisions and actually wage the war, but those who must endure it and the "widows" and "orphans" whom they leave behind them.[46]

And in one case, Bernard acted as a man of the Spirit who was free and exempt from all partiality by successively reproaching two parties who refused to come to terms: Pope Innocent II and King Louis VII.[47] Only a prophet would thus dare to raise his voice—and with such vehemence! —against the two highest powers on whom he was dependent. His role was not to make political decisions, but to make consciences aware of their duties, to denounce evil, and point toward the good—or at least that which appeared to him as good. Certainly a war can be lawful; but only as a last resort, when all other means of checking a conflict have failed, and when the motives for waging war have been sufficiently examined. For example, if the Duchess Adelaide of Lorraine discovered that the castle for which she wanted to wage battle did not actually belong to her, she should refrain from launching an attack; if the motive of justice was not a sufficient deterrent, she

43. Ep 97, 1, PL 182:230.
44. Ep 97, 2, PL 182:230.
45. Ep 222, PL 182:389.
46. Ep 221, 1, PL 182:386.
47. Texts are cited by P. Lorson, "S. Bernard devant la guerre...," pp. 793-94.

should act "for love of God," since it is charity which enforces the observance of justice.[48]

Finally, there were wars among Christians which were religious not only because they involved matters of morality, but because the unity of the Church was at stake. Such was the case in times of schism and revolt against the pope, as happened when the anti-pope Anacletus set himself up against Innocent II. At such moments, Bernard surmounted his spontaneous repugnance toward violence: "It is not my place to exhort to combat," he wrote to the Emperor Lothar.[49] But in such a situation, he believed that it was his duty to do this, or, more precisely, once again to urge those who held political power to reflect on their obligations toward the papacy. He said to the king of England, Henry I Beauclerc: "Justice is on our side. Still, this does not seem to carry any weight with the inhabitants of Rome. By the justice of our cause, we appease God; and by force of arms, we inspire fear in the enemy. . . ."[50] They are not so much our personal enemies, but the enemies of God, he explained. And to Conrad III, successor to Lothar, he insisted on the defensive character of the armed intervention which he requested against the Roman rebels: both the temporal and the spiritual powers must defend themselves—*invicem se defendant.*[51] When, on the occasion of this same schism, the inhabitants of Genoa and Pisa wanted to break the peace treaty which Bernard had urged both sides to accept only with great difficulty, he replied in substance: If you must fight—*quod si militare placet, arma probare delectat. . .*—at least let it be for some worthwhile cause, that is, against the enemies of the Church, not against your neighbors. Only in such an instance would conquest be "honest" and "just."[52] There is nothing in any of these positions held by Bernard which is not traditional and consistent with the doctrine proposed by Anselm of Lucca.

48. Ep 120, PL 182:265-66.
49. Ep 139, 1, PL 182:294.
50. Ep 138, PL 182:293.
51. Ep 244, 1, PL 182:441.
52. Ep 129, 3, PL 183:284.

3. *Wars against Non-Christians*

A. The Jews

From the most ancient times, Jews were traditionally considered among the top-ranking enemies of the Church. The only time that Bernard had to adopt a practical line of conduct was when he took on their defense in the Rhineland where, on the occasion of the Second Crusade, a pseudo-hermit was trying to rouse Christians against them. Bernard acted for several reasons: faith in the mystery which they represented, charity toward them as persons, and hope of their eventual conversion. The arguments which he brought forth at the time were not original. But besides this, he reacted against the disorder wrought by this false monk who provoked men to violence: it should never be introduced into society by idle young soldiers or by pseudo-clerics who managed to escape all institutional control. The best move for either type would have been to enter a monastery and stay there.

B. Heretics

There was no lack of heretics in Bernard's time. They were mostly Cathari who went by various names, according to their leaders or the regions where they spread their doctrine; there were some in the Rhineland, in the south of France, and elsewhere. With regard to these also, Bernard's instructions were very clear. In the first of the *Sermons* which he composed at the request of Eberwin, provost of the Premonstratensians at Steinfeld in the diocese of Cologne, to refute the heretics, he declared: "...We must lay hold of them by rational arguments and not by force of arms."[53] Eberwin had complained not only of their doctrinal errors, but of the troubles and violence which they instigated: "The

---

53. SC 64, 8, *Opera*, 2:170. In the phrase "*capiantur, dico, non armis, sed argumentis,*" the first of these words is used by Bernard in reference to his writings on the *Song of Songs*, 2, 15, *Capite nobis vulpes parvulas . . .*, which are commented on later, SC 65, 4, *Opera*, 2:175.

people, animated by an excess of zeal, have seized their
teachers and, despite our efforts to forbid them, have burned
them at the stake."[54] The situation was aggravated by the
fact that in the same region, the heretical sects were fighting
among themselves.[55] It seemed to require the wielding of a
pen and the use of spiritual "armaments." Eberwin asked
Bernard to play the role of the "peaceful warrior," *bellator
pacificus:* the same role that the abbot of Clairvaux had once
attributed to the religious of the Premonstratensian Order of
which the provost of Steinfeld was a member.[56] For his part,
Bernard thought that, here again, it was a case of the "necessary" and "arduous defense" of the Church; he himself used
these words in speaking of the protection required by the
entire body of Christian people.[57]

And after having done everything possible toward this end,
he reaffirmed the fact that faith is not something to be imposed: *fides suadenda est, non imponenda.* If "coercion" and
even "persecution" seemed required, it would not be incum-
bent upon the ardent passion of the masses, but rather the
duty of the "temporal princes," those who rightfully bore
the sword and who should know how to use it with the least
amount of violence.[58] The word "persecute" which Bernard
used again with regard to the heretics from the region of
Toulouse,[59] had a precise juridical meaning which was already
evident in the writings of Anselm of Lucca: it referred to the
prevention of wrong-doing and a subsequent coercion in
favor of good conduct.[60] But it seems that the depth of St

---

54. *Epistola ad s. Bernardum (inter s. Bernardi, 472)*, 2, PL 182:677. Concerning Eberwin and this correspondence with Bernard see *Recueil d'études sur S.
Bernard* (Rome, 1962), I, 196-97, and *Opera*, 3:71.

55. Ep 472, 4, PL 182:678.

56. See above, note 25.

57. SC 65, 1, 8, *Opera*, 2:172, 177.

58. SC 66, 12 and 14, *Opera*, 2:187. Concerning the long debated question as to
who, in Bernard's opinion, had the right to wield the temporal sword, an excellent
restatement may be found in P. Zerbi, "Riflessione sul simbolo delle due spade in
San Bernardo di Clairvaux," *Raccolta di studi in onore di G. Sorranzo* (Milan,
1967), pp. 1-18.

59. Ep 242, 1, PL 182:436.

60. On this meaning of the word *persecutio* see A. Stickler, "Il potere coattivo
materiale della Chiesa nella riforma gregoriana secondo Anselmo di Lucca," *Studi
Gregoriana,* 2 (1947), 239.

Bernard's yearning for non-violence was most evident when, even while permitting recourse to the use of arms, he could not refrain from preaching kindness. Soon after encouraging the people of Toulouse to defend themselves, he exhorted them to practice "hospitality" toward "pilgrims, indigents, the poorly-clad, the sick, prisoners," all those in whom the person of Christ could be welcomed.[61] And it was just before refuting the heretics of the Rhineland that he wrote one of his most beautiful hymns to love:

> Oh, great force of love!...What is more violent? It overcomes God himself. And what is more non-violent? It is love. I ask you: what is this power, so violent with a view to victory, so subdued in its own use of violence?

All of this is verified in Jesus Christ, in his voluntary humiliation; he is the perfect model of non-violence motivated by love. As the expression comes from Bernard's pen: *Quid tamen tam non violentum?* [62]

C. The Wends

The Wends were a Slavic people who lived on the northeastern frontier of the Empire, and, to use Bernard's term, they were "pagans": they were not Christians and, indeed, adhered to no known religion. They threatened to be an obstacle to the Second Crusade which had Bernard's ardent support. Following a diet of prelates and princes which met at Frankfurt on March 13, 1147, the abbot of Clairvaux wrote in one of the drafts of his encyclical on the Crusade:

> We declare that the Christian forces should be armed against them and must take up the sign of salvation—that is, the Cross—to destroy these nations entirely or, indeed, to convert them.[63]

61. Ep 242, 2, PL 182:437.
62. SC 64, 10, *Opera*, 2:171.
63. Ep 457, PL 182:651. Concerning the relationship of this text with other accounts of the call to the crusades see "L'encyclique de S. Bernard en faveur de la croisade," *Revue bénédictine,* 81 (1971), 303-304.

Ad delendas penitus, aut certe convertendas nationes illas:
these few words provoked contradictory interpretations, and
the sayings of the chronicler Helmold do not contribute to any
clarification of the matter:

> This holy man [Bernard] advised by some unknown ora-
> cles, began to exhort the princes and the people to jour-
> ney to Jerusalem in order to subdue the barbarian nations
> of the East and make them submit to Christian laws; he
> said that the time was near when all nations would enter
> [the Kingdom of God] and thus all Israel would be
> saved.[64]

Even in Helmold's statement, the conversion of pagans is
associated with their submission which was considered as a
means of allowing them to "enter" the Kingdom—if there
were no other way to accomplish this. The phrase quoted
above can also be logically translated as follows: "Christians
should arm themselves and take up the sign of their salvation
to exterminate, *or preferably*, to convert the nations."[65]

We saw that Bernard had spoken of the conversion of the
Jews. He avoided any apocalyptic prophecy with regard to
other nations. But, because of Helmold's testimony and that
of others in the same vein, as well as the statement from
Bernard himself which has been translated above, some historians have attributed to him the idea of a "forced conversion" of the Wends. Others have asked themselves whether the
Crusade launched against them was a war of conquest and
domination, or a missionary expedition. It becomes more and
more evident that the alternatives are not that clear-cut.
There are few explicit documents available which might
permit a definite answer. And actually it is not a matter of

---

64. *Helmoldi presbyteri Bozoviensis cronica Slavorum*, I, 59 (ed. B. Scheidler;
MGH, Script. rer. Germ.), pp. 114-15. Even this formulation of the idea attributed to Bernard was not unprecedented; proof lies in the fact that it immediately
found a corresponding echo among the princes, the bishops, the knights, and the
common people, and that to the extent that Helmold described it as "incredible."

65. This is the translation adopted by P. Dérumaux, *S. Bernard et les infidèles:
Essai historique et doctrinal* (Diss. Institut catholique, Paris, 1943), p. 408; the
words *aut certe* take on the meaning of "or preferably."

resolving the problem here, but of trying to understand St. Bernard's attitude. In the light of what we know of his reaction in other conflicts, it seems just to adopt the opinion of one of the foremost specialists on the subject of this Crusade: "We believe that we can class this appeal as a part of a strictly missionary concept."[66]

D. The Mohammedans in the Holy Land

We know more about Bernard's participation in the Second Crusade summoned by Eugenius III against the Saracens of Palestine. When Bernard was commissioned by the pope to take charge of it, he saw it as a defensive operation and, paradoxical as it may seem, oriented toward the reestablishment of peace. He would say as much after the failure of the venture: "We announced peace and other good things, and instead we have only troubles."[67] Nevertheless, his attitude in this war was dictated by motives which were a part of his life even before the expedition; these are the ones which are appropriate to consider at the start.

1. *The Vocation of the Templars*

Before the great military campaign was launched in 1146, after the fall of Edessa during the previous year, the Frankish kingdom in the East had known a long period of armed peace. Bernard was already involved in this through the publication of his *In Praise of the New Militia, for the Templars.* The vocation of these knights was to guarantee the security and tranquillity of Christians living in the Holy Land, as well as those who went there on pilgrimage. The treatise written for them is divided into two parts: the second is a series of meditations on the mysteries which had once unfolded in the Holy Places; the first justifies the vocation of the Knights

---

66. H. D. Kahl, "Slaven und Deutsche in der brandenburgischen Geschichte des 12. Jahrhunderts," in H. Beumann, *Heidenmission und Kreuzugsgedanke* (Darmstadt, 1963), p. 282. See also B. Flood, "St. Bernard's View. . .," pp. 134-35.

67. Csi 2, 1, *Opera*, 3:411.

Templar both in their own eyes and in Christian public opinion.[68] Two ideas are dominant. They were not invented by Bernard, but he gives them a quality of literary expression rooted in his own fervor and talent. The first is that a defensive war, in Palestine as elsewhere, is lawful. The second is that, even in such a case, violence must be reduced to a minimum.

Once again 'Bernard affirmed that everything depended on the motivation: if the intention were good, the result of the combat, whatever it was—victory or defeat, death inflicted or suffered—would be legitimate.[69] But this is rarely the case; nearly all wars waged in society were evil and, according to a play on words which the abbot of Clairvaux was fond of using: "they are not *militia*, but rather *malicia*."[70] He insisted on this contrast between so many frivolous, avoidable, and useless battles, and those to which the Templars could be devoted. The first were works of the devil, the author of hatred and violence; they could lead to victory which would be a misfortune—*infelix victoria*—if the success were the crowning point of a struggle inspired by pride and anger. On the contrary, both the life and death of the Templars were meritorious if their purpose was the maintenance or reestablishment of peace. The Lord's precursor did not condemn those who made profession of arms; he merely asked them to use the least possible violence. Thus Bernard accepted violence as an evil present in the world, inherent in the society in which he and his contemporaries lived. But he tried to set limitations; the Templars did not have the right to kill pagans unless it was impossible to do otherwise. According to another play on words, it was a distinction between *homicida* and *malicida*.[71] This was based on the assumption that if one

68. *Recueil d'études sur S. Bernard* (Rome, 1966), II, 96-99. John R. Sommerfeldt, "The Social Theory of Bernard of Clairvaux," *Studies in Medieval Cistercian History* . . ., pp. 35-48, has given a nuanced judgment on the idea which Bernard had of the society of his times. For the Templars see pp. 45-46.

69. Tpl, 2, *Opera* 3:215. A French translation of Tpl by E. de Solms has appeared under the title, *S. Bernard: Textes choisis et presentés par D. J. Leclercq* (Namur, 1958), pp. 149-91.

70. Tpl, 3, *Opera* 3:216.

71. Tpl, 4, *Opera*, 3:217. These ideas are developed up to p. 219.

had suffered an act of agression from some malefactor, one may defend oneself by the means at one's disposal. The responsibility fell on those who had provoked the battle and who, as it is written in the psalm, "wanted war."[72]

Other than the style, what is particularly new in this theory on the vocation of the Templars is Bernard's insistence on the mystery of death. Whether it is suffered or inflicted, it is the occasion of an encounter with God. It is the same, during times of peace, for all men. But war obliged the Christian knights to keep it always in perspective. The greatness of the profession of arms lies in the risk of death, and this consideration helped Bernard to orientate war toward something other than itself, toward the passage into a world beyond where each will be judged according to his intentions. At the very beginning of his treatise, Bernard introduced this consideration of death,[73] which confers a very solemn and hopeful character on all the rest: the knight should not fear death,[74] his position is secure. He is even more certain of his salvation if he is killed than if he kills: *securus interimit, interior securior*; it is better to be the victim of violence than the instigator, to endure it rather than take the initiative.[75] The words which describe this hopeful security—*secura* and *tuta*—are repeated.[76] "Therefore go forth in all security, *securi ergo procedite. . . .*" Bernard had written this in the

---

72. Tpl, 5, *Opera*, 3: 218; in 7 there is an allusion to Psalm 67, 31: *"Dissipa gentes quae bella volunt."* The most recent general discussion of the spirituality of the Templars is that of Desmond Seward, *The Monks of War: The Military Religious Orders* (London, 1972); ch. 2. "The Birth of a New Vocation," pp. 11-34, gives a good picture of the part played by St Bernard who "defined a new vocation" which was that of the *milites*. The fact that the Templars shared to some extent Cistercian spirituality helped humanize war. Once again, Bernard created the theory and even the theology of an already existing fact: that of knights living a religious life in the Holy Land. In the same way he gave a doctrinal interpretation of the "Cistercian fact" which existed before he spoke of it, as I have shown in an essay, "The Intentions of the Founders of the Cistercian Order," *The Cistercian Spirit* (CS 3; Spencer, Massachusetts, 1970), pp. 101-116.

73. Tpl, 1-2, *Opera*, 3:214-15.

74. Tpl, 4, *Opera*, 3:217.

75. *Ibid.*

76. Tpl, 2, *Opera*, 3:215.

introduction, before singing a hymn to the death of a Christian who is guided only by his faith and his will to serve the Lord; thus everything bespeaks "glory," "joy," "exultation," and "beatitude."[77]

The second part of the treatise, which is twice as long as the first, is consecrated to the prayer of the Templars who should contemplate the mysteries to which the Holy Places bear witness. There could be no clearer demonstration of the fact that war is subordinate to these higher realities; nor could one do more to spiritualize the military profession. Undoubtedly Bernard proved to these professional soldiers that their function was a service to the Church. However, the originality of his teaching did not consist in explaining that the armed combat which they were carrying on in the Holy Land as a continuation of the First Crusade was a holy war. They already knew this. The point of his treatise was to demonstrate the relative aspect of the military profession by uniting it, and even subordinating it, to a life of prayer; the "new militia" had for its goal not only war, but also prayer. The latter was even the more important, and, by means of it, this new category of knights, like the monks, could reconcile the activities of two social "orders" within their lives. The monks, some of whom came from families of the fighting profession, accomplished the functions of the other two orders: praying and working. The Templars were those who both fought and prayed; they were the soldier-monks.

2. *Contemporary Opinion Regarding the Templars*

In order to pass judgment on Bernard's ideas with regard to this program, we can compare them to those found in other documents dating from the same period. First, a letter which was probably written by the first master of the Templars, Hugh of Payns. He was a relative of Bernard and this document seems to have stimulated Bernard to write his *Praise of the New Militia*. The knights were tempted—in the

77. Tpl, 1, *Opera*, 3:214-15.

strongest sense of the word—to regard their profession as "illicit and pernicious." But it was not so:

> During times of peace, you struggle against your own flesh by means of fast and abstinence. . .; during times of war, you wage armed combat with the enemies of peace who injure you or wish to do so. . . .The devil suggests to you that, if you kill an enemy in a fit of hatred and rage, if you plunder his goods, it is done through greed; whereas, in fact, you seek to drive away your assailant: you kill without malice, you plunder without illicit lust. . . .What you hate is wickedness, not the man himself; whatever you take away from your adversaries because of their sins is just payment for your labors; you risk your lives to save your neighbor—does that not merit a reward?

Hugh also considered it a matter of good intention and he too insisted on the importance of prayer and humility.[78] We should recognize that the arguments he used to justify the profession of arms were valid and consistent with tradition; but they did not reach the heights—or, if one prefers, the depths—of St Bernard's writings, that quality of personal solemnity which engaged all human destiny.

The pacifist objection must not have been rare. For, toward the middle of the twelfth century, we see a patriarch of Jerusalem had consulted the provost of the cathedral at Troyes, a learned cleric who was known as Peter Manducator. His reply began with these words:

> You seek to know whether Christians are permitted to fight the pagans and kill them, since the Lord says in the Law: "Thou shalt not kill," and in the Gospel: "He who wields a sword will perish by the sword." It would seem that the Christian, especially if he has made religious profession and wears the habit, should tolerate injustices rather than seek vengeance. . . .[79]

78. The text is presented and edited in *Recueil d'études sur S. Bernard,* II, 87-96.

79. The text is presented and edited under the title "Gratien, Pierre de Troyes, et la seconde croisade," *Studia Gratiana,* II (1954), 585-93.

Then he cited six relevant verses from Scripture, with special attention given to the precept to "turn the other cheek." His interpretation was borrowed from St Augustine who, among other things, had declared:

> Jesus himself, when struck on the cheek, did not present the other one, but instead asked: "Why did you strike me?" St Paul, struck by the high priest, cursed him saying: "May the Lord strike you down, you whitewashed wall. . . ."

There followed twenty other "authorities" in support of the same thesis. Peter of Troyes ended with an appeal to the argument based on good intention; legitimate defense, disinterested service to the interest of Christ and not that of the fighter, obedience to the pope as "vicar" of Christ, the willingness to risk a death which, in such a case, would be a martyrdom as meritorious as that of the martyrs in the primitive Church. The conclusion was explicit: "Therefore, act in a manly way, with an easy conscience; spill the blood of Christ's enemies, *funde sanguinem inimicorum Christi. . . .*" All of this is irreproachable from the point of view of tradition. But how the tone differs from the words of St. Bernard! At any rate, Peter of Troyes had not introduced anything new, since all of his quotations were taken from the recent *Decretum* of Gratian which was full of ancient texts.

Later John of Salisbury would say of the Templars: "They are virtually the only men who are engaged in legitimate warfare."[80] For his part, Isaac of Stella, a Cistercian, would

---

80. *Polycraticus,* C. VII, ch. 21 (ed. C.C.J. Webb; Oxford, 1909), II, 198: "Milites quoque Templi . . . quorum fere professio est humanum sanguinem fundere, Non equidem eos viros sanguinum dicam, qui pene soli inter homines legitima gerunt bella." The most recent study of historical sociology on the subject of the Templars and other orders of knights is that of R. Hostie, *Vie et mort des ordres religieux* (Paris, 1972), pp. 105-112; Helen C.R. Laurie, *Two Studies in Chrétien de Troyes* (Geneva, 1972), p. 215, writes: "St. Bernard's ideal of the Knight devoting his life to the crusading movement may not be less relevant for Chrétien [de Troyes] than the practical concern of a John of Salisbury who interprets for a secular society in need of practical renovation the meaning of a committed life. All three impress one as belonging to the same Christian civilization, each striving to influence men in the furtherance of a Kingdom of God on earth."

later write of the years when he had been a young cleric. He was otherwise known to be a great admirer of Bernard and venerated him as a "saint"; but he included in one of his sermons a page which some would interpret as a condemnation of the Templars and a critique of what the abbot of Clairvaux had written about them.[81] If the passage is read in context, we can see that the preacher's purpose was to exhort his audience of monks to moderation, prudence in all things, and a distrust of any thoughtless infatuation with what is "new." There had recently been some innovators in the field of theology and Isaac seems to refer to Abelard without naming him. There had also been innovations on a practical level, such as this "new militia" which was really a "new monstrosity"—that is, something unprecedented—since it aimed to

> . . .force unbelievers into the faith by blows with sword and stick; those who did not bear the name of Christian could be justly deprived of their property, and it was a religious act to kill them. Those who died in this venture of depopulation were called martyrs. . . .How would such behavior compare with the patience of Christ, his gentleness, and his manner of preaching?

This description of the new military orders is closer to the sayings of Hugh of Payns and Peter of Troyes than those of St. Bernard who had carefully avoided mention of spoliation. On the contrary, he had preached voluntary poverty and disinterestedness,[82] and he had merely alluded to martyrdom,[83] whereas Peter of Troyes had further developed the theme.

Be that as it may, Isaac of Stella passed no peremptory judgment on the Templars:

81. Isaac of Stella, *Sermon 48,* PL 194:1853-54. On Isaac's veneration for St Bernard, see G. Raciti, "Isaac de l'Etoile," *Dictionnaire de spiritualité,* VII/2, col. 2018. There are some who have thought—and the idea should not be excluded— that here Isaac has in view, not so much the Templars, as the knights of the Order of Calatrava, approved in 1164 by Alexander III as Cistercian warriors, since they have "made profession in the Order of Citeaux," as has been shown by Joseph F. O'Callaghan, "The Order of Calatrava and the Archbishops of Toledo, 1147-1245," *Studies in Medieval Cistercian History* . . ., pp. 65 and 83.

82. Tpl, 7, *Opera,* 3:220.

83. Tpl, 2, 1, *Opera,* 3:215.

Do we condemn these knights, as well as the scholars mentioned above? We do not condemn one or the other, but neither do we praise them: not that what they do is altogether evil, but because it can become the occasion of evil. It is a wretched fact: nearly all evils have sprung from things that were initially good.

That is the lesson which the preacher wished to inculcate:

My dear friends, we need to exercise great caution and circumspection. . . .When something may be lawfully done, will we not be tempted to do it for mere pleasure?

Here we find again the problem of right intention and the necessary limits inherent in even lawful violence. Isaac agreed with the principles of all those who had broached the subject before him. The little that he did say is enough to make us appreciate the ample spiritual doctrine which St. Bernard had added to that of the moralists; these latter had been content to establish what was permissible and to warn against the temptation of abusing armed force.

3. *The Moslems Threaten the Holy Places*

The Templars had been founded for a time of armed peace. But when the Saracens launched an attack, it was open war and a new army had to be raised. Such was the case when the fortified city of Edessa fell to the Moslems in 1145. This defeat persuaded the prince of Antioch, Raymond of Poitiers, to request aid from Emperor Manuel of Byzantium, and then, in the face of his refusal, from the West in the person of Eugenius III. The latter decided on a crusade and commissioned Louis VII to organize it; he in turn begged the pope's assistance in raising the necessary army. The pontiff and the king held the actual power, but it was Bernard who could speak with authority; he was asked to come to Vézelay and, on the following 31st of March, he was at the king's side when the expedition was announced. He had not taken the initiative in this levy of troops, nor in his own role in the affair. But, with his usual extreme fervor, he devoted himself to the execution of the pope's order and obedience to God: *te iubente, immo per te Deo*, as he would say to Eugenius III. [84] The first task assumed by him was the dispatch of an encyclical in which he explained the theology and morality of the crusade as he conceived it. Since I have already devoted two articles to this document, I will merely summarize relevant portions from these works and others.

In order to situate this encyclical historically, we must study it on several levels. First there is the basic written tradition and the textual criticism. It seems that Bernard suggested various ideas and phrases to his secretary. From these it was possible to reconstruct different texts addressed respectively to princes, prelates, and to all the Christian people, in the East and especially in the West. Each one included those reflections which were valid for all, as well as other useful material which pertained to the specific circumstances in a given country. [85]

Another level is that of literary criticism. Here it seems evident that Bernard succeeded in manipulating the already ancient themes in such a way as to compose a masterpiece which was so beautiful and so original that it was destined to eclipse all the other encyclicals on the subject, both present and future, and even those which emanated from the Holy See. Once again he had given new life to a literary genre. The thoughts which he developed were mainly of a doctrinal nature, and notably christological; they were but an extension of what he had previously written with regard to the Templars. [86]

On the level of political history, Bernard not only was an innovator, he enlarged—doubtless unwittingly—the field of mobilization, and this was, in fact, contrary to the intentions

---

84. Csi, 2, 9, *Opera,* 3:411. On the political and military context—extremely complex! —of Bernard's intervention, there is a good overall view in F. Cognasso, *Storia delle crociate* (1967), pp. 403-470: "La crociata di S. Bernardo."

85. "L'encyclique de S. Bernard sur la seconde croisade," pp. 303-304; and "A propos de l'encyclique de S. Bernard sur la croisade," *Revue bénédictine,* 82 (1972), 312.

86. "Pour l'histoire de l'encyclique de S. Bernard sur la croisade," forthcoming in the *Mélanges offerts à E. R. Labande,* I, III, and IV.

of the pope. Whereas the latter conceived of a venture which would mainly involve the people of France, Bernard wished to engage all of the Christian nations. As a monk, he was under the illusion that he could succeed in uniting princes with divergent interests for the sake of a common cause; instead, they carried their private dissensions with them into the Holy Land, which weakened the forces and led to their defeat.[87]

Finally, on the level of Bernard's attitude toward war—which is our main consideration here—it is noteworthy that, in his encyclical, he merely took what had previously been the teachings of tradition, as well as his own, and applied them to a particular defensive war, but one which had assumed an exceptionally religious character. He did not need to invent the idea of a just war, nor that of a holy war. Anselm of Lucca, writing a short time before, had not envisioned a crusade, but he had laid down its doctrinal foundations; Gregory VII had perhaps considered the practical consequences of these principles. But it was Gregory's second successor, Urban II, who drew on them seven years after Gregory's death when he launched the First Crusade in 1095. In studying the history of justifiable violence, to pass directly from St Augustine to St Bernard without mentioning Anselm of Lucca would be to ignore a decisive link in the chain.[88]

Nevertheless, even while allowing this type of violence, Bernard sought, as he had done all his life, to minimize it and accentuate its relative worth by "personalizing" the military expedition into the Holy Land; more than others, he insisted on the interior conversion which should be at the heart of every departure. He did not confer any sacred character on the fighting itself, for it was already known that this was a "holy" war; but he emphasized the ascetic and expiatory nature of the struggle. He thus created a kind of Crusader mystique, just as he had elaborated the spirituality of the Templar; this aspect of his teaching has been examined a

87. *Ibid.,* part II.
88. As does J. M. Muller, *L'évangile de la non-violence,* pp. 79-80.

number of times.[89] Here again he revealed his monastic bent;
just as a knight of the Temple was—or should be—a soldier-
monk, so Bernard imagined, not without a new element of
illusion, that the Crusader would be a voluntary penitent,
solely preoccupied with his salvation and his eternal hap-
piness. He applied motives inspired by the feudal society to
the service of Christ in the country which belonged to Him;
since Palestine was "His land," His vassals were bound to
come to the aid of their Lord under the banner of the
Cross.[90] The idea that this pilgrimage fraught with risks and
suffering would obtain "indulgences," that is, remission of
sins and the punishment due, was not a new one; Bernard's
only original note was his insistence not on the juridical
value, but on the effects on conversion of the heart.

Among the many arguments used to persuade the noble
knights, and especially the young ones, that they should set
out, Bernard congratulated them on their bravery. Have we
the right to maintain that he "flattered" them, as if to seduce
them with motives that were too human and a bit too
"sympathetic"?[91] Recent works have shown that, during this
period of demographic growth, there were many idle cadets
of families who indulged in fighting or even creating disorder
within the society.[92] The Church had tried to regulate this
bellicose fervor by setting up an organization of knights and
proposing an ideal; this had been largely ineffective.[93]
Bernard knew well all of the generous resources concealed in

89. Y. Congar. "Henri de Marcy, abbé de Clairvaux, cardinal-évêque d'Albano et
légat pontifical," *Analecta Monastica,* 5 (1958; *Studia Anselmiana,* 2nd ed., 43)
77-82; B. Flood, "St Bernard's View of the Crusade"; H. Dörries, *Wort und
Stunde,* (Göttingen, 1967), II, 62-63; P. Rousset, "Les laïcs dans la croisade," pp.
435-43; E. Delaruelle, "L'idée de croisade chez S. Bernard," *Mélanges S. Bernard*
(Dijon, s.d. [1954]), pp. 53-67.
90. On this aspect see B. Flood, "St Bernard's View . . .," p. 133.
91. P. Lorson, "S. Bernard devant la guerre . . .," p. 799. We now know that
Bernard's praise of the Bavarians was really addressed to all the peoples to whom
Bernard appealed; "L'encyclique de S. Bernard," pp. 293-300.
92. Bibliography in "Pour l'historie de l'encyclique," p. 2.
93. P. Rousset, "S. Bernard et l'esprit chevaleresque, *Nova et vetera,* 45 (1970),
28-29.

such effervescent youth.[94] For those who did not enter the "army of Christ" which was monasticism, he suggested another way of devoting oneself to the service of the Lord: among the Templars, and then among the crusaders.[95] In the one case in which he wrote a letter of recommendation on behalf of a young nobleman who wished to be armed as a knight, he advanced two qualifications: this son of the count of Champagne was to be ready to fight "against the enemies of the Cross of Christ" and to submit himself to the "dignity of military discipline." [96] Once again, this episode reveals the prime importance of intention and an insistance on that ascetism and self-control which would permit one to use force only within the limits fixed by moral law.

Finally, we can ask to what extent Bernard was concerned with the conversion of the Moslems. This is an immense problem; in order to resolve it, we would need to examine the whole mystery of the "salvation of the infidels" as it is laid down in his doctrine.[97] There have been attempts to excuse Bernard's lack of "missionary spirit" based on his ignorance, and that of his contemporaries, with regard to non-Christian peoples and all those who were situated on the fringe of the little Mediterranean and European world which was familiar to them.[98] And there is some truth in this explanation; research into the geography and cartography of the twelfth century would confirm this point of view.[99] However, during

94. "Le rôle des jeunes d'après S. Bernard," *Vie religieuse et vie contemplative* (Gembloux, Paris, 1969), pp. 40-52.

95. See A. Dimier, *S. Bernard, pêcheur de Dieu* (Paris, 1953), pp. 62-63; p. Rousset, "S. Bernard et l'esprit chevaleresque," pp. 32-33.

96. Ep 468, PL 182:672-73.

97. The subject has been treated at length in the voluminous dissertation of P. Derumaux cited above, n. 65, a summary of which has appeared under the title "S. Bernard et les infidèles," *Mélanges S. Bernard*, pp. 68-79.

98. J. Lecler, "S. Bernard, le prophète de la chrétienté," *Etudes*, 277 (1953), 297-98.

99. "Monastic Historiography . . ." cited above (n. 5), p. 67. A map of the world—*Mappa Mundi*—contemporary with St. Bernard's youth (it dates from 1109-1110) and coming from the Benedictine monastery of Thorney in England—is reproduced in R. W. Southern, *Western Society and the Church in the Middle Ages (Pelican History of the Church*, 2; Harmondsworth, Baltimore: Penguin, 1970), pl. III. All of Africa is pushed into a corner south of Europe, and Asia

this same period, a man like Peter the Venerable took the trouble to "invite" the Moslems to salvation—yet surely not without some self-deception.[100] On this point Bernard seems to have been more realistic. He saw the situation as it was. In his encyclical on the Crusade, after advising that the conversion of the Jews should be patiently awaited, since they were subject to Christian princes in the West and could not stand as obstacles, he added:

> If the Gentiles were similarly subject, I would say that we should be patient with them also rather than pursue them with swords. But since they have instigated acts of violence against us, those who rightfully bear the sword [that is, in the language of Paul, the princes] are obliged to drive back their forces. (*Cum in nos coeperint esse violenti, oportet vim repellere. . . .*)

Therefore, this required an army which would not "submit to their violence"— *violentiam sustinere.*[101] The words are clear and consistent with Bernard's teachings in all other circumstances: never instigate the violence, but when others have taken the initiative, use it in self-defense. This did not preclude the possibility of leading the adversaries to the Christian faith when circumstances permitted.

In speaking of the Crusade, we could also pose the question of Bernard's attitude toward the Christian "schismatics" of the East. In 1149 and 1150, after the failure of the military expedition into the Holy Land, he accepted a project which had already been germinating in certain minds, an attack on

---

Minor is in the extreme north and less wide than the Bosporus. Already in 1145 Otto of Freising related that a bishop, Hugh of Jabala, brought back to Europe from the Holy Land a legend of a vast Christian state in cental Asia ruled by a certain Prester John. It was only some years later that a letter attributed to Prester John and addressed to the emperor at Constantinople began to circulate in the West. The aim of this letter may have been to urge people to set out on a crusade. But the description it gives of the unknown kingdom leaves too much room for the marvellous to have contributed to a better knowledge of Asia. The problems raised by this letter and its consequences have been studied by Robert Silverberg, *The Realm of Prester John* (Gardon City, New York, 1971).

100. "Pierre le Vénérable, L'invitation au salut," *Témoins de la spiritualité occidentale* (Paris, 1965), pp. 245-62.

101. "L'encyclique de S. Bernard," p. 299.

Constantinople by the Western forces (the idea was eventually thwarted by the divisions among the princes).[102] However, it was a matter of conquering them, not as schismatics, but as the political adversaries of the Crusaders. Bernard recognized that their political separation from Rome constituted a violent situation, an absence of peace—*iuncti fide, pace divisi.* He reminded Eugenius III of his responsibility as universal pastor.[103] Bernard desired reconciliation.[104] Once again, in this area, Christian politics prevented the realization of the evangelical ideal.

This whole survey of the mentality of the times explains the attitude adopted by Bernard in this Second Crusade. Are these facts sufficient justification? In the eyes of one who would judge from a distance of several centuries, were not Bernard's actions imprudent? His true weakness was not his religious motivation, but his lack of information and political realism.

> The modern historian can do no more than point out the fervor with which this great relgious leader used his tremendous moral influence to send armies to their deaths (whether from sickness or from combat).[105]

Bernard himself was perhaps aware of his error in tactics, if not his fault; he did feel the need to justify himself.[106] At any

102. Ep 380, PL 182:583-84; Dérumaux, *S. Bernard et les infidèles* [diss.], pp. 433-36.

103. Csi 3, 4, *Opera*, 3:433-34.

104. L. Grill, "Bernard von Clairvaux und die Ostkirche," *Analecta Sacri Ordinis Cisterciensis*, 19 (1963), 165-88; B. Flood, "St Bernard's View . . .," p. 142, n. 77, has indicated certain texts which show that the hostility of the western Christians, which continued from the time of the First Crusade, increased because of the fact that they were considered responsible for the failure of the Second.

105. M. D. Knowles, *Nouvelle histoire de l'Eglise*, II, *Le moyen âge* (Paris, 1968), p. 263.

106. Csi II, 1-4, *Opera*, 3:410-13. On Bernard's reaction to the failure of the Crusade, see Giles Constable, "A Report of a Lost Sermon by St Bernard on the Failure of the Second Crusade," *Studies in Medieval Cistercian History . . .*, pp. 49-54. The author shows that for Bernard the Crusade was as much an occasion for personal and moral improvement as for political victory. We have already seen (n. 71) that a victory could be "unhappy"; in the same way a defeat could be the occasion of spiritual benefit because of the repentance and humiliation to which it gave rise (Constable, p. 52).

rate, he suffered reproaches for it which entailed some practical consequences for him and his community; not only did people stop making generous donations to the monastery of Clairvaux, but some even demanded the restitution of lands which they had previously offered.[107] He said nothing about this. The only suffering which he expressed in his "Apologia"[108] was the awareness that a military enterprise conceived by the pope and by himself, directed against the enemies of Christ, had turned into a fight among Christians. In deploring the situation—for we have seen that he always did his utmost to avoid it—he remained consistent with a conviction which had continually animated his life.

CONCLUSIONS

Limitations of a Saint Engaged in Politics

When, with a view toward writing this account, I re-examined the dossier of sources and bibliography which pertained to Bernard's attitude toward war, I was prepared to admit that there were contradictions in him, in his behavior, in his ideas. And, after all, these would only have served to make him more human and closer to the majority of us. And yet, at the end of my investigation, Bernard appeared consistent; fundamentally he was a man of peace. During the last nine years of his life, he found himself involved, without having sought to be, in two wars undertaken against non-Christians, the Wends, and the Moslems of the Holy Land. And in these circumstances as before, he knew that violence was a fact of life whose total abolition was not within his power; thus he tried to establish certain limits by imposing conditions as to its use and motivation.

However, these general conclusions invite certain complementary considerations, no longer with a view toward understanding Bernard's attitude, but for the purpose of forming a

107. "St. Bernard and the Contemplative Community," p. 73.
108. *Apologia super consumptionem Icrosolymitarum:* this is the title at the beginning of c. II of Csi, *Opera,* 3:410.

critical judgment. In the first place, in these texts on the subject of war as in all the rest—his critique of Cluny or Abelard's trial—we must allow for his use of rhetoric; it usually involved a certain amount of exaggeration which would not have deceived his contemporaries. We should read these works intelligently and admire them for what their style and teachings are worth. Their beauty and human depth account for the fact that they have outlived in the memories of generations so many other documents—papal encyclicals, canonical tracts—which only today's scholars have redeemed from oblivion; here too we can catch a glimpse of ideas like Bernard's, and sometimes they are expressed with greater precision and moderation. But they lack the tone, the fervor which characterized all that he said and which touched the human heart. He was the one who promulgated the ideas that Anselm of Lucca had expressed before him. Unless we are specialists in medieval studies, we can be forgiven for our knowledge of Bernard's texts and our lack of familiarity with the author of the *Liber canonum*, as well as Peter of Troyes and Hugh of Payns. It is less excusable for us to quote a few phrases from these texts and attempt to isolate them from the historical, psychological, and literary context which gives them meaning and determines their impact. Bernard himself dealt only with the essentials; there are nuances, but he does not present all of the traditional justifications which would have supported his assertions. What Anselm of Lucca had developed in three books, one of which contained no less than twenty-nine chapters, Bernard summarized in a few pages. By this very fact, he was transmitting it to posterity. Just as his *Praise of the New Militia* remained relevant even after the supression of the Templars—one could always draw from it a teaching on Christian death and the mysteries of salvation—so his encyclical on the Second Crusade was continually copied, translated, and meditated on long after the last Crusade.

Then too, in order to appreciate Bernard's texts, it is necessary to recall the circumstances in which they were composed:

They were partially written at a moment of collective, and perhaps individual, psychosis: when preparations for the Crusade were in full swing. Their aim was propaganda—almost publicity.[109]

The violent society of his time in which everything—even violence—was "sacralized," accepted a violent writing style; in fact, it was necessary.

Furthermore, Bernard could not refrain from being himself. This man of the Church was steeped in the monastic way of life.[110] He projected onto the whole Christian order the idea and image which he held of his own Cistercian life. He preferred religious life to the profession of arms; he conceived of war, when it was unavoidable, as an exercise in asceticism. In his service to the causes which he adopted, he employed all of the natural gifts that he had received. He could thus become the first victim of his style and his eloquence, his fervor and his charm.[111] There was in him, alongside a capacity for intransigence, a need to be cordial. Thus, in the area of doctrine, and especially with regard to Abelard and Peter the Venerable, he could sometimes prove to be violent. But even then, he aimed at friendships; he sought a personal encounter with his adversaries with a view toward reconciliation.

Finally, we would be guilty of an error in perspective if we judged Bernard's attitude toward war solely according to his treatise on the Templars or his intervention in the Crusade; the latter was merely one episode in his life, as it was in the history of the eleventh and twelfth centuries. It marked the occasion for a practical manifestation of two realities which were already deep and permanent: a great desire for peace on the part of churchmen, and their vivid awareness of their inability to abolish violence. They aspired to the ideal of a just and tranquil society, without yielding to a utopian idealism. Their attitude was one of Christian realism, which

109. P. Lorson, "S. Bernard devant la guerre . . .," p. 800.

110. See Y. Congar, "L'ecclésiologie de S. Bernard," *Saint Bernard théologien* (*Analecta Sacri Ordinis Cisterciensis*, 9 [1953], fasc. 3-4; 2nd ed., Rome, 1955), pp. 177-81.

111. *S. Bernard et l'esprit cistercien* (*Collection "Maîtres spirituels,"* 36; Paris, 1966), pp. 59-63.

acknowledges the existence of sin but is not resigned to it; it seeks to change the heart of man, stimulate his conversion, even when the "institutions of peace" admit their ineffectiveness. Bernard did not seem particularly interested in the "truce of God." It was not in this area that he wished to act. Nor did he situate himself outside of the normal living conditions of his time; he stood to one side, on the fringe, even at a slight distance, but without being so aloof that he could no longer intervene. Monasticism for him was not the equivalent of a "counter-culture" but a milieu which was capable of exercising a moderating influence; we have as proof his own actions and the counsel he offered to other monks and abbots in cases of local or national conflicts.[112]

Did he always know how to find the most appropriate means to an end? He experienced the difficulty of being torn between the exigencies of the Gospel and the cultural factors within his society which established certain restrictions. At times, a combination of violence and non-violence existed in him, but he always accorded preference to the latter. He was marked by the mentality of his time. We can rightly contest his political sense, but we cannot refuse him the merit of having retained a genuine concern for individuals, a gift of patience, and a great respect for the possible evolution of his adversaries and an eventual reconciliation with them. His correspondence bears witness to the tremendous network of friendly relations that he had woven. In this particular century—whatever may have been the case in other periods of history—there was no pure political theory, that is, one which could not be compromised according to the culture and given circumstances. Bernard accepted the risks which are always present for one who is committed to an idea. But at the same time, he taught that such risks should be run with moderation, such positions held with caution. His writings on the subject of war reveal both the religious ideal of the man of God and his limitations in the field of politics.

112. For example in Ep 80, PL 182:201-202, where he recommends that the abbot of Molesmes deal with malefactors according to this counsel given in the *Rule* of St Benedict and inspired by the Epistle of St. James (2:13): "Let mercy prevail over justice."

RHETORIC AND STYLE IN THE
DE CONSIDERATIONE

ELIZABETH T. KENNAN

The Catholic University of America

ST BERNARD WAS A POET as well as a theologian and a politician. The superb polish of his language, sermons which scan, letters that persuade with figures, arguments that proceed by antithesis or sentences interlocked by chiasmus bedazzle the reader. But it is especially when one approaches St Bernard as a translator that one bows—indeed almost quails—before his rhetorical power.

St Bernard's rhetoric bedevils the translator because so much of the appeal and power of his argument comes from the relationship of the Latin words he employs: from their rhythm or their rhyme or their resemblance as cognates. To preserve that power in English is almost impossible. Even more difficult, however, is to render words which he seems to have compounded himself to fit the rhetorical rather than the logical demands of his passage. When in the first book of the *De consideratione*, for example, he speaks of the papal responsibility personally to judge some of the lawsuits pending before the Curia, he urges Eugene, "diligenter sed breviter decidere . . . frustratorias et venatorias praecidere dilationes."[1] The Latin is felicitous; the English is problematical. Eugene should avoid delays in court which are vain and which—remind one of the hunt? "Venatorias" was clearly chosen or compounded to complement "frustratorias" in scansion and assonance. But the exact meaning of the word is elusive; Bernard seems to have been the only Latin writer to

1. Csi, 1, 13, *Opera* 3:408.

40

have used it. It comes, of course, from "venator," or "hunter," and may most appropriately evoke a tableau of hunting with traps or snares and so, by extension, cunning or contrivance. But this is only supposition; we can never exactly know what associations Bernard intended to imply.

Fortunately for the translator's peace of mind, it is seldom that St Bernard resorts to such unusual language to balance a phrase. Occasionally, literal meaning is stretched when a word is chosen for scansion or sound, values which simply cannot be rendered in the English. But in most cases a derivative sense is fairly apparent. The only loss is in elegance or force of statement.

But there is another situation in which the loss of the rhetorical setting is serious. Even within a single treatise like the *De consideratione*, St Bernard constantly modulates his language to reflect the cast of his argument or the subject of his exposition. His most highly wrought passages, for example, occur when he is speaking of matters fraught with majesty. Although he certainly uses rhetorical devices when arguing or urging a point, still the most densely rhetorical section of the *De consideratione* occurs in the fifth book when he discusses his vision of God and the heavenly hierarchy. When he tells of the ranks and the functions of the spiritual powers, Bernard plays on his language almost like an organ. Epanaphora provides a constantly repeated base note: "cernere est, cernere est" or "putemus, putemus." Within each sentence or group of phrases, repetitions and variations of sound, be they assonance, parachesis, or paronomasia, provide a kind of lyric. Repetition of individual words, anadiplosis, forms an obligato. A truncated passage may give you some idea of the technique. Bernard is describing the characteristics and functions of the spirits within the hierarchy:

> Cernere est in his, qui Seraphim appellantur, quomodo amet qui unde amet non habet. . . . Cernere est in Cherubim, qui plenitudo scientiae dicuntur, Deum scientiarum dominus esse, qui solum solam nesciat ignorantiam . . . . Cernere est in Thronis. . . . qui circumvenire nolit, circumveniri non possit . . . cui insit amor, error absit, absit et perturbatio. . . .²

2. Csi, 5, 10, *Opera* 3:474.

There is epanaphora with the "cernere est"; anadiplosis with "amet:" anastrophe with "absit"; polyptoton with "scientiae" and "scientiarum"; paronomasia with "insit" and "absit," "scientia," and "nesciat"; assonance with "amet" and "habet." Cognates and interlocking sounds are never allowed to cross the logical structure. There is an interlocking framework for each grade in the hierarchy which both unifies the logic and emphasizes the uniqueness of each subject under discussion. Loss of these unities in translation is serious.

Recognizing the almost baroque ornamentation employed to describe heaven, one is somewhat shocked to discover the stark economy of language Bernard uses to present the Trinity in the same book. The discussion was apparently provoked by questions Gilbert Porreta had raised about the relationship of the Trinity to some separate essence called "divinity."[3] St Bernard was anxious to reaffirm traditional conceptions. Yet by reopening the matter which had already been dealt with at the Council of Reims in a widely circulated letter, Bernard risked criticism for daring to discuss the ultimate Christian mysteries in a public forum; a charge which he had laid against Peter Abelard earlier with singular venom.[4]

Whether or not concern on this score made him stylistically cautious we will never know, but it is nonetheless striking that he took great care to express himself with the utmost solemnity. He achieved that solemnity by rhetoric, but a rhetoric which simplifies, almost liquefies the prose. Sentences are short, almost staccato in their lack of subordinate clauses. The language is higly repetitious both of words and of sound:

> Non est formatus Deus: forma est. Non est affectus Deus: affectio est. Non est compositus Deus: merum simplex est. . . .Trinitas est tamen Deus. Quid ergo? Destruimus quod dictum est de unitate, quia inducimus trinitatem? Non; sed statuimus unitatem. Dicimus Patrem, dicimus Filium, dicimus Spiritum Sanctum, non tamen tres Deos,

---

3. Nicholas M. Häring, "Notes on the Council and Consistory of Rheims," *Medieval Studies*, 28 (1966), 39-59.
4. Ep 188, PL 182:1-354.

sed unum. Quid sibi vult iste, ut sic loquar, absque numero, numerus? . . . quid numerasti? Naturas? Una est.
Essentias? Una est. Substantias? Una est. Deitates? Una
est.[5]

Grammatical parallels underline logical parallels. The language is full of anadiplosis. When individual words are not
repeated, their sounds are. The total effect is hymnodic, giving
a prayerful quality to statements which might otherwise seem
simple assertions. The language professes the author's awe
and humility in such a way that he does not need to state
them outright. The translator is hard pressed not to lose that
sense of the language.

It is much simpler for a translator to catch Bernard's intention when he is expressing awe of some earthly majesty. His
technique when glorifying the pope or praising an extraordinary legate is not nearly so subtle. He usually builds an extended catalog of powers or virtues consisting of a series of
short parallel clauses moving to a logical if not a linguistic
climax. The mighty invocation with which he opens his discussion of the papal office, "You are the prince of the
bishops, you are the heir of the Apostles," is the finest and
most famous of these passages. But it is only one of many in
the *De consideratione*. There are moments, indeed, when
Bernard amplifies to the point of danger. He closes his treatment of the papal office, for example, with a sequence which
almost exhausts the listener:

> For the rest, consider that you ought to be a model of
> justice, a mirror of holiness, and exemplar of piety, a
> preacher of truth, a defender of the faith, the teacher of
> the nations, the leader of Christians, a friend of the Bride-
> groom and attendant of the Bride, the director of the
> clergy, the shepherd of the people, the instructor of the
> foolish, the refuge of the oppressed, the advocate of the
> poor, the hope of the unfortunate, the protector of
> orphans, the judge of widows, the eye of the blind, the
> tongue of the mute, the support of the aged, the avenger
> of crimes, the terror of evil men, the glory of the good,

5. Csi, 5, 17, *Opera.* 3:480-81.

the staff of the powerful, the hammer of tyrants, the father of kings, the moderator of laws, the dispenser of canons, the salt of the earth, the light of the world, a priest of the Most High, the vicar of Christ, the anointed of the Lord and, finally, the god of Pharoah.[6]

Although the papal office is Bernard's favorite subject for cataloging, he can use the device to exalt or condemn any group. Good legates come in for an extended list of virtues.[7] The sins of the Romans are visited on them in a short but pungent variation on the series:

Before all they are wise to do evil, but they do not know how to do good. They are detested on earth and in heaven, they are hostile toward both; irreverent toward God, disrespectful toward holy things, quarrelsome among themselves, envious of their neighbors, discourteous to strangers. Loving no one, no one loves them, and since they strive to be feared by everyone, they must fear everyone.[8]

The technique of the climaxing catalog in Bernard's hands has extreme power. But it cannot be used too frequently at the risk of wearying the reader. For most of the *De consideratione* the traditional devices of rhetoric are used, repetition of words or sounds, balancing or chiastic structures, simple amplification, and so on. It would be tedious to try to enumerate them here, but it is impossible to pass on without a few examples of Bernard's virtuosity.

6. "De cetero oportere te esse considera formam iustitiae, sanctimoniae speculum, pietatis exemplar, assertorem veritatis, fidei defensorem, doctorem gentium, christianorum ducem, amicum sponsi, sponsae paranymphum, cleri ordinatorem, pastorem plebium, magistrum insipientium, refugium oppressorum, pauperum advocatum, miserorum spem, tutorem pupillorum, iudicem viduarum, oculum caecorum, linguam mutorum, baculum senum, ultorem scelerum, malorum metum, bonorum gloriam, virgam potentium, malleum tyrannorum, regum patrem, legum moderatorem, canonum dispensatorem, sal terrae, orbis lumen, sacerdotem Altissimi, vicarium Christi, christum Domini, postremo deum Pharaonis." Csi, 4, 23, *Opera* 3:466.
7. Csi, 4, 12, *Opera* 3:457.
8. "Ante omnia sapientes sunt ut faciant mala, bonum autem facere nesciunt. Hi invisi terrae et caelo, utrique iniecere manus, impii in Deum, temerarii in sancta, seditiosi in invicem, aemuli in vicinos, inhumani in extraneos, quos neminem amantes amat nemo, et, cum timeri affectant ab omnibus, omnes timeant necesse est." Csi, 4, 4, *Opera* 3:452.

When verbally flagellating the ambitious lawyers who crowded the Curia, Bernard packed six variations on the root *struere* into a single sentence:

His sunt qui instruunt a quibus fuerant instruendi, adstruunt non comperta, sed sua, struunt de proprio calumnias innocentiae, destruunt simplicitatem veritatis, obstruunt iudicii vias.[9]

The Latin defies duplication. We have had to be satisfied with the far more mundane logical sense of the sentence:

These are men who instruct those by whom they should have been taught, who introduce not facts but their own fabrications, who heap up calumny of their own invention against innocent people, who destroy the simplicity of truth, who obstruct the ways of justice.

When discussing the competence of the papal court, Bernard makes a distinction between spiritual and civil cases. As a general rule, he insists that ecclesiastical courts confine themselves to spiritual matters. To make his point, he asks in a sentence of arresting rhetorical power:

Quanam tibi maior videtur et dignitas et potestas, dimittendi peccata an praedia dividendi?[10]

The last phrase, with its two alliterative nouns surrounded by assonant participles, compels attention and forces comparison of its two elements. Yet Bernard follows it with the clipped phrase, "Sed non est comparatio." In English, one can take the sequence only at face value:

Tell me, which seems to you the greater honor and greater power: to forgive sins or to divide estates? But there is no comparison.

In the Latin, however, the last sentence has the full force of irony since the comparison has already been made in the language of the previous sentence, if not in its logic.

9. *Opera* 3:408.
10. *Opera* 3:402.

In his sermons, St Bernard makes rich use of rhetorical figures. In the *De consideratione* he is somewhat more restrained. He uses the common metaphors freely, of course; the bishop as shepherd or steward or friend of the Bridegroom. But he economizes in the use of extended metaphor with the result that the images he does evoke have added impact. They often create a visual dimension of great freshness in the midst of an otherwise tense argument. When, for example, he is persuading Eugene to consider himself apart from his office, to face his nature as man and not as official, he combines litotes with metaphor in a delicate passage:

> Were you born wearing the mitre? Were you born glittering with jewels or florid with silk or crowned with feathers, or covered with precious metals? If you scatter all these things and blow them away from the face of your consideration like the morning clouds which quickly pass and rapidly disappear, you will catch sight of a naked man who is poor, wretched, and miserable.[11]

When asserting the definition of papal office as a trusteeship, Bernard asks:

> Does your throne flatter you? It is a watchtower; from it you oversee everything, exercising not dominion but ministry through the office of your episcopacy. Why should you not be placed on high where you can see everything, you who have been appointed watchman over all? In fact, this prospect calls not for leisure but readiness for war.[12]

Figurative rhetoric in the *De consideratione* can both relieve tension and heighten the persuasiveness of an argument. But

---

11. "Numquid infulatus? Numquid micans gemmis, aut floridus sericis, aut coronatus pennis, aut suffarcinatus metallis? Se cuncta haec, veluti nubes quasdam matutines, velociter transeuntes et cito pertransituras, dessipes et exsuffles a facie considerationis tuae, occurret tibi homo nudus, et pauper, et miser, et miserabilis." Csi, 2, 18, *Opera* 3:425-26.

12. "Blanditur cathedra? Specula est. Inde denique superintendis, sonans tibi episcopi nomine non dominium, sed officium. Quidni loceris in eminenti, unde prospectes omnia, qui speculator super omnia constitueris? " Csi, 2, 10, *Opera* 3:417.

the device of antithesis, of which Bernard was master, can both climax an argument and provide a framework for it. In its simplest form, antithesis catches the reader's attention and forces home a point. When warning Eugene against flatterers, for example, Bernard observes that petitioners should

> be put in the same class as the man who flatters and speaks so as to please everyone, even if he asks for nothing. It is not the face of the scorpion that you should fear; he stings with his tail! [13]

Again, when discussing the misuse made of appeals, he notes:

> Appeal is permitted not when you want to injure others, but when you are injured. ....Appeal is not a subterfuge but a refuge! " [But now] appeals are made beyond what is just and right, contrary to custom and order. No account is taken of place, means, time, cause or person.....The antidote has been turned into poison! [14]

Used with great subtlety, antithesis can condense into a single phrase an intricate position on papal government. The *De consideratione* is famous for its elliptical arguments in this genre. The first of them occurs at the very outset of the treatise. Bernard rails against the prevailing conditions at the Curia where disputes over civil and territorial claims had been allowed to engulf every other activity. The saint's scorn for this situation is caught in a single phrase:

> Oh yes, every day laws resound through the palace, but they are the laws of Justinian, not of the Lord.[15]

In Rome, bribery had crept into the very fabric of the papal court. Rather than fulminate against an obvious abuse, Bernard impaled it on an antithesis:

13. "Adulantem et ad placitum cuiusque loquentem, unum de rogantibus puta, etiamsi nihil rogaverit. Scorpioni non est in facie quod formides, sed pungit a cauda." Csi, 4, 9, *Opera* 3:455.

14. "Appellare, non ut graves, sed si graveris, licet. . . . Non est autem suffugium appellatio, sed refugium. . . . Praeter vis et fas, praeter morem et ordinem fiunt. Non locus, non modus, non tempus, non causa discernitur aut persona. . . . Antidotum versum in venenum." Csi, 3, 7, *Opera* 3:436.

15. "Et quidem quotidie perstrepunt in palatio leges, sed Iustiniani, non Domini." Csi, 1, 5, *Opera* 3:399.

> Few look to the mouth of the lawgiver, all look to his
> hands. But not without reason: they carry out all the
> papal business.[16]

When antithesis is extended through a whole argument it
gives powerful scope for irony and for dramatic heightening
of conclusions. Bernard uses it to achieve these effects in a
scalding critique of contemporary bishops:

> Bishops have more than enough people on hand to whom
> they can entrust souls, but they find no one to whom
> they can commit their paltry possessions: obviously they
> have made the best evaluation of the situation—they have
> great concern for the least matters, little or no concern
> for the greatest. . . .Each day we carefully review the ex-
> penses of the day, but are unaware of the continual losses
> of the Lord's flock. There is a daily dispute with the
> servants concerning the price of food and the number of
> loaves of bread; rarely indeed is a meeting convened with
> the priests concerning the people's sins. An ass falls and
> there is someone to raise her up; a soul perishes and there
> is no one who gives it a thought.[17]

Antithesis survives translation, so does figure. But in many of
the rhetorical structures outlined here the *De consideratione*
is untranslatable. In this sense, the translator owes an apology
to St Bernard.

---

16. "Pauci ad os legislatoria, ad manus omnes respiciunt. Non immerito tamen:
omne papale negotium illae agunt." Csi, 4, 4, *Opera* 3:451.
17. "Satis superque episcopi ad manum habent, quibus animas credant; et cui
suas committant facultatulas, non inveniunt: optimi videlicet aestimatores rerum,
qui magnam de minimis, parvam aut nullam de maximis curam gerant. . . .
Quotidianas expensas quotidiano reciprocamus scrutinio, et continua dominici
gregis detrimenta nescimus. De pretio escarum et numero panum cum ministris
quotidiana lis est; rara admodum cum presbyteris celebratur collatio de peccatis
populorum. Cadit asina, et est qui sublevet eam; perit anima, et nemo qui
reputet." Csi, 40, 20, *Opera* 3:463-64.

THE MONASTIC LIFE ACCORDING TO
SAINT BERNARD

BEDE K. LACKNER, O CIST

University of Texas in Arlington

THE IMPOSING LITERARY LEGACY of St Bernard of Clairvaux has inspired numerous studies, scholarly as well as popular writings; this paper seeks to outline the basic ideas of the *doctor mellifluus* on the monastic life, a subject hardly explored thus far. Reasons for such an undertaking are therefore abundant; not least among them is the desire, very apropos today, to gain a better understanding of the early Cistercian ideals which certainly shaped Bernard's thinking.

Bernard decided early in life that to save his soul in a world filled with dangers and with insufficient protection against temptations, he must become a monk. But he did not join one of the new reform orders or even Cluny, then still *in floribus*. Feeling that he was a carnal man surrounded by the realities of sin and convinced that his soul needed a stronger medicine, he came to the conclusion that he must leave the world unreservedly.[1] Accordingly his choice fell on the re-

---

1. "Different remedies are prescribed for different illnesses; the more serious the illness, the more drastic the remedy." Apo IV, 7, PL 182:903, *Opera* 3:87. For an English translation of this treatise see *Apologia to Abbot William (The Works of Bernard of Clairvaux,* I; *Treatises* I; CF 1; Spencer, Massachusetts, 1970), pp. 33-69, esp. p. 42. This work will hereafter be cited *An Apologia.* Early Cîteaux was succinctly described in *Sancti Bernardi vita prima auctore Guillelmo olim Sancti Theodorici abbate,* III, 7 and IV, 19, PL 185: 231 and 237f. See also *St Bernard of Clairvaux: The Story of His Life as Recorded in the Vita Prima by Certain of His Contemporaries* (trans. Geoffrey Webb and Adrian Walker; Westminster, Maryland, 1960), pp. 34 and 37. This work will hereafter be cited *Life.*

49

cently founded New Monastery (Cîteaux) which practiced apostolic poverty and led a stricter, holier, and more secluded life than other monasteries. It assured effective remedies against human pride and, shielded from the sight of men, it offered safety, recollection, and peace under the yoke of Christ. While praising other religious institutes as holy and legitimate,[2] Bernard opted for the Cistercian ideal as the only one open to him and expedient. As he said, "I am attached to all the orders by love, but it is in one alone that I find my work."[3]

Motivating his resolve was, one may safely assume, his dissatisfaction with the Cluniac way of life, based on less than authentic usages, and his preference for cenobitic monachism at a time when contemporary reforms tended to stress eastern eremitic principles.[4]

For St Bernard's views on "conversion" see Anselme Dimier and Bede Lackner (trans.), "Der hl. Bernhard und die 'Conversio,'" *Anima*, 8 (1953), 66-72. According to some authorities, Bernard entered Cîteaux because he knew some of its members and because the New Monastery was noted for its Marian devotion. Jean Marilier, "La vocation," *Bernard de Clairvaux*, (Paris, 1953), pp. 29-37.

2. "It may equally be asked why I do not join all orders since I praise them all. For it is a fact that I do praise them all and love any that live good and virtuous lives in the Church," Apo IV, 8, PL 182:905, *Opera* 3:88, *An Apologia*, p. 43. "I am a Cistercian myself, but this does not mean that I reject the Cluniacs. On the contrary, I am very fond of them; I praise and extol them." *Ibid.* "I ought not pass over those holy men who, being dead to the world, lead a better life to God alone; their life is hidden with Christ in glory, where they zealously seek and, doubtless, find what is the pleasure of God, and their only care is to please him." These are "the Camaldolese, Vallombrosians, Carthusians, Cluniacs, the brethren of Marmoutier . . . the brethren of Caen, Tiron and Savigny." Ep 126, 10, PL 182:278. English translation by Bruno Scott James, *The Letters of St Bernard of Clairvaux* (Chicago, 1953); hereafter cited *Letters*. For Letter 126, see p. 197.

3. Apo IV, 8, PL 182:905, *Opera* 3:88; *An Apologia*, p. 43. Elsewhere Bernard added, "You might ask why don't you join them [the Cluniacs] if you think so highly of them? My reply is this: because, as the apostle says, 'Everyone should remain in the vocation in which he was called.' " Apo IV, 7, PL 182:905, *Opera* 3:87, *An Apologia*, p. 42.

4. For more on the subject, see Bede K. Lackner, *The Eleventh-Century Background of Cîteaux* (CS 8; Spencer, Massachusetts, 1972), chapters II and VI, and Jean Leclercq, "L'eremitisme et les Cisterciens," *L'Eremitismo in Occidente nei secoli XI e XII (Miscellanea del Centro di Studi Medioevali*, IV; Milano, 1965), pp. 573-76. In Pre XVI, 46, Bernard himself noted the polarity between the Cluniac *instituta* and *consuetudines* and the Cistercian ideal of *paupertas* and *Regulae puritas*; PL 182:886, *Opera* 3:285. English translation, *On Precept and Dispensation*, in CF 1, pp. 105-150. Hereafter cited *On Precept*.

Eremitic life, of course, had its attractions. In Bernard's description, the solitary ate only once a day, avoided all conversation with women, and supported himself by the work of his own hands.[5] Such abnegation and frugality and the resultant freedom to devote more time to prayer than in a monastery offered undeniable advantages: in the absence of riches, of human crowds or worldly concerns, and secular recreations, the "desert" was apt to silence carnal desires and material interests and thus frustrate the designs of the devil.[6] But Bernard also realized that one's spiritual life was not necessarily safer in the "desert," for if the solitary yielded to weakness the "desert" would by its very nature conceal such wrongdoings and keep them from others. Thus no one will challenge an evil act since it has not witnesses. In the absence of warnings and corrective remedies the tempter, who has the advantage of seeing his victim while he himself remains invisible, will grow bolder and evil is liable to happen more frequently. It is indeed a fact that a great many generous souls who had become solitaries had failed the test; they were disowned by the "desert" and rejected as strangers since they had lost their fervor. And even if they had chosen to remain solitaries, they violated the law of the "desert" which abhors dissolute, that is, incompatible, elements.[7]

In view of such very real hazards, Bernard sought stronger and safer weapons: the company of experienced warriors. In

---

5. Ep 404, PL 182:616. According to J. Leclerq, Bernard encouraged Albert, the addressee of this letter, to persevere in his vocation even though he did not counsel Albert to become a solitary. *L'Eremitismo in Occidente*, p. 575.

6. PP I, 5, PL 183:408, *Opera* 5:191. In Bernard's description, advocates of the desert felt they must "flee from riches, crowded towns, and delicate meats." They said to themselves, "modesty is safer in the desert where I can live in peace with a few others or quite alone, so as to please him alone to whom I have pledged myself." Ep 115, 1, PL 182:261, *Letters*, p. 179.

7. "If you, a little sheep, penetrate the shadows of the wood alone, you are offering yourself as a prey to the wolf." Ep 115, 2, PL 182:262, *Letters*, p. 180. See also Circ III, 6, PL 183:138f., *Opera* 4:287, and SC LXIV, 4, PL 183:1085, *Opera* 2:168. J. Leclercq therefore concludes, "Instead of recognizing the possible advantages of eremitism, Bernard ascribes nothing but dangers and inconveniences to it. He one-sidedly insists on the conditions laid down by the author of the *Rule* of St Benedict for passing to a hermitage, without adding the praises voiced by the same author for the anchorites." *L'Eremitismo in Occidente*, p. 575.

a cenobitic monastery, he reasoned, one can easily discover the will of God. Also, by the very nature of community life and the laws of human association the brethren have an obligation to give mutual assistance to each other. Thus, taught by his commilitants, the monk will learn how to be beneficial to others: no one will hinder him in his pursuit of perfection and the performance of good works. Also, a good example will impress others and inspire them to similar actions. On the other hand, the monk will not find it easy to give in to evil even if he were tempted to do so. For as soon as the brethren notice his predicament they will approach him, reason with him, and, ultimately, cause him to remain steadfast.[8]

Like the hermit, the cenobite must completely break with the world. To join a monastery involves struggles and major sacrifices. The monk already has won one important battle: he has renounced the whole world with all its blessings—family ties, kinship, and legitimate joys—and has evaded the snares of the devil by locking himself into the confinement of the monastery where he has surrendered his own will to the rule of other men.[9]

Thus he is free from the multitudinous concerns of a

8. "By the very law of brotherhood and human association, we owe counsel and help to our brethren in the community. And we expect the same from them: counsel, to enlighten our ignorance, and help, to aid our weakness." Adv III, 5, PL 183:45f., *Opera* 4:178f. See also Pl. 7, PL 183: 364, *Opera* 4:332f.; PP I, 4, PL 183:407, *Opera* 5:190; Ep 115, 2, PL 182:262. But, the right kind of cenobitic life will always be based on *spiritual solitude:* "Sit solitary, like the turtle-dove; withdraw yourself from people . . . . Get away, then, I tell you, not physically, but in mind and in intention, in spirit and devotion; for the Lord Christ is himself a spirit, and it is spiritual solitude that he requires of you, though bodily withdrawal is not without its uses . . . . Be quite clear that the only solitude required of you is that of mind and spirit. You are alone in spirit, if you are not thinking about ordinary matters, if you are not interested in things present, if you reject worldly values, if you keep out of quarrels, if you do not resent injuries or hug grievances. Otherwise you are not really alone, even when you are alone in body." SC XL, 4, PL 183:983f., *Opera* II, 26f. See also *Saint Bernard On the Song of Songs* (trans. Religious of C.S.M.V.; London, 1952), p. 121 (hereafter cited *On the Song of Songs*). See also Div XLII, 4, PL 183:663, *Opera* 6/1:258 and, very importantly, *Vita prima*, V, 35, PL 185: 24-28.

9. Ep 385, 4, PL 182:589. To Bernard the monastery is also a prison: "We monks . . . have scorned the world, renounced the affection of our parents, shut ourselves up in monastic prisons." PL 182:589, *Letters*, p. 492. This is a "hard

layman's life, free to engage in an undisturbed *vacatio* in the monastery. He is on a safer road than married persons: he is free from the responsibilities involved in the raising of children and need not worry about how to please a wife. He gives no thought to affairs in the market place or any other secular business. He need not even be preoccupied about food and clothing, for all this is given to him by the monastery. Unburdened by any such distracting obligation, he can wholly devote himself to his real, that is, spiritual, vocation.[10]

Bernard often listed the constitutive elements of this vocation. They are, briefly—if one looks at his classical description in the letter *ad monachos Alpenses*[11]—communal prayer, fasts, vigils, the *lectio divina*, obedience to the *Rule* of St Benedict, to the abbot and the brethren, voluntary poverty, manual labor, and a faithful perseverance in the cultivation of the monastic virtues.[12]

Theoretically this specification can be applied also to the other contemporary Benedictine houses; in practice, however, there was an all-important difference between the Black Monks and the Cistercian reformers. The guiding principle of the Cistercians was, as Bernard attested, *puritas Regulae*,[13]

---

prison" (Ep 227, PL 182: 396), yet by no means a confinement: "What greater miracle is there than to see so many young men, adolescents, noblemen, and all the rest, held as it were in an open jail without chains, bound solely by the fear of God? " Ded I, 2, PL 183:519, *Opera* 5:371.

10. "The cenobites are converts of the heart. They are not bothered by temporal concerns but are free to repose so that they may experience how good the Lord is." Div II, 4, PL 183:566, *Opera* 5:378. See also Div II, 1, PL 183:542, *Opera* 5:375-76.

11. "Our order is abjection, is humility, is voluntary poverty, obedience, peace, and joy in the Holy Spirit. Our order is to be under a master, under an abbot, under a Rule, under discipline. Our order is to cultivate silence, to train oneself in fasts, vigils, prayers, manual labor, and above all, to keep that 'more excellent way' which is [the way of] charity; furthermore, to advance day by day in all these things, and to persevere in them until the last day." Ep 142, 1, PL 182:297.

12. Ep 1, 3-4, 11, PL 182:71f., 77; Ep 68, 4, PL 182:178; Ep 87, 8, PL 182:215; Ep 143, 2, PL 182:299; and SC IX, 2, PL 182:815f., *Opera* 1:43.

13. "If a monk of the Cluniac observance wishes to embrace the poverty of the Cistercians choosing the purity of the Rule rather than those customs . . . I would discourage him, at least if he did not have the consent of his abbot." Pre XVI, 46, PL 182:886, *Opera* 3:285, *On Precept*, p. 139. See also Ep 7, 19: "If there should be any who wish to change the purity of the Rule . . . ." PL 182:104, *Letters*, p. 37.

whereas in other monasteries the *Rule* of St Benedict had undergone a definite evolution codified in various custom-aries (*consuetudines*) or else been given strongly eremitic features. The White Monks decided to keep the *Rule sic et simpliciter*. Their principle was: nothing more, nothing less, and nothing otherwise than prescribed by the *Rule*.[14]

In this conception the abbot could not claim exemptions from the *Rule*. He is not above the *Rule*, he is not a *grand seigneur*, he must not aspire to the *pontificalia*.[15] To be abbot is not a vocation, but a necessity. Since the abbot professed the *Rule*, he remains subject to it. Never seeking to impose his own will on his charges, he must see to it that the *Rule* be observed in all its particulars. From his monks he may claim only such an obedience which is in accord with the *Rule* they have professed. He has no right to keep his monk from doing what he has professed or to demand more than he has promised. For he is not the agent but merely the witness of the monk's profession.[16]

While the Black Monks had their customaries and variety of observances, the Cistercians strove to keep the *Rule* in the

14. Pre IV, 10-11, PL 182:866f., *Opera* 3:460f., *On Precept*, p. 112f.; Circ III, 11, PL 183:142, *Opera* 4:290f. In Ep 7, 16, Bernard clearly states: "the day on which I begin to live by other rules, which may God forbid, and other habits, to keep other obeservances, to introduce new things and follow different customs, on that day I shall no longer keep my vow . . . ." PL 182:102, *Letters*, p. 35. See also Ep 7, 19, PL 182:104, and Ep 96, PL 182:229. The objection that to defend the *puritas Regulae* principle the Cistercians actually went against the *Rule* (they refused oblates but accepted *conversi*, etc.) is resolved by Bernard's explanation in Pre IV, 9-10, PL 182:806f., *Opera* 3:259f.

15. "They claim the pontifical insignia for themselves, using mitre, ring and sandals after the manner of prelates. But . . . the monk's profession clearly abhors this." Mor IX, 36, PL 182:832. See also *ibid.*, IX, 34, PL 182:831. Adalbero of Laon (died 1030) graphically described such a monastic potentate, "King Odeylo" of Cluny, in *Carmen ad Rotbertum regem*, PL 141:771-86.

16. "In our regular profession while stability is explicity promised, there is no mention at all of being subject to the abbot." Ep 7, 15, PL 182:102. "We make our profession solemnly and according to the Rule in the presence of the abbot, but only in his presence, not at his pleasure." Ep 7, 17, PL 182:103, *Letters*, p. 35f. The letter has also other references: nn. 2, 12, 14-18, in PL 182:94f., 100, and 101-104. See also Ep 73, 2, PL 182:187; Pre IV, 9-10, PL 182:865-67, *Opera* 3:259f.; Csi II, 6, 9, 11, 13, PL 182:747-50, *Opera* 3:416-18; *ibid.*, IV, 4, 11, PL 182:780, *Opera* 3:457; Adv III, 5-6, PL 183:45f., *Opera* 4:178-80; Div XXXV, 1, PL 183:634, *Opera* 5:288-89; and SC XXXI, 3-4, PL 183:941f., *Opera* 1:221.

manner they professed it, namely, *ex integro ad litteram.*[17] In defense of the *puritas Regulae* they admitted no other rules, habits, observances, innovations, or customs. Since they took the same vows, they wished to observe the *Rule* and their usages (customs) uniformly in every monastery. This applied to the chant, the *lectio,* the divine office, and even to matters of food and clothing. Adherence to the common customs of the Order foreclosed harmful private judgments, strange innovations, particular interests, and—it seems—even papal favors apt to cause disparity; more importantly, it guaranteed steadfastness in unity.[18]

The question has often been raised whether this determination implied an absolute literalism on the part of the early Cistercians, and experts still disagree when attempting to discern the mind of St Bernard. The great abbot did of course use the expression *integrally, according to the letter*, for to him any observance which did not harmonize with the purity of the *Rule* was unsafe. But, he also admitted that there is a certain hierarchy in the precepts of the *Rule.* Some, for instance the provisions on the virtues, are absolutely unchangeable. Others, however, are minor regulations which could admit exceptions in emergencies: then the letter of the law yielded to the law of love, but never in satisfaction of someone's personal will.[19] As Bernard expressed it:

17. "Do they, for instance, profess the usages of Cluny at Mont Majeur or these perhaps their rites or else in both places the literal distriction of the Cistercians? . . . The Cistercians . . . live not so much according to the Rule, but seek to keep it integrally and purely to the letter, as they believe they professed." Pre XVI, 48-49, PL 182:886., *Opera* 3:286f., *On Precept,* p. 141f. More recent studies on the subject are Kolumban Spahr, "Die Regelauslegung im 'Neukloster,' " *Festschrift zum 800-Jahrgedächtnis des Todes Bernhards von Clairvaux* (Vienna, 1952), pp. 22-30; Basil Pennington, "Toward Discerning the Spirit and Aims of the Founders of the Order of Cîteaux" *The Cistercian Spirit* (CS 3; Spencer, Massachussets, 1970), p. 13f., and Louis Lekai, "The Rule and the Early Cistercians," *Cistercian Studies,* 3 (1970), 243-51. However, the final word has not yet been spoken on this point.
18. "So long as I stand fast in unity, I am not preferring my private judgment to the common observances . . . . I say my conscience is clear because I have not broken the bond of unity." Ep 7, 16, PL 182: 102f., *Letters,* p. 35. See also Ep 4, 6, 7, 359, PL 182:89, 92, 93, and 560f.
19. Pre I, II, 3, VII, 13-14, XVI, 49, PL 182:861f., 869, 887, *Opera* 3:254f., 256, 262f., 286f. See also Ep 7, 3, and 6, PL 183: 95-97, and Div XLI, 3, PL 183:655, *Opera* 6/1: 246-47.

Who would doubt that a person absorbed in prayer is conversing with God? And yet, we are called away, we are forced away from it at the command of love, for the sake of our brethren who need a helping hand or a word of consolation. How often does quiet contemplation yield to the whirl of duties? How often is a book put down with a good conscience to give way to the toils of manual labor? How often are we omitting even [the conventual] Mass, in order to do justice to farming needs? This is an inverted order, but necessity knows no law.[20]

The Cistercian differed from his traditionalist neighbors in yet another important field: he embraced *voluntary poverty* which to him meant abjectness and destitution. In imitation of the apostles and the first Christians, he left the world to become a *pauper Christi* who called nothing his own in the monastery where he was simply *a pauper inter pauperes*. Such poorness is more than poverty in the ordinary sense; Bernard calls it *voluntary poverty*, one which rejects everything that is superfluous. This kind of poverty is a genuine martyrdom which entitles the monk to greater rewards than accumulated and warranted by his labors.[21]

As a sign of humility the White Monks wore, in imitation of the poor Christ, cheap and simple clothes. Two *cucullae* and two tunics sufficed for the most part since, in addition to its

---

20. SC L, 5, PL 183:1022f., *Opera* 2:79f. See also *On the Song of Songs*, p. 159.

21. "The same reward is promised to the poor and to martyrs . . . because voluntary poverty is truly a type of martyrdom. The prophet says: happy the man who does not seek gold, or money, or treasures. Who is he that we may praise him? For he did marvelous things in his life. But what is more marvelous, what martyrdom is greater than to hunger during meals, to shiver while clad in many costly vestments, and to be oppressed by poverty amid all the riches offered by the world, displayed by the devil, and desired by the senses? For will not he who fought in this manner—rejecting the world with its promises, deriding the enemy and his temptations, and, what is more glorious, winning the victory over himself and crucifying his restless curiosity—rightly be crowned? . . . The kingdom of heaven is promised to the poor and to the martyrs." OS I, 15, PL 183:461f., *Opera* 5:341. See also Ep 7, 2, PL 182:94; Ep 46, PL 182:153; Ep 55, PL 182:160; Ep 106, 2, PL 182:242; Ep 144, PL 182:301; Ep 173, PL 182:321; Ep 299, PL 182:501; Ep 349, PL 182:554, *Letters*, p. 461; Apo X, 24, PL 182:912f., *Opera* 3:101; Circ I, 4, PL 183:134, *Opera* 4:275; and Div XXV, 4-5, PL 183:635, *Opera* 6/1:189-91.

natural purpose of covering the body, clothing was to be an instrument of virtue. To foster such spiritual fervor they drastically reduced the traditional monastic wardrobe, rejecting such accepted additions as linen shirts, long sleeves, wide hoods, and, in general, articles made of finer material. They remained totally unconcerned about color, cheapness, and style; they felt clothing must not adorn the body but arm the soldiers of Christ for the heat and the cold of the spiritual combat.[22]

Poverty also demanded that the monks keep a frugal and simple diet and eat only the produce of their own labors.[23] Accordingly the White Monks' diet consisted of bread—more of grit than grain—of salt, all kinds of vegetables, and cooked dishes prepared without oil or fat. If wine was served by exception, it was always mixed with much water.[24] Unlike the Cluniacs, the Cistercians rejected honeyed and pulverized wine and preferred simple dishes in their natural flavor, that is, without additional seasoning—pepper, ginger, cumin, sage—and without ingenious culinary experimentations.[25] They avoided whatever was apt to stimulate the palate and ate with moderation, knowing that repletion would dull the

22. Ep 1, 3, 5, 8, 11, PL 182:72-77; Apo X, 24, PL 182:912f., *Opera* 3:101; Div XXI, 2-3, PL 183:594f., *Opera* 6/1:169-70; and Miss IV, 10, PL 183:85, *Opera* 4:55f.

23. "Our profession and the example of the early monks prescribe that we live by the labor of our hands and not from the sanctuary of God." Ep 397, 2, PL 182:607. See also SC LIII, 5: "We must eat our bread in the sweat of our brow." PL 183:1035, *Opera* 2:98.

24. "Wine and white bread, honey-wine and pittances benefit the body, not the soul . . . . Vegetables, beens, roots and bran bread and water may be poor for one living at his ease, but hard work makes them taste delicious." Ep 1, 11-12, PL 182:77f. Bernard's biographer similarly stated, "The monks' diet matched the simplicity of their dwellings. The bread was produced by the toil of the brethren from the almost barren earth of that desert place, and it seemed to be made more of grit than grain, and as with all the other food they ate it almost had no flavor." *Vita prima,* VII, 36, PL 185:248, *Life,* p. 60. See also Apo VI, 12 and IX, 19, PL 182:906f. and 909f., *Opera* 3:91f., 96f.; Abael VIII, 19, PL 182:1068; and Humb, 3, PL 183:515, *Opera* 5:442-43.

25. Ep 1, 11, PL 182:77; Apo IX, 20-21, PL 182:910f., *Opera* 3:98f., *An Apologia,* pp. 55-57. Even if Bernard wrote in a satirical vein (*An Apologia,* p. 16f.), he did not simply talk in the abstract. See, for instance, PL 149:726ff. where Udalric of Cluny furnishes some pertinent details.

senses and thus hamper prayer and meditation. They also kept regular fasts, to follow the example of the Fathers and the martyrs and to mortify their bodies and senses.[26] They worried little about the possible effect of their monotonous diet; as Bernard said, a monk must not be apprehensive about his complexion, but only about his profession.[27]

Voluntary poverty also called for manual labor. Work is everyone's lot. Since clerics are in the service of the altar—they baptize, bury the dead, visit the sick, bless marriages, instruct the ignorant, reprove delinquents, excommunicate evildoers, absolve the reformed, and reconcile the repentent—they have a right to live from parish revenues. But monks have an altogether different vocation: they do not cultivate the Lord's vineyard, they do not tend the flock; hence they cannot claim tithes which rightfully belong to the secular clergy. Hence they must work and become self-supporting. The monastic profession, the *Rule* of St Benedict, and the example of the early monks clearly enjoin this obligation.[28] For the Cistercians this meant the restoration of manual labor, that is, agriculture, animal farming, the practice of all kinds of skills in the monastic workshops,[29] and, with the help of their *conversi,* economic autarky.[30]

26. Apo IX, 21, PL 182:910f., *Opera* 3:98f.; Adv III, 2, PL 183:44, *Opera* 4:176; Quad III, 1, 3, 4; Quad IV, 1 and VII, 1, PL 183:174-76 and 184f., *Opera* 4:364-78; QH VII, 8, PL 183:282, *Opera* 4:417f.; OS V, 7, PL 183:479, *Opera* 5:365-66; and V And 1-2, PL 183: 501f., *Opera* 5:423-24.

27. SC XXX, 11-12, PL 183:939f., *Opera* 1:127. Bernard lists some complaints of monastic self-tormentors: "Vegetables inflate, cheese stuffs the stomach, milk causes headache, water is bad for the lungs, cauliflower induces depression, leeks excite to anger, and fish from the pond or from muddy water discolor one's complexion."

28. "It is the clerics' business to administer the altar and to live by the altar." Ep 397, 2, PL 182:607, *Letters* 499. See also Ep 385, 4: "Whether we wish it or not, our life is one of toil." PL 182:589; Div II, 1, Div XXXIX, 1, Div LV, 2-3, PL 183:542, 577, 645, 678, *Opera* 6/1:80-81, 5:220-21, 6/1:281-82; and QH *Praefatio,* 1, PL 183:185, *Opera* 4:383.

29. QH IX, 1, PL 183:216, *Opera* 4:435; Div I, 7, Div XV, 1, Div XXI, 2-3, Div XXVII, 1, PL 183:540f., 577, 594, 612, *Opera* 6/1:77-78, 140-41, 169-70; SC XXIV, 8, SC XXVI, 7, PL 183:898, 908, *Opera* 1:164f.

30. Ep 79, 3, Ep 306, 2, PL 182:201, 508; Asc III, 6, PL 183:307, *Opera* 5:134-35; and Ben 7, PL 183:379, *Opera* 5:6-7.

From this follows that the monk was not to engage in pastoral care or in any other work outside the monastery. He was not to care for others and neglect his now soul.[31] Since the construction and the maintenance of the ark of Noah, that is, the care of souls, is the exclusive business of clerics, it is neither fitting nor expedient nor lawful for a monk—who is, anyway, unlearned and untrained—to preach; this would be an outright usurpation.[32] Equally reprehensible is to see monks run around in cities and castles or scheming about possible foundations in the Holy Land. For the Holy Land needs crusaders, not monks whose place is in the monastery.[33]

31. "If I have just a little oil for my own use, do you think I ought to give it to you and myself go empty? No, I keep it for mine own anointing, and will not bring it forth save at the prophet's bidding. If some of you, esteeming me as other than I am, importune still, I shall reply, 'Not so, lest there be not enough for us and you; but go ye rather unto them that sell, and buy for yourselves.' But 'Charity seeks not her own,' you say? Do you know why? Because she does not lack it! Nobody seeks what they already have; and charity is always in possession of her own—this is to say, of the things needful to salvation." SC XVIII, 3, PL 183:860, *Opera* 1:104, *On the Song of Songs*, p. 45.

32. "It is clear and beyond doubt that it is not proper for a monk to preach in public." SC LXIV, 3, PL 183:1084f., *Opera* 2:168. Elsewhere Bernard added, "Not teaching but lamenting is the duty of the monk I am supposed to be and of the sinner that I am. There could not be anything more silly than for an untaught man such as I confess I am to presume to teach what he knows nothing about. An untaught man is not competent to teach, a monk does not dare to do so, and a penitent does not want to do so. It is in order to avoid this that I have flown far away and dwelt in solitude." Ep. 89, 2, PL 182:294f., *Letters*, p. 138. See also Ep 242, 3, PL 182:437; Ep 365, 1, PL 182:570; Asspt III, 5, PL 183:423f., *Opera* 5:241-42; Div XXXVI, 3, PL 183:638f., *Opera* 5:215-16; and SC XLI, 6, PL 183:987, *Opera* 2:32.

33. Ep 359, PL 182:560, *Letters*, p. 23. See also Ep 399, PL 182:612: "It is the vocation of a monk to seek not the earthly but the heavenly Jerusalem, and he will do this not by setting out on his feet but by progressing in virtue." Similarly, "to a monk towns must be prisons and the wilderness a paradise." Ep 365, 1, PL 182:570, *Letters*, p. 465. For, "What concern have they with crowds? . . . What have they do with wandering about the countryside when they are professed to lead a life in solitude? Why do they sew the sign of the Cross on their clothes, when they always carry it on their hearts so long as they cherish their religious way of life? . . . If any monk or lay-brother should leave this monastery to go on the expedition, he will place himself under sentence of excommunication." *Letters*, p. 469. For other references see Div XCIII, 2, PL 183:716, *Opera* 6/1:349-51; Miss IV, 10, PL 183:85, *Opera* 4:56; and QH VII, 13-14, PL 183:203f., *Opera* 4:421-24.

In the house of God the monks must either follow the example of the biblical Martha, imitate Mary's contemplation, or else engage in Lazarus' penitential exercises. This raises an explosive subject: the question about the respective merits of the active and the contemplative life. To Bernard the best part is, briefly, excellence in both action and contemplation—*vacare Deo et proximo ministrare*—but always *within* the monastery. In the monastery one will not follow his own inclinations but endeavor to do the will of God.[34]

The question of spiritual reading (*lectio*) poses a similar problem, namely, whether monks ought to cultivate secular learning. According to Bernard, all knowledge based on the truth is good in itself. The Church benefits from such studies and from such learning, for they enable her to refute her opponents and to enlighten the ignorant. The liberal arts are therefore an ennobling and useful study—but they are not for monks whose vocation is to advance in virtue. For one may lead a virtuous life without any education in the liberal arts, as can be seen from the example of the apostles who, though not versed in rhetoric and philosophy, became outstanding vehicles and instruments of divine grace. Monks should rather study Scripture and the Fathers. They must not seek knowledge which puffs up but cultivate subjects which contribute to spiritual growth. Such a study will seek the right *order*, that is, the truths necessary for salvation; such a study will have the right *ardor* (zeal), since it leads to the practice of love and charity; finally, it will have the right *intention*, for it seeks our own spiritual and moral improvement and the edification of our neighbor. Full realizing that the time is short, monks must work on their salvation with fear and trembling and establish the right priorities. Hence the importance of acquiring above all a better knowledge of God and of oneself.[35] To a young man anxious to complete his studies be-

34. Asspt III, 2-5, PL 183:422-24, *Opera* 5:239-42; Ep 397, 2, PL 182:607. An outstanding example of this ideal is Bernard's brother Gerard, portrayed in a masterly fashion in SC XXVI, PL 183:903ff., *Opera* 1:171-78.

35. SC XXXVI and XXXVII, PL 183:967-74, *Opera* 2:1-14. According to Bernard's biographer, "It was his [Bernard's] great delight to pass hours in reading [that is, studying] Scripture." *Vita prima*, IV, 24, PL 185:241, *Life*, p. 42. Anoth-

fore joining the monastery Bernard wrote: "Do not put forward any excuses. If you still have your heart set on study, if you still wish to learn and be under a master, the Master himself is here and calls you, the Master in whom all the treasures of wisdom are stored. He it is who teaches man all that man knows."[36] He teaches the monk not to satisfy his curiosity or his desire for personal fame, but to work on his perfection and thus benefit his fellow men.

The monastic life, the Cistercian life thus far described, makes heroic demands but offers little or no physical comfort to its champions. Tender souls may therefore become frightened about the rigor of the Order, the severity of the *Rule*, the hardship caused by the renunciation of the world, the conflict between virtues and vices, the long vigils, the unchanging routine of the choir, and the pains of frequent fasting.[37] But one must not lose courage. Monks are not followers of Hippocrates who seeks to save man for this world; they are disciples of Christ who teaches man to give up and lose his earthly life. This is also what the prophets and the apostles did, this is what the Gospel demands.[38] To the—

---

er source of Bernard's knowledge was meditation and reflection. As Bernard himself stated, "Believe me who have experience, you will acquire much more in the woods than you ever will in books. Woods and stones will teach you what you can never hear from any master." Ep 106, 2, PL 182:241, *Letters*, p. 155. On the other hand, writing will cause a great many distractions even if it is about purely spiritual matters: "You say that all this [writing] can be done in silence. I am surprised that you can seriously mean this. How can the mind be quiet when composing a letter and a turmoil of expressions are clamoring and every sort of phrase and diversity of meanings are jostling one another? When words spring into the mind but just the word one wants escapes one; when literary effect, meaning, and how to convey a meaning clearly, and what should be said and in what order it should be said, has to be carefully considered; all the things which those who understand these matters scrutinize carefully? And do you tell me there is any quiet in all this? Can you call this silence, even if the lips are not moving? " Ep 89, 1, PL 182:220, *Letters*, p. 137. See also Apo *Praefatiuncula*, 1, PL 182:987, *Opera* 3:81; and Div XXXIV, 1, PL 183:630f., *Opera* 6/1:228-29.

36. Ep 412, PL 182: 621, *Letters* p. 509.

37. Div XCV, 2, PL 183:719, *Opera* 6/1:354.

38. " 'Mine own vineyard have I not kept.' I have used these words to express my own imperfection. But they can be used also in the same sense as our Savior's words in the Gospel, 'He that loseth his life for my sake shall find it'; and he who can say them in this sense will be perfect. He will moreover be a really fit person

Cistercian—monk the choice is clear, for he knows: "the
rougher the thistle, the softer the cloth."[39]

to be made keeper of the vineyards, for the care of them will never hinder his
keeping of his own! Such an one was Peter, such an one was Paul. And you, too,
can show yourself an imitator of Paul and a disciple of Christ, if you give up your
own will and make complete renunciation of your bodily desires, crucifying the
flesh with its vices and lusts. You will be wiser if you thus lose your life in order
to keep it, than if you lose it by keeping it." SC XXX, 10-12, PL 183:938-40,
Opera 1:216-18, *On the Song of Songs*, p. 87. See also Div XXXVI, 1, PL
183:637f., *Opera* 5:214.

39. Ep 322, 1, PL 182:527, *Letters*, p. 449.

SAINT BERNARD ON THE DUTIES OF THE CHRISTIAN PRINCE

WILLIAM O. PAULSELL

Atlantic Christian College

BERNARD OF CLAIRVAUX has captured the interest of many historians because he successfully united the contemplative and active lives in his own career. David Knowles says that "it is difficult to name any other saint in the history of the Church whose influence, both on the public life of an epoch and on the consciences of a multitude of individuals, was, during his lifetime so profound and so pervasive."[1] Father Lekai writes of a time when "St. Bernard stood literally in the center of European politics."[2] Bernard's writings reveal both a deep human tenderness and a severity that few men could resist. Yet, as Louis Bouyer says, "In his tenderness as in his severity, Bernard was the same, that is to say always passionate, because passionately human in the superhuman violence of the efforts which he made to attain the ends he believed himself bound to pursue."[3]

Always affirming his love for Clairvaux, Bernard frequently complained about being called from the monastery to deal with worldly matters. Even while in the monastery he corresponded with many of the princes of Europe, instructing them on matters of Church and State. This paper is based on a survey of the letters Bernard wrote to the rulers of Europe in which he taught them their duties and demanded their obedience. As one reads through this body of correspondence, a

1. David Knowles, *The Monastic Order in England* (Cambridge, 1963), p. 217.
2. Louis J. Lekai, *The White Monks* (Okauchee, Wisconsin, 1953), p. 36.
3. Louis Bouyer, *The Cistercian Heritage* (London, 1958), p. 25.

63

number of principles about political duty appear. Although
Bernard was often pragmatic and sometimes, as Bruno Scott
James says, a party to subterfuge,[4] he did advocate a rather
traditional medieval viewpoint.

I

First, Bernard supported the Pauline injunction that men
must obey the powers that be because they are ordained by
God. To Louis the Younger he wrote:

> Though all the words were to combine in making me at-
> tempt something against your royal Majesty, yet I would
> fear God and not dare to oppose the king whom he had
> ordained. I know where it is written, "He that resisteth the
> power, resisteth the ordinance of God."[5]

To Conrad, king of the Romans, he said that the Empire
should be obedient and honor the teaching of Paul.

> I have never wanted the king to be dishonoured or the
> empire to be diminished, and my soul hates those who do,
> for I have read, "let every soul be subject to the higher
> powers," and "he that resisteth the power resisteth the
> ordinance of God."[6]

However, he also instructed Conrad to obey the pope, who is
an even higher power ordained by God.

II

Second, Bernard felt that a primary duty of the Christian
prince was to defend the Church. Writing to Conrad, urging
him to put down a rebellion against Pope Eugenius III, he
argued that as Christ was both King and High Priest, Crown
and Church were inseparably united in Him. Each was related
to and dependent upon the other.

> May I have no part in the counsels of those who say either
> that the peace and liberty of the Church will suffer from

4. Bruno Scott James, *The Letters of Bernard of Clairvaux* (London, 1953), pp.
363, 366. All quotations from Bernard's letters in this paper are taken from this
translation. References are also given for those letters that appear in PL 182. The
numbering of the letters in James and PL do not agree; in the references that
follow James' number appears first.
5. Letter 186, p. 257; Ep 152.
6. Letter 226, p. 304; Ep 183.

the empire, or that the prosperity and glory of the empire will suffer from the Church. For God, who founded both, did not unite them for their mutual destruction but for their mutual support.[7]

When the Church is under attack, said Bernard, it is the duty of the Christian prince to rally to her side. In fact, if the Prince does not, God will protect the Church in His own way, possibly at the expense of the Prince.

> The arm of the Lord is not shortened, nor has he become powerless to deliver his people. Even now he will surely save his bride whom he has redeemed with his blood. . . .He will deliver her, I say, and if necessary by another's hand. It is a matter for the consideration of the princes of the realm whether this would be to the king's honour or the benefit of the kingdom. Of course it would not.[8]

III

Third, the item most frequently dealt with in these letters was that of recommendations for various religious. In one letter Bernard argued that Count Theobald might benefit his own soul by helping a certain monk known for "his poverty and holy way of life."

> Help him, if not for his sake at any rate for your own, because, if his poverty makes you necessary to him, his holy way of life makes him just as necessary, if not more so, to you.[9]

Theobald was reminded that when doing things for monks he was helping Christ.

> But I can briefly and truthfully say that whatever it may please you of your liberality so confer on him as a true servant of Christ, you may be sure you have conferred on Christ himself.[10]

A similar admonition was given to King Henry I about Cistercians in England.

---

7. Letter 320, p. 394; Ep 244.
8. *Ibid.*
9. Letter 42, p. 74; Ep 40.
10. Letter 46, p. 76.

Help them as messengers of your Lord and in their persons fulfil your duties as a vassal of their Lord. And may he for his honour, the salvation of your soul, and the health and peace of your kingdom, bring you safe and happy to a good and peaceful end.[11]

The same point is made in another context. The duke and duchess of Lorraine had established a policy of remitting all tolls and other dues for Cistercians passing through their area. However, some of the duke's servants had been exacting such tolls anyway, and Bernard asked the duke and duchess either to change their policy or to instruct their servants not to exact the tolls. It is obvious, however, that Bernard would prefer to see the old policy enforced. Naturally, such action had great spiritual benefits.

Without doubt your reward for all this will be very great in heaven, if we believe those words of our Lord in the Gospel: "As long as you did it to one of the least of my brethren, you did it to me."[12]

On one occasion Bernard complained to Count Ebal of Flore that he was mistreating a Benedictine monastery built by his mother. Bernard told him to

confirm the gift as it was made by your mother to these holy brothers, yet so that they promise to keep there as many monks as may conveniently and wholly maintain the life, while you and your mother undertake to provide food and clothing so that the monks may be supported in the service of God.[13]

Bernard praised the King of Scotland for his interest in Cistercians. In particular was he grateful for the king's aid to the monks of Rievaulx.

You opened to them the treasury of your good will and anointed them with the oil of your compassion and kindness, so that the house of the King of heaven was filled with the odour of your ointments.[14]

11. Letter 95, p. 142; Ep 92.
12. Letter 123, p. 183; Ep 119.
13. Letter 233, p. 311.
14. Letter 172, p. 242.

He also asked for the King's good will toward the group of monks who had left St Mary's at York in order to follow a more strict Cistercian life.

IV

Fourth, Bernard frequently exhorted princes to have respect for the clergy and the Church. In one letter he criticized William, count of Poitiers, for expelling the clergy of St Hilary from their city. The only effect of this would be to arouse the wrath of God against the count.

> Turn back, I pray you, turn back, or you too will be cut off. Turn back, I say, and restore peace to your friends and their church to your clergy, or you will irrevocably alienate him "that is feared by awestruck princes, feared amongst the kings of the earth."[15]

Pope Innocent II had called a Council to meet in Pisa in 1135. King Louis "le Gros" refused to allow the French bishops to attend on the grounds that the weather would be too hot. Bernard wrote him a heated letter, stating that the bishops were not made of ice, although the hearts of some might be frozen as far as the good of the Church is concerned. He assured the King that if the Council did anything contrary to the interests of the French crown, all of the French delegates to the Council would work to have it changed.

Bernard's basic argument, however, was that the king's disobedience to the Church would not go unnoticed by God. "The kingdoms of this world and their prerogatives will certainly only remain sound and inimpaired for their lords so long as they do not contravene the divine ordinances and dispositions."[16]

On the matter of a papal schism, Bernard wrote the emperor Lothair, praising him for his support of Innocent II.

> Blessed be God who has raised you up to be a sceptre of salvation amongst us for the honour and glory of his name, to restore the Imperial dignity, to support the Church in an evil hour, and finally to work salvation even now upon the earth. It is his doing that the power of your crown spreads

15. Letter 130, p. 199; Ep 128.
16. Letter 133, p. 203; Ep 255.

and rises more each day, ever increasing and growing in dignity and splendour before God and men.[17]

It is the duty of the prince, said Bernard, to save the Church from the "mad fury of schismatics."[18]

V

A fifth item about which Bernard corresponded was the question of disputed episcopal elections. Shortly after the healing of the papal schism, Bernard was approached by the archbishop of Lyons and several others for assistance in choosing a new bishop for Langres, Bernard's own diocese. A procedural agreement was made, but the archbishop ignored it and chose a monk of Cluny for the office. The king of France invested him with the temporalities of the see and the new bishop was consecrated. Upon a request from Bernard, the pope declared the election invalid. Bernard himself was then elected, but he declined the office. Finally, Bernard's prior at Clairvaux, Godfrey de la Roche, was appointed to the office. The king, however, having already invested the previous candidate, did not want to countermand that action and invest someone else.

In a letter to Louis the Younger, Bernard stated that the new bishop had been properly elected and that he wished to hold his lands under the king of France. The king should act swiftly that the new bishop might be properly confirmed and order restored to the Church.[19]

Another disputed election involved the see of York. After long negotiation William Fitzherbert, the son of the king's sister, was chosen. Opposition to him developed, and after a lengthy dispute, Pope Eugenius III, the first Cistercian pope, deposed William and ordered another election in which Henry Murdac, a Cistercian of Clairvaux and also a Yorkshireman, was chosen. However, a majority of the clergy, supported by the king, refused to recognize him.

17. Letter 142, p. 210; Ep 139.
18. *Ibid.*
19. Letter 186, pp. 257-59; Ep 170.

Bernard wrote to King Stephen of England that his troubles were a manifestation of divine chastisement, and for that reason he ought to submit to the will of God.[20] He also wrote to Queen Matilda, asking that she use her influence to see that episcopal elections remained free.

> . . . . If you could arrange that the king should abjure before his bishops and princes the sacrilegious intrusion on the liberty of the chapter, so that it alone should have the decision to which it alone is entitled, know that it would be greatly to the honour of God, the well-being and security of the king and his friends, and to the profit of the whole realm.[21]

Bernard likewise urged King Louis of France not to interfere with the election of the bishop of Auxerre. More than one election had been held, and the pope had appointed an investigative commission on the whole affair. Louis refused to support the outcome on the grounds that he had given approval only for the first election. Bernard reacted:

> It would not have entered anyone's head that, once your consent had been given, it ought to have been sought a second time, especially when there had not been another election after that one. Must the favor of the king be obtained every time the clergy differ amongst themselves? [22]

VI

Sixth, one of the traditional duties of the medieval prince was to administer justice. In a series of letters to Theobald, Bernard pleaded for justice tempered with mercy. A certain Humbert had been accused of a crime, but in Bernard's eyes was innocent. Theobald refused to recognize this because all legal procedures had not yet been exhausted. Bernard warned the count that he stood under the judgment of God, and should take care how he handled the case.

20. Letter 197, p. 267.
21. Letter 198, p. 268.
22. Letter 348, p. 427; Ep 282.

Do you not fear that "as you have judged, so you will be judged"? Do you not realize that God can disinherit Count Theobald quite as easily as Count Theobald has disinherited Humbert? [23]

Theobald did hear Humbert's case and dismissed the accusations against him. However, Bernard criticized the count for having promised to restore Humbert's possessions and then not actually doing so. As a result an innocent man and his family have been reduced to poverty. Theobald, said Bernard, had strayed from his reputation for honesty.[24]

In another case Bernard asked the count to show mercy to the wife of a criminal. "Be merciful to her that you may obtain mercy."[25] In the same letter he mentioned the case of a man who had lost a duel, and, under orders from the count, had his eyes put out and his goods confiscated.

It is only right, if you will be so pleased that enough of his goods should be returned for him at least to support his miserable life. And the sin of the father ought not to be visited on his innocent sons, so that they cannot inherit the family property, if there is any.[26]

VII

Seventh, there are several references in the letters to the prince's duty to look after the welfare of the needy. Bernard instructed Melisande, in her role as queen of Jerusalem, to "Take care of the pilgrims, the needy, and especially the prisoners, for God is gained by such sacrifices."[27] In another context he reminded her of Paul's admonition that a good widow should bring up children, give shelter, wash the feet of saints, minister to those who suffer tribulation, and follow "every good work."[28]

23. Letter 39, p. 71; Ep 37.
24. Letter 40, pp. 72-73; Ep 38.
25. Letter 41, p. 73; Ep 39.
26. *Ibid.*
27. Letter 272, p. 345; Ep 206.
28. Letter 274, p. 348; Ep 289.

In a letter to Roger, king of Sicily, in which he recommended a monk, Bernard said that Roger would do better to serve the needy rather than the greedy. The needy will be more grateful to him and will glorify him more.[29]

VIII

The eighth and final point concerns war. Although Bernard did preach the Second Crusade, his letters contain numerous admonitions against war and violence. For example, he wrote to Duke Conrad of Zähringen who was contemplating war against the count of Geneva. Bernard pointed out that the count was willing to submit to justice and do satisfaction for any evil he might have done to Conrad. Therefore, the duke should avoid provoking the wrath of God.

So if . . . you set out to invade his territory, destroy churches, burn homesteads, and shed human blood, there can be no doubt at all that you will seriously anger him, who is the "father to the orphan and gives the widow redress."[30]

If God is angry it makes no difference how strong one's army may be; God's purposes will triumph. Bernard asked the duke to work out a full treaty or at least an armistice until the basis for a lasting peace could be agreed upon. It is impossible, he said, for two armies to clash without "terrible slaughter on both sides, which is what I fear so much."[31]

Many of Bernard's statements on peace are found in the correspondence about the controversy between King Louis the Younger of France and Count Theobald over the attempt by the King's seneschal, Ralph, to divorce Theobald's niece. Bernard stoutly defended the interests of Theobald and took the case to the pope, who submitted it to a council that upheld the first marriage of Ralph. An interdict was laid on Ralph's territory, and Louis invaded Theobald's realm bringing devastation and suffering upon the land.

29. Letter 276, p. 349; Ep 207.
30. Letter 97, p. 143; Ep 97.
31. *Ibid.*

In order to save his land, Theobald attempted to have the interdict lifted. This made Bernard furious, and he condemned Louis for using violence in this manner.

> Do you not realize how great was your offence in obliging Count Theobald, by the violence of the war you waged against him, to take an oath contrary to God and all justice that he would not only seek but also obtain an undeserved and unlawful absolution of the interdict on Count Ralph and his lands? Why do you want to add one sin upon another and heap up the wrath of God against yourself? [32]

Chiding the king for resisting good advice, Bernard warned Louis not to blame his violent and agressive policies on Theobald. The count, for his part, has been ready and willing to make peace.

> But you will not receive any peaceful overtures or keep your own truce or accept sound advice. On the contrary, by some mysterious judgment of God, you insist on turning everything round so perversely that you deem disgrace to be honour and honour to be disgrace and fear what is safe and scorn what you should fear. [33]

Bernard also criticized Louis for his evil associations.

> I shall not withhold the fact that you are again trying to make common cause with excommunicated persons, that I hear you are associating with robbers and thieves in the slaughter of men, the burning of homesteads, the destruction of churches, and the scattering of the poor.... Moreover you billet your brother and his soldiers, archers, and cross-bowmen in the houses of the bishops against all right and justice, thereby rashly exposing the property of the Church to be squandered in disgraceful uses of this kind. I tell you, you will not remain long unpunished if you continue in this way. [34]

Although Bernard called upon princes to make peace and avoid war, he did preach the Second Crusade with vigor and

32. Letter 296, pp. 363-64; Ep 220.
33. Letter 297, p. 365; Ep 221.
34. *Ibid.*

deep conviction. He described the occupation of the Holy Land by infidels and said:

> Alas, if there be none to withstand him, he will soon invade the very city of the living God, overturn the arsenal of our redemption, and defile the holy places which have been adorned by the blood of the immaculate lamb.[35]

God, of course, could send down twelve legions of angels and save His land, said Bernard, but He wanted to test His people. Furthermore, He has had mercy in that He is offering the Crusade as a means of salvation.

> How great a number of sinners have here confessed with tears and obtained pardon for their sins since the time when these holy precincts were cleansed of pagan filth by the swords of our fathers. The evil one sees this and is enraged, he gnashes his teeth and withers away in fury.[36]

Now, men of the present generation must rise to the occasion.

> Your land is well known to be rich in young and vigorous men. The world is full of their praises and the renown of their courage is on the lips of all. Gird yourselves therefore like men and take up arms with joy and with zeal for your Christian name, in order to "take vengeance on the heathen, and curb the nations." O mighty soldiers, O men of war, you have a cause for which you can fight without danger to your souls; a cause in which to conquer is glorious and for which to die is gain.[37]

Although Bernard spoke harshly about the necesity of destroying pagans, he insisted that Jews were "not to be persecuted, killed or even put to flight."

> The Jews are for us the living words of Scripture, for they remind us always of what our Lord suffered. They are dispersed all over the world so that by expiating their crime they may be everywhere the living witness to our redemp-

35. Letter 391, p. 461.
36. *Ibid.*
37. *Ibid.*, p. 462.

tion. Under Christian princes they endure a hard captivity, but "they only want for the time of their deliverance." Finally we are told by the Apostle that when the time is ripe all Israel shall be saved. But those who die before will remain in death. If the Jews are utterly wiped out, what will become of our hope for their promised salvation, their eventual conversion.[38]

And, in a letter to the archbishop of Mainz, Bernard said, "Is it not a far better triumph for the Church to convince and convert the Jews than to put them all to the sword? "[39]

However, Bernard took a very hard line against non-Jewish pagans. In a letter about a crusade against pagans in Eastern Europe Bernard wrote:

We utterly forbid that for any reason whatsoever a truce should be made with these peoples, either for the sake of money or for the sake of tribute, until such a time as, by God's help, they shall be either converted or wiped out.[40]

In summary, Bernard affirmed the Pauline injunction that Christians should obey the powers that be. He felt that princes should defend the Church, provide for the needs of monks and monastic communities, respect the clergy and the Church, avoid interference in episcopal elections, administer justice, look after the welfare of the needy, and avoid war except in the case of the Crusades when the cause, he felt, was just. The manner in which a prince ruled had a direct relationship to his salvation. He wrote to the king of France, "So may you administer your kingdom of France, great and mighty king, as to obtain the Kingdom of heaven."[41]

38. *Ibid.*, pp. 462-63.
39. Letter 393, p. 466; Ep 365.
40. Letter 394, p. 467.
41. Letter 210, p. 286; Ep 457.

PETER ABELARD'S *LETTER 10* AND CISTERCIAN LITURGICAL REFORM

CHRYSOGONUS WADDELL, OCSO

Abbey of Gethsemani

I SUSPECT that Peter Abelard's *Letter 10*[1] will never receive even a small fraction of the attention which generations of scholars have lavished upon the *Historia calamitatum* and the subsequent correspondence between Peter and his Heloise. *Letter 10* admittedly contains not the slightest element of love-interest for the romantically inclined; and the theologian can find much more substantial material to work

1. Number 10 in the Migne version, PL 178:355-40—the edition here followed. The *editio princeps* of 1616 (*Petri Abaelardi, Filosofi et Theologi, Abbatis Ruyensis, et Heloissae Coniugis eius, primae Paracletensis abbatissae, Opera, nunc primum edita ex mss. codd. v. illust. Francisci Amboesii*, Parisiis, sumptibus Nicolai BVON . . . M.DCXVI) contains first the Abelard-Heloise exchange of letters, then a separate series: *Aliae Mag[istri] Petri Abaelardi Nannetensis Epistolae*. In this letter series, our Letter 10 appears as *Epistola* V.

The manuscript tradition is tenuous in the extreme. Only a single late and very poor MS version is known to be extant—Paris, Bibliothèque nationale, ms. latin 13057. This paper MS, which still bears the *ex libris* of St-Germain-des-Prés, has been described in detail by J. Monfrin, *Abélard: Historia Calamitatum* (Paris, 1959), p. 28 where the editor takes exception to a few of the details given in the parallel description of the MS by J. T. Muckle, "Abelard's Letter of Consolation to a friend *(Historia Calamitatum)*," in *Mediaeval Studies*, 12 (1950), 167. Victor Cousin considered this MS too defective to be used for his two-volume edition of Peter's *Opera—Petri Abaelardi Opera hactenus seorsim edita . . . recensuit, notas, argumenta, indices adjecit Victor Cousin, adjuvantibus C. Jourdain et E. Despois* (Paris, 1849-1859). Cousin's text, as well as that printed in PL 178 in 1855 depend, then, on the *editio princeps* begun by Françoise d'Amboise but completed and given its final shape by André Duchesne. (For a discussion of the dual editorship of this 1616 edition, see J. Monfrin, *Abélard*, pp. 31-39.) Unfortunately, neither d'Amboise nor Duchesne specify which MS or MSS they used for *Letter 10*. The Migne version departs from the *editio princeps* only in matters of spelling, punctuation, and a few insignificant details.

with in Peter's other writings. Still, theologians as well as historians, musicologists, and liturgists have frequently referred to this letter, if only in passing, and often without any real insight. No serious introduction to this minor but remarkable document can be attempted within the limits of so brief a paper as the present one; and I shall touch on only a few points without attempting to prove anything. My chief concern will be to suggest one or two ideas which might deserve further study and development, and to encourage others to give this letter the attention it deserves.

Letter 10 was sparked by a passing remark made by Bernard of Clairvaux on the occasion of his visit to Heloise and her community at the nunnery of the Paraclete sometime in the early 1130s.[2] Bernard had met with an embarrassingly enthusiastic reception, and even "la très sage Héloise" seems to have been left a bit giddy by the visit. Bernard, she told Peter *cum summa exsultatione*, had spoken more like an angel than like a mere mortal man. He had made one negative remark, but this he had confided (*intimavit*) to Heloise in private (*secreto*). The fact is that the Abbot of Clairvaux had been a trifle taken aback (*aliquantulum commotum*) to hear the words "daily bread" changed to "supersubstantial bread" when the Lord's Prayer was said aloud at Lauds and Vespers. Abelard—for he was the one responsible for this innovation—felt obliged to justify this initiative of his, particularly, he wrote, since Bernard had apparently given signs of a special love for Abelard (*ea caritate, qua me praecipue amplectimini*); and there was no one whom Peter more wanted to avoid offending than the Abbot of Clairvaux,

2. The precise date is uncertain, but practically everyone is agreed on some year between 1131 and 1135. Typical are: Arno Borst, "Abälard und Bernhard," *Historische Zeitschrift,* 186 (1958), 504; Commission d'Histoire de l'Ordre de Cîteaux, *Bernard de Clairvaux* (Paris, 1953), p. 582; Ezio Francischini, "S. Bernardo nel suo secolo," *S. Bernardo: Pubblicazione nell'VIII centenario della sua morte* (Milan, 1954), p. 18; M. Huglo (ed.), "L'innario ambrosiano e l'innario cisterciense," *Fonti e paleografia del canto ambrosiano (Archivio Ambrosiano,* VII; Milan, 1956), p. 95; E. Vacandard, *Vie de saint Bernard, abbé de Clairvaux* (Paris, 1910), II, 120; Lorenz Weinrich, "Peter Abelard as Musician," *The Musical Quarterly,* 55 (1969), 299; Watkin Williams, *Saint Bernard of Clairvaux* (Westminster, Maryland, 1952), p. 299.

whom he styled not only "Venerable" but "most dear"
(*dilectissimo*).³
Abelard's defense of his version of the Lord's Prayer was

3. PL 178:335 BC. Was Peter being a bit fulsome in his *exordium?* Bernard's
Letter 77 (de baptismo), written in answer to a request from Hugh of St-Victor
around 1126, was possibly aimed at positions expressed either by Peter or by
Peter's disciples, who at that time were flocking to the Master in his retreat at
Quincey. However, Abelard remained un-named both in Hugh's letter and
Bernard's reply, and it is far from certain that Bernard really knew just whom he
was refuting. See Damien Van den Eynde, *Essai sur la succession et la date des
écrits de Hughes de Saint-Victor (Spicilegium Pontificii Athenaei Antoniani,* 13;
Rome, 1960), pp. 132-37; see also S.M. Deutsch, *Peter Abelard, ein kritischer
Theologe des 12. Jahrhunderts* (Leipzig, 1883), pp. 466-72; L. Ott, *Untersuchun-
gen zur theologischen Briefliteratur der Frühscholastik (Beiträge zur Geschichte
der Philosophie und der Theologie des Mittelalters,* 34; Münster, 1937), p. 497.
    Again, Bernard has usually been identified as one of the "two new apostles"
who, according to Peter, writing in his autobiographical *Historia calamitatum,*
journeyed to and fro stirring up persecution against the long-suffering, much
misunderstood Peter—pp. 202-203 of the edition by J.T. Muckle; p. 97 of the
edition by J. Monfrin. In a lengthy Appendix (pp. 212-13), J.T. Muckle questions
the identification of Bernard as one of Abelard's persecutors at this early date.
For his part, Damien Van den Eynde, in his study, "Détails biographiques sur
Pierre Abélard," *Antonianum,* 38 (1963), 221-22, finds Father Muckle's arguments rather weak; but he seems to have overlooked the important article by
Arno Borst, "Abälard und Bernhard," *Historische Zeitschrift,* 186 (1958), where
the author presents a good (though not absolutely conclusive) case against identifying Bernard as one of the *novi apostoli* (pp. 501-503). All in all, it might be a
bit rash to insist that Bernard and Peter were already on the warpath as early as
1131-1135. As for the precise basis for Peter's friendly, even reverential form of
address, we can only conjecture. It seems certain that they had had a personal
encounter early in 1131, when both were present among the retinue of Pope
Innocent at the monastery of Morigny (near Étampes); see the *Chronicon Mauri-
niacensis monasterii,* MGH, SS, 26, 40-41. Abelard, who at that time was trying
(unsuccessfully) to reform the recalcitrant community of St Gildas de Rhuys, in
Brittany, probably received no small measure of encouragement from Bernard;
and perhaps—though this again is a matter of conjecture—Bernard had put in a
good word for Heloise and her community, whose possession of the Paraclete was
confirmed by the pope in 1131. At any rate, even on the eve of the fateful
Council of Sens (1140—though some scholars have made out a case for 1141),
Abelard had to admit that, whatever Bernard's overt machinations might now be,
up to that time the abbot of Clairvaux had given every appearance of being not
only a friend, but a most dear friend: " . . . *hucusque amicum immo amicissimum
simulavit.*" See the recently published letter written by Peter to a group of sym-
pathizers; edited in part by J. T. Muckle, p. 213; and in its entirety by Jean
Leclercq, *Etudes sur S. Bernard et le lexte de ses écrits (Analecta Sacri Ordinis
Cisterciensis,* 9; Rome, 1953), pp. 104-105; and by R. Klibansky, "Peter Abailard
and Bernard of Clairvaux: A Letter by Abailard," *Medieval and Renaissance
Studies,* 5 (1961), 22-32.

based chiefly on an argument from authority. The New
Testament gives the Lord's Prayer in two rather different
versions—the one in the Gospel according to St Matthew, the
other in the Gospel according to St Luke; and St Matthew's
version, Peter insisted, was by far the more authoritative one,
and on several counts: (1) Matthew had heard it from our
Lord's own lips, while Luke had got his version from St Paul,
who had not even been present when the prayer had been
formulated by the Lord; (2) the Matthaean version had been
given to the apostles on the summit of the mount where the
Sermon on the Mount was given; the Lukan version had been
given to the mere *hoi polloi* down below on the plain; (3) St
Matthew's text included seven petitions (which obviously
suggested the fullness of grace given by the Holy Spirit with
his seven-fold gifts), while St Luke's text had only five petitions (and five stands, of course, for our five physical senses);
(4) further, St Matthew's version had been given to the
twelve apostles, while St Luke's version had been given in
answer to the request of a single disciple who had ambitioned
nothing higher than praying even as the disciples of John the
Baptist had prayed. Therefore, the Lord's Prayer as given in
Matthew 5 was more authoritative than the parallel version in
Luke 11. But if this was so, why should one substitute the
term "daily bread" (which is in the Lukan version) for
"supersubstantial bread" (which is in the Matthaean version,[4]
and which also has the support of the Greek tradition)?
The "standard" version of the Lord's Prayer accordingly corresponded neither to the Matthaean version nor the Lukan
one. And was it not outrageously presumptuous to modify
the *ipsissima verba* of Christ himself? Peter, then, merely
adopted the authentic text of the more authoritative version
of the Lord's Prayer. Let others follow common custom if
they cared to do so, so long as they accept the principle
which Peter now explained: in cases of conflict between the

4. But only in the Vulgate. Though Peter refers to the authority of the Greek
text of Mt 6:11, where *epioúsion* corresponds to the latin *supersubstantialem*, he
seems unaware of the fact that the Greek text of the Lukan version likewise
employs *epioúsion* (Lk 11:3).

two, reason (*ratio*) is to be preferred to common practice (*usus*), truth (*veritas*) to custom (*consuetudo*). And at this point Peter cribbed a whole series of texts from Ivo of Chartres—texts lifted in turn by Ivo from the *Codex Iustinianus*,[5] from St Augustine's *De baptismo contra Donatistas*,[6] from the frequently quoted letter of Gregory VII to Bishop Guitmund of Aversa;[7] and Peter closed this series with a quotation from the yet more famous letter of Gregory the Great to Augustine of Canterbury.[8] Essentially the same series of *auctoritates* was used by Peter in the Rule he had written for Heloise and her nuns, in a passage where he laid down the categorical imperative: "We absolutely forbid that custom should ever be preferred to reason, or that anything should be defended simply on the score of its being customary. . . ."[9]

At this point in Peter's argumentation, more than one nodding scholar has concluded that Peter was attacking Bernard and his colleagues for preferring custom to reason.[10] On the contrary, the whole thrust of Peter's thought leads into an *ad hominem* argument: How dare *you*, of all people,

5. *Liber* VIII, 52 (53), 2, ed. P. Krüger, *Codex Iustianus* (Berlin, 1877), p. 792. The text appears in Ivo, *Decreti pars IV,* cap. 202.

6. *Liber* IV, 5, 7, in PL 43:157 = Ivo, *Decreti,* cap. 235. In point of fact, Augustine himself was here quoting St Cyprian's *Epistola 73 ad Iubaianum,* PL 3:1117.

7. *Epistola 69* (of which only a fragment remains among Gregory's *Epistolae extra Registrum Vagantes)* = Ivo, *Decreti,* cap. 213. The text has been studied in detail, and exegeted with the brilliance synonmous with the name of G. B. Ladner, "Two Gregorian Letters: On the Sources and Nature of Gregory VII's Reform Ideology," *Studi Gregoriani per la Storia dei Gregorio VII e della Riforma Gregoriana,* 5 (1956), 221-42.

8. *Epistola 64,* 3rd response, in PL 77:1187.

9. T. P. McLaughlin, "Abelard's Rule for Religious Women" [= *Letter 8*], *Mediaeval Studies,* 18 (1956), 265-66: "Omnino enim prohibemus ut numquam consuetudo rationi praeponatur, nec umquam aliquid defendatur quia sit consuetudo, sed quia ratio, nec quia sit usitatum, sed quia bonum, et tanto libentius excipiatur quanto melius apparebit . . . ."

10. Ezio Franceschini serves as a horrible example when he writes ("S. Bernardo nel suo secolo," p. 19, n. 2): "Ecco di fronte i due termini antitetici: l'*usus* e la *consuetudo* alla *ratio* e alla *veritas*. Bernardo sostiene che per nessun motivo può essere violata la *consuetudo* . . . . Tutta l'opera di Bernardo è sotto questo segno e questo principio d'intransigenza."

accuse *me* of novelty, when you and your fellow Cistercians are notorious for flaunting tradition and custom and common practice so often as you have to choose between reason and custom?

Peter thereupon produced an elenchus of Cistercian liturgical novelties adopted in the name of fidelity to reason and to the text of the *Holy Rule*.

The novel Cistercian hymnal leads the list of *admiranda*. The Cistercians, Peter wrote, reject the standard hymn-repertory, and instead sing unfamiliar hymns of foreign importation—hymns so few in number that they fail to provide for the needs of the liturgical year. Indeed, on 365 days of the year, one and the same hymn (*Aeterne rerum Conditor*) is sung in season and out of season at Vigils.

Peter might also have added that, on many feast days, a single hymn had to do triple service at First and Second Vespers and at Lauds. The reason for this anomalous situation is to be found in several texts of the *Holy Rule*, where Benedict had used the term *ambrosianum* instead of *hymnus*.[11] A standard interpretation current in the twelfth century was that *ambrosianum* really meant a hymn composed by St Ambrose. For the White Monks, then, with their program of fidelity to the Holy Rule as they understood it, there was nothing one could do but adopt the archaic Milanese hymnal, which provided only a single non-variable hymn for the Night Office.[12]

Peter's jibe must have found like-minded Cistercian readers. I recently had the good fortune to identify a sheaf of hymn-texts from the early Cistercian hymnal, but bound into a breviary MS of a somewhat later date.[13] Many of these hymns were divided into two sections, thus making it possible to sing the first division at Vigils, the second division at

11. In the Hanslik edition (CSEL 75): cap. 9, 4 (p. 54); cap. 12, 4 (p. 60); cap. 13, 11 (p. 62); cap. 17, 8 (p. 67).

12. For further details and bibliographical references, see Chrysogonus Waddell, "The Origin and Early Evolution of the Cistercian Antiphonary," *The Cistercian Spirit* (CS3; Spencer, Massachusetts, 1970), pp. 204-206.

13. Troyes, Bibliothèque municipale, ms. 1467—a twelfth-century breviary from Clairvaux.

Lauds, and the entire hymn at First and Second Vespers. This practice eliminated the monotonous daily chanting of the inevitable *Aeterne rerum Conditor*, and also made for a bit more variety at Lauds and Vespers. At a somewhat later date, but before 1147, some lynx-eyed Cistercian must have noted that Benedict had used the term *ambrosianum* only with reference to Vigils, Lauds, and Vespers. This opened the door to a large body of popular and utterly standard hymns which were then assigned to Terce and Compline. At the same time, some of the more archaic, esoteric-sounding Milanese hymn-tunes were re-written or else replaced by newly composed Cistercian melodies of great verve and exuberance. The upshot was that, as regards the hymnal, Peter had much of his ammunition taken away from him, since this revised hymnal achieved a fine balance between what the *Holy Rule* seemed to require and what seemed to be the exigencies of legitimate *usus* and *consuetudo.*

A second Cistercian novelty was their rejection of the lengthy suffrages of the saints—an appendage to the Office not specifically mentioned in the *Holy Rule* and consisting of *blocs* of antiphons, versicles, and collects in honor of Our Lady, the Holy Cross, St Benedict, Sts Peter and Paul, various local patron saints. Abelard found it especially surprising that the Cistercians, despite their devotion towards Mary, omitted even *her* commemoration. A number of Cistercians must have shared this view because, in 1152, the General Chapter introduced a daily commemoration of Our Lady at both Lauds and Vespers.[14] As for other saints, their commemorations were not entirely neglected. Some 104 saints received Office commemorations on their memorial day—though only as something of an extra tacked onto the Office after the dismissal verse had been sung.

Likewise remarkable was the reduced number of processions. At the date of Peter's writing, solemn processions were limited to Candlemas Day and Palm Sunday; and it was only in 1151 that the General Chapter, in answer to the urging of

14. *Statuta* I, 46-48 (1152, 6, 7, and 19).

Bernard himself, authorized an Ascension Day procession.[15] Processions began proliferating only in the thirteenth century.

Again, by continuing to chant alleluias throughout the Septuagesima season, the Cistercians went clean contrary to western medieval practice. True, the preliminary acts of the First Synod of Aachen (816), as well as parallel statutes issuing from the same reform,[16] forbade the alleluia after Septuagesima; but the Cistercians had made profession according to the *Rule* of St Benedict, and not according to the statutes of Aachen. Since Benedict had prescribed alleluia-antiphons at Vigils *usque caput Quadragesimae;* that was that—at least for the Office.[17] As for the Mass, the Cistercians followed the general practice, since Benedict has nothing to say about the alleluia of the Mass; and Bernard himself on one occasion referred to the dropping of the *solemn* alleluia (that is, the Mass-alleluia) as of Septuagesima Sunday.[18]

Abelard was on still shakier ground when he claimed that the White Monks, contrary to the custom followed elsewhere, omitted the Apostles' Creed connected with Prime and Compline. Though the *Holy Rule* makes no mention of this text, which was recited *secreto*, the Cistercians followed the general practice, since the Creed was said either *before* the Office (Vigils and Prime), or else *after* the Office (Compline). Strictly speaking, it was not an element *within* the Office. The earliest redaction of the Cistercian *Usages*, roughly contemporaneous with Peter's *Letter 10*, clinches the matter.[19]

Peter also had a word to say about doxologies. The Cistercians used them for certain Night Office responsories

15. Thus Helinand of Froidmont, in his *Chronicon*, PL 212:1057. For other references to Bernard's role in the introduction of this procession, see Bruno Griesser, "Die *Ecclesiastica officia Cisterciensis Ordinis* des Cod. 1711 von Trient," *Analecta Sacri Ordinis Cisterciensis*, 12 (1956), 172.

16. *Corpus Consuetudinum Monasticarum* I, (1963), 436, 447, 465, 522, 549, 558.

17. Cap. 15, 2 (Hanslik edition, p. 63).

18. " . . . In luctu paenitentiae Septuagesima praesens agitur. Unde et reticetur interim alleluia sollemne . . . ." Sept, I, concluding section, *Opera* 4:349.

19. Griesser, "Die *Ecclesiastica officia*," pp. 174-75 for the dating of the MS; for the details about the Apostles' Creed, cap. (XCI) LXVIII, p. 230; cap. (XCII) LXIX, p. 234; cap. (CV) LXXXII, p. 246.

(since Bendict had specifically prescribed this),[20] but omitted them for the short responsories of the other Hours (since Benedict had been silent on this point).

More serious was the peculiar Cistercian Office for the last three days of Holy Week. All other monks conformed with the Western Church in celebrating these Offices according to an extremely archaic form of the non-monastic Roman Office; only the Cistercians insisted on retaining the ferial-day monastic Office-structure for these days—surely because Benedict apparently had provided for no exceptions. But this does not mean the Cistercians rejected the Roman Office-structure *in toto*. They themselves used the Roman Office of the Dead, and there was no problem about this: after all, this Office was celebrated *over and above* the canonical Office prescribed by the *Holy Rule*.

Though the facts alleged by Peter are a bit tendentious as regards this or that detail, the thrust of his argument is absolutely sound: the Cistercians *were* as bad as he was when it came to flaunting custom in the name of reason and authority. But Peter concluded with a new development—a plea in favor of variety as regards the use of texts. We are back to the question of his (and Matthew's) version of the Lord's Prayer. St Paul, Peter wrote, was not opposed to new or novel words, but only to words profane and contrary to the faith. Further, the emergence of new heresies justified the forging of a new vocabulary; and non-biblical words such as *persona, trinitas* and *homo-ousion* were cases in point. Finally, the ancient sees of Lyons and Milan allowed their suffragan dioceses freedom to follow other usages; and even in Rome, the customs of the Lateran Basilica—Head and Mother of all churches—were followed by no other Roman church. The message of Pentecost was that God wants to be worshipped in divers tongues: and, if in divers tongues, why not in divers forms of prayer and liturgy? Let others do as they like. Peter will pray the Lord's Prayer as the Lord himself prayed it.

I rather doubt that Bernard really had any quarrel with

20. Cap. 9, 6; cap. 11, 3 (Hanslik edition, pp. 55 and 57).

Peter regarding the legitimacy of variety of custom. Though
the principle of a relative uniformity was enforced *within* the
Cistercian Order, Bernard was all for pluralism. Long before
Peter wrote his *Letter 10,* Bernard had already rejoiced in the
multiplicity of graces and forms of religious life, and he made
this one of the major themes of his *Apologia ad Guillelmum
abbatem.*[21] No one has spoken more strongly than Bernard in
favor of the Benedictine principle, *alius quidem sic, alius vero
sic.*[22]

And the whole thrust of the Cistercian reform was similarly
based on the principle defended by Peter: mere custom must
always yield to the exigencies of reason and the authentic. A
decade or so before Peter wrote his *Letter 10,* William of
Malmesbury had sketched a remarkable pen-portrait of
Stephen Harding, in which Stephen summed up the Cistercian position along these lines: God creates and governs
according to the divine *ratio.* All genuine authority is rooted
in the divine *ratio,* and is meant to bring fallen man back to
the true *ratio* and order of things. This is specifically the
function of the *Holy Rule. Authority* and *reason* can never
be in conflict—so long, of course, as the authority is genuine
and the reason is truly reason. Therefore, so often as the *Rule*
is explicit on any point, even though the matter at hand
seems difficult to understand, it is reasonable to follow the
Rule's authority, since this authority is rooted in the divine
ratio. As regards matters not covered by the *Rule,* one is free
to opt for anything conformed to reason and not contrary to
the *Rule.*[23] It was not a question of the *Rule* and nothing but
the *Rule* but rather a question of the *Rule* and whatever else
was reasonable and helpful for the observance of the *Rule.*

Thus, in the area of chant reform, Bernard and his colleagues, sometime before 1147, re-wrote the melodies of the
entire Cistercian chant repertory. Their study of the theorists
had convinced them that their chant failed to conform with

21. Apo, III, 6-IV, 9, *Opera* 3:86-89.

22. *Regula Benedicti,* cap. 40, 1 (Hanslik edition, p. 101). The ultimate source
is I Cor 7:7.

23. *Gesta regum Anglorum,* IV, n. 344, in PL 179:1287-88.

the nature of chant as described by the standard theorists such as Regino of Prüm, Berno of Reichenau, [Pseudo-] Odo of Cluny, Guido of Arezzo, and John Cotton.[24] The reformed antiphonary was admittedly unlike any other antiphonary, but this was because the Cistercian antiphonary was based on *ratio* and not mere *usus*. Abelard would have applauded.

Of course, I do not wish to suggest that Peter and the Cistercians were completely at one as regards the tension between custom and reason or authority. My general impression is that, in practice, the Cistercians tended to make authority an absolute norm for reason; while Peter, at least on occasion, tended to use reason as the instrument for discerning whether what passed as authority was really authoritative.

I do not know if Bernard ever treated specifically Peter's defense of the "supersubstantial bread"—phrase in the *textus receptus* of the Lord's Prayer. But perhaps Bernard's position is contained in a remarkable passage from his Third Sermon for Christmas Eve:

> The Church. . .has the counsel and the Spirit of her Spouse and her God, in whose bosom her Beloved rests, possessing her and preserving her as the seat of His heart. Undoubtedly it is she who sounded His heart, and looked with the eye of contemplation into the very abyss of God's secrets, to make a permanent dwelling for herself in His heart, and for Him in her own. Whenever, therefore, she either changes the words in divine Scripture or gives them a new application, the new sense of the words is even stronger than their former sense. The new sense may perhaps be said to excel the original by as much as reality excels the image, light excels shade, the mistress excels the servant.[25]

---

24. For an excellent presentation of this aspect of the chant reform, see Solutor Marosszéki, "Les origines du chant cistercien: Recherches sur les réformes du plain-chant cistercien au XIIe siècle," *Analecta Sacri Ordinis Cisterciensis,* 8 (1952), 47-90.

25. Bernard, *The Nativity* (Chicago, Dublin, London, 1959), p. 17; Latin text in *Opera* 4:212.

Whatever might be the difference of emphases with regard to the tension between *consuetudo-usus* and *ratio-auctoritas*, I tentatively hold that Peter and Bernard were not so very much at odds with one another. Nor was their common attitude particularly unique. I suggest that their attitude simply reflected something of the climate of the Gregorian reform, and that both Peter and Bernard could have said Amen to the words of Gerhard Ladner:

> The question is. . .whether or not a custom is in conformity with the truth and its truthful tradition. If it is not, it must be reformed. This reform is not an innovation which would violate tradition. . .but it is the undoing of such innovations in favor of customs which are in accordance with truth and tradition. To build a bridge from the old truth to acceptable customs of the present across half a millennium of inveterate "bad customs," was in fact the problem and aim of the Gregorian reform.[26]

26. Ladner, "Two Gregorian letters," p. 242.

THE SOURCE OF THE *CAPITULA* OF SENS OF 1140

EDWARD F. LITTLE

Claremont, California

I PROPOSE TO SUMMARIZE recent discussion of the sources and authenticity of the propositions proferred against Peter Abelard at the council of Sens, June 3, 1140. Some recent discussions with Father Jean Leclercq on this subject will be given special attention.

Let us begin with the article of Jean Rivière, "Les capitula d'Abelard condamnés au concile de Sens" in *Recherches de théologie ancienne et médiévale,* V (1933), 5-22. It is a good starting point, because (1) it reviewed the various lists and texts of the *capitula* to that time, (2) it made use of the text of the nineteen *capitula* given in the *Apoligia ne juxta Boetianum* of Abelard, discovered and edited by Paul Ruf and Martin Grabmann three years before,[1] and (3) it was widely accepted as establishing definitely the number and texts of the *capitula.*[2] Even though there was some confusion in the article in references to other lists and texts, these will be passed over now as thoroughly obsolete.[3]

Rivière referred to a lost list of propositions which accompanied *Letter 190* of St Bernard of Clairvaux. In 1953, in an article, "Autour des capitula d'Abélard," Jean Leclercq pointed out that this so-called lost list "is conserved in more

---

1. Paul Ruf and Martin Grabmann, "Ein neuaufgefundenes Bruchstück der Apologia Abaelards," *Sitzungsberichte der Bayerischen Akademie der Wissenschaften,* phil.-hist. Abteilung, 5 (1930), pp. 3-41.

2. For example, Denzinger-Schönmetzer, *Enchiridion Symbolorum* (33rd edition, Barcelona, Freiburg, Rome, New York, 1965), nos. 721-39, pp. 236-37, denominates this text as the principal text.

3. For example, earlier editions of the *Enchiridion Symbolorum,* Portalié's article in the *Dictionnaire de théologie catholique,* etc.

than 25 manuscripts.'"[4] Although he did not then give a text of this list of propositions, he pointed out the possibility of doing so. He also called our attention to certain peculiarities: the presence of signs (crosses or asterisks) before certain of the propositions and gradual disappearance of the list in the manuscript tradition (although not in some of the oldest manuscripts).

In 1961 Leopold Grill published a text of this list attributed to St Bernard, from MS Heiligenkreuz 226, in an article, "Die neunzehn Capitula Bernhards von Clairvaux gegen Abälard."[5] He also took up the problem of the signs that accompanied the *capitula* and he proposed an explanation of their meaning. Where Jean Leclerq had suggested[6] that these little signs had originally been used to signify a selection of propositions that had been discussed by the council, Leopold Grill (reading *respondemus* instead of *respondimus*) proposed that they had been used to signify a selection of propositions that would be (in the future) responded to by the council. Of course this meant that the text was of preconciliar date.[7]

In any case we had placed at our disposal another text of the nineteen *capitula* apparently of an early date and connected in some way to St Bernard, different in some details from Rivière's text taken from the *Apologia* of Abelard.[8] Whatever the significance of the asterisks, the question of fixing the text of the nineteen propositions was paramount.

In 1967, Eligius Buytaert presented arguments for the

---

4. Jean Leclercq, "Autour des capitula d'Abélard," *Analecta sacri ordinis Cisterciensis*, 9 (1953), 101-105.

5. *Historisches Jahrbuch der Görresgesellschaft*, 80 (1961), 230-39.

6. Jean Leclercq, "Autour des capitula," footnote 3.

7. Grill, footnotes 46 and 49, also suggests the possibility that the words, *Ad capitula tantummodo ista respondemus, quae signo tali* * *nota sunt* and *Bernardus* were marginal insertions.

8. Most important of all, they differ in the numbering, since the list attributed to St Bernard by Grill combines two of the list cited by Rivière from Abelard's *Apologia* (ed. Ruf), combining no. 9 and no. 10 in no. 9; and vice versa, combining no. 2 and no. 3 in no. 2. In addition there are many differences in wording. These I have summarized in a table of comparison in *The "Heresies" of Peter Abelard*, pp. 380-81.

dating of Abelard's *Apologia*, the basis of the Rivière text, prior to the council.[9] Although not thoroughly compelling, as Buytaert's modest language seems to admit, his conclusions have been convincing to many of us.

In a dissertation on *The "Heresies" of Peter Abelard*, presented in 1969 to the Université de Montréal, Institut d'Etudes Médiévales, I followed the aforesaid chronology and argued that the *Apologia ne juxta Boetianum* was a response to the charges in St Bernard's *Letter 190*. Because of its anteriority, the list from *Letter 190* was adopted in that dissertation as an original and canonical list of the *capitula*. Since Grill's edition was the only printed one, it was the text used.

In 1968, Jean Leclercq published an article in the *Revue Bénédictine* on the sucessive forms of St Bernard's *Letter 190*, in which he questioned the authenticity of the complementary dossier, that is, the nineteen *capitula*.[10] This led to an exchange of views between us: (1) in an appendix prepared for the defense of the dissertation (subsequently incorporated in part in footnote 27 to chapter three, in a revision of the text), and (2) in a reply written by Jean Leclercq which is to appear shortly in the *Bulletin de philosophie médiévale* of the S.I.E.P.M. It is unnecessary to repeat the details of this exchange here, and furthermore it might only serve to confuse the important matters. Suffice to say that I am in agreement with Jean Leclercq's rebuttal to my arguments, as well as with the confidence he places in the originality of the Signy MS (Charleville 67) of *Letter 190*, and with the text of *capitula* which he gives.[11] I am pleased

---

9. Eligius Buytaert, "Thomas of Morigny and the *Apologia* of Abelard," *Antonianum*, 42 (1967), 45-64; see also recapitulation of his arguments in *Petri Abalardi opera theologica (Corpus Christianorum continuatio mediaevalis,* XI; Turnhout, 1969), I, 352-55.

10. Jean Leclercq, "Les formes successives de la lettre-traité de saint Bernard contre Abélard," *Revue Bénédictine,* 78 (1968), 87-105; also summarized in "Notes Abélardiennes," *Bulletin de philosophie médiévale,* 8-9 (1966-1967), 59-60.

11. "Les formes successives," pp. 94-97, 103-104.

that "although my arguments were not entirely convincing, he agrees that it is very likely that St Bernard had some part at least in the transmission of this list, and that this list is attested in a not-negligible part of the manuscript tradition, and he has decided to reproduce the critical edition following the edition of *Letter 190*, contrary to his previous intention."[12]

What may we conclude then with respect to the *capitula* associated with the council of Sens?

(1) TEXT. The text given by Jean Leclercq in the *Revue Bénédictine* differs only in insignificant variations of spelling, word choice, and word order from the text edited by Leopold Grill.[13]   A critical edition, based upon all the manuscripts of *Letter 190* in which it appears, is, as we have just seen, forthcoming soon. It should approximate these two cited here. Thus we now have something very close to, and shortly will have a definitive text of the *capitula* bringing a long history of confusion to an end.

(2) AUTHENTICITY. Although the list is not a part of the manuscript of *Letter 190* in what now seems to be its earliest form (MS Charleville 67), and although it appears to have been prompted by William of St Thierry, indeed even possibly written by him, it seems to have been made a part of the letter at an early date. Whether or not St Bernard was the first to write it in its form in this text, he seems to have adopted it, and in this sense it is authentically his. It appears in many early manuscripts of his letter. Abelard clearly regarded him as his accuser with these nineteen propositions, as his two *Apologies* explicitly indicate. St Bernard was a leader in this affair.

Perhaps the senses of the word "authenticity" need distinction. If the nineteen *capitula* are not authentically St Bernard's by initial composition, as Jean Leclercq's analysis

12. Letter from Jean Leclercq, 8/13/71, with text of the forthcoming article in the *Bulletin de philosophie médiévale*, which is quoted with slight syntactical revision.

13. Proposition no. 4: "i"-s are used in place of "j" and "y"; no. 6: *aliquod* for *aliquid*; no. 7: *possit Deus* for *Deus possit*; no. 8: *contraximus* for *traximus*; no. 9: *adscribendum* for *ascribendum*; no. 11: *etiam* for *et*; no. 12: *melior* and *peior* are reversed in order; *homo* is added; no. 15: "i" is used in place of "y" in *diabolus; sive*, in place of *vel*.

of the Signy MS seems to suggest, they are authentically his by assumption of responsibility for them and inclusion in a subsequent edition of his letter.

William of St Thierry's influence on St Bernard is beyond doubt. (If St Bernard picked up *stultilogia*, for example, from Thomas of Morigny, it could have easily been by way of William). Nevertheless, William's suggestions, even where literally taken over by St Bernard, do not absolve St Bernard of authorship. As in a world of cases, wherever we get ideas or words (and few of us are as original as we would like to think), once we put them down we assume responsibility for them. It is in this sense that St Bernard must be regarded as an author of the text of the nineteen *capitula*. Their inclusion in *Letter 190* is, in this sense, authentic, the earliest known list, and list proposed for some kind of public consideration.

(3) THE ASTERISKS. There remains the problem of the asterisks, or signs, which indicated a selection of certain propositions that were (or were to be) responded to by the council. In "Autour des capitula" (1953) Jean Leclercq identified these propositions as numbers 1, 2, 4, and 13 in Rivière's list. This looks like a slip of the pen, inasmuch as those would correspond to different numbers in the list appended to *Letter 190* (Rivière's list was Abelard's list, not St Bernard's). But tabulation of the asterisks, or signs, as noted in the *Revue Bénédictine,* pp. 101-102, clearly favors numbers 1, 2, 4, and 13 in Bernard's list. This latter identification is confirmed explicitly by Jean Leclercq in "Notes Abélardiennes" (1966-1967), p. 60.

The question of the reading of *respondimus* or *respondemus* in the manuscripts, and its significance in determination of the status of the four specially marked *capitula,* still needs clarification. It seems likely that these are a reduced list of the *capitula,* which received some sort of final emphasis. It would be ironic to say that, after all these years of confusion, the list of nineteen was discovered to be meaningless at the very moment that its text was established with some certainty. But this hardly seems to be the case: the entire history of the affair and the full list of the *capitula* should remain of interest to us.

THE CHAPTER OF SOISSONS (1132) AND THE AUTHORSHIP OF THE *REPLY OF THE BENEDICTINE ABBOTS TO CARDINAL MATTHEW*

STANLEY CEGLAR, SDB

Hamilton, Ontario

IN 1894, Dom Ursmer Berlière, as an Appendix to his study on the "General Chapters of Benedictine Monasteries," republished three documents[1] which have a close connection with the activity of Abbot William of Saint Thierry at the first two general chapters of Benedictine abbots of the region of Reims. The first of the documents,[2] which Berlière with good reasons dated during the Council of Reims in October 1131,[3] contains the acts of the first general chapter of some Benedictine abbots of the province of Reims: (a) they established an association of prayers for the deceased brethren, (b) introduced some changes in the divine office (*Capitulum de diligentia psallendi*) in order that it might be performed with greater devotion (*ut morose et cum devota distinctione regulares horae dicantur*), (c) decreed that fast and abstinence be observed according to the *Rule* of St Benedict, and (d) that silence in the cloister be observed by all.[4] Among the signatories were three abbots who had come

---

1. Dom Ursmer Berlière, *Documents inédits pour servir à l'histoire ecclésiastique de la Belgique* (Maredsous, 1894), I, 91-110: "I. Premier chapitre provincial de Reims (1131)," pp. 91-93; "II. Lettre du cardinal Mathieu d'Albano aux abbés bénédictins du chapitre de Reims (1131-1132)," pp. 93-102; "III. Réponse des abbés bénédictins (1131-1132)," pp. 103-110. See also *idem*, "Les chapitres généraux de l'ordre de S. Benoît avant de IVᵉ concile de Latran (1215)," *Revue bénédictine*, VIII (1891), 255-64, especially pp. 256-61.

2. *Documents inédits*, I, 92-93, and "Les chapitres généraux," pp. 260-61.

3. *Documents inédits*, I, 92.

4. *Ibid.*, p. 93: "In claustro vero silentium a toto conventu teneatur." It seems that the phrase "according to the *Rule* of St. Benedict" *(Secundum regulam beati Benedicti)* used in the previous sentence in regard to fast and abstinence, was meant also for the next sentence dealing with silence. What the abbots meant by this prescription is explained in their reply to Matthew: " . . . Ubi vix aliquando

out of St Nicaise, Simon of St Nicolas, William of St Thierry, and Drogo of St John in Laon. Geoffrey, who from 1121-1131 had been abbot of St Medard of Soissons, does not appear among them, since shortly before the Council of Reims he was elected bishop of Châlons-sur-Marne.[5]

In these acts, with their insistence on the *Rule* and disregard of certain Cluniac customs, Cardinal Matthew, at the time papal legate in France, saw an attack on the Cluniac traditions and way of life, which was the apple of his eye.[6] In a rather lengthy letter he first praised their zeal, and then chided them for the changes introduced.[7] He made several slighting allusions to the Cistercian observances[8] and compared the abbots to the scribes and pharisees of the gospel.[9] This must have reminded William of the open letter of Peter the Venerable to St Bernard, written some seven or eight years previously.[10] But if Cardinal Matthew thought that with his letter the matter would be closed and that the abbots would repentantly return to the Cluniac observances, he was mistaken. They were deeply hurt by the letter that misinterpreted their intentions and, in part at least, distorted the

---

invenimus tale colloquium, cum bona eorum voluntate exigimus silentium, non perpetuum tamen, sicut vos calumpniamini, sed sicut posse singulos intelligimus." *Ibid.*, p. 107.

5. Luc d'Achery (ed.), *Spicilegium sive collectio veterum aliquot scriptorum qui in Galliae bibliothecis delituerant* ... Nova editio priori accuratior ... lectiones V. C. Stephanus Baluze, ac R. P. D. Edmundus Martene collegerunt, expurgata per Ludovicum-Franciscum-Joseph De la Barre, Tornacensem (Paris, 1723), II, 486-92: "Chronicon S. Medardi Suessionensis"; p. 488: "MCXXXI ... Gaufridus, ... Abbas Ecclesiae beati Medardi, Episcopus Catalaunensis effectus est."

6. M. D. Knowles, *Cistercians & Cluniacs* (London, 1955), pp. 24-25. On Cardinal Matthew of Albano, see: U. Berlière, "Le cardinal Matthieu d'Albano (c. 1085-1135)," *Revue bénédictine*, 18 (1901), 113-40, 279-303; and also: Stanislaus Ceglar, S.D.B., *William of Saint Thierry: The Chronology of His Life with a Study of His Treatise "On the Nature of Love," His Authorship of the "Brevis commentatio," the "In lacu," and the "Reply to Cardinal Matthew"* (Washington, D.C., 1971), pp. 121-24, 400-413.

7. *Documents inédits*, I, 94-102; and Knowles, *Cistercians & Cluniacs*, p. 24.

8. *Documents inédits*, I, 100-101: "Quia vero illa ruralia et manualia opera, hoc in tempore, multis in locis, nec decet, nec expedit facere, ... "; p. 102, ll. 26-28: "Vosque de manuum vestrarum labore vivetis, quia tunc primum et tunc vere, secundum quod quidam opinantur et somniant, monachi eritis."

9. *Ibid.*, p. 96, ll. 29-35, and p. 100, ll. 13-20.

10. Dom Martin Marrier (ed.), *Biliotheca Cluniacensis* (Mâcon, 1915), col. 660E; PL 189:116B: "O, o, Pharisaeorum novum genus, rursus mundo redditum! ..." S. Ceglar, *William of St Thierry*, pp. 85, 86 (note 69), and 87.

facts.[11] The abbots deemed it proper that Matthew's open letter should receive an open answer from them, and they replied with a letter of about the same length.[12] Berlière pointedly remarks that the abbots paid him back in his own coin.[13]

The question arises as to who wrote the open *Reply of the Benedictine Abbots.* It is obvious that groups as such do not write letters. The individual members may express their opinions and propose what should be said, but then they delegate one of the members to write it. The choice will naturally be someone skillful in writing. Among the group of abbots, beside William, Drogo is the only one known to have written anything, some sermons, and even those are close imitations of Bernard's,[14] but they were probably written later than the Council of 1131. The most likely, and practically the only suitable candidate to be entrusted with composing the reply to Matthew was therefore Abbot William of St Thierry. The internal evidence of the *Reply* not only supports such an inference, but makes it practically certain. It is not so much evident in the first part of the *Reply* where the author followed Matthew's criticisms very closely, point by point, and refuted them. It becomes increasingly clear toward the end where he felt free to introduce ideas and expressions of his own, which are typically William's in thought and style. The following passage is the most characteristic:

11. For instance, he accused them of having imposed a "perpetual" silence in their cloisters, and this for others but not for themselves. *Documents inédits,* I, 95, 1. 30: "... Cur in claustris vestris *perpetuum* [silentium] imposuistis ..."; p. 100, 11. 1-2: "... Ne in sermone offenderent, subditis vestris *perpetuum* imposuistis silentium ..."; p. 100, 1. 30: "Vestro *perpetuo* silentio imposito"; p. 100, 11. 11-16: "Si vos ipsi post completorium generali silentio studere deberetis, quod *vos,* quemadmodum relatum est, omnino *renuistis et refutastis.* Unde satis miramur quod *ea, quae dicitis, non facitis,* nec istud tantillum digito movere vultis, ... *vos* autem *docere semper, nihil unquam facere vultis.*" (Italics mine.)

12. *Ibid.,* pp. 103-110.

13. *Ibid.,* p. 94, 1. 17: "Ces abbés, il faut le reconnaître, lui rendirent la monnaie de sa pièce," M. D. Knowles, *Cistercians & Cluniacs,* p. 25.

14. Jean Leclercq, *Recueil d'études sur saint Bernard et ses écrits* (Rome, 1962), I, 95-111, especially p. 97.

15. William of St Thierry, *Deux traités de l'amour de Dieu (De la contemplation de Dieu, De la nature et de la dignité de l'amour)* (ed. and trans. M.-M. Davy; Paris, 1953); and *Un traité de la vie solitaire, Epistola ad fratres de Monte-Dei* (ed. and trans. M.-M. Davy; Paris, 1940), offers better editions than those in the PL 184.

Resp Matt:

In Ieremia, "Sedete," inquit Godolias ad filios Israël, "in domibus vestris et urbibus vestris et comedat unusquisque de vite sua et ficu sua ceterisque bonis terrae, *ego vero respondebo pro vobis Babyloniis!* " . . . Da talia omnibus invidentibus nobis, talia ut videant et intelligant si forte vel *sola vexatio intellectum dabit auditui* (Is 28: 19). . . .[16] *Martha solebat conqueri* in iudicio Domini *de Maria* quod secum non laboraret, quod, satagente illa circa f r e q u e n s *ministerium,* quieta ipsa ad pedes Domini resideret nec audiebatur. *Nunc* in iudicio vestro *Maria* conqueritur et *murmurat quod* non *permittitur* laborare, *quod sedenti iuxta pedes Domini* quies et silentium indicitur, et a vobis defenditur. *Miseremini, miseremini saltem vos* qui talia estis experti, miseremini do-

Nat am:[15i]

In Ieremia populo Israël Godolias legitur praedicasse: "Ego pro vobis respondebo Chaldaeis qui veniunt ad nos. Vos autem colligite frumentum, vinum et oleum in vasis vestris, et *habitate securi in urbibus vestris."* (Davy, p. 106, 1. 23; PL 184: 395D.) . . . Donec longa et patiens experientia *intellectum* super his *dabit auditui.* (Davy, p. 80, 1. 32; PL 184:384D.)

Med XI:
Ubi est hodie *querela Marthae,* quod sola dimittitur *ministrare?*
Nonne *hodie Mariae* potius *murmur* totam replet domum *quod permittitur ad pedes Domini sedere?* [17]
(PL 180:240B.)
. . . *Miseremini* mei *saltem vos,* domini mei, servi Dei mei (Job 19:22).
(PL 180:238D.)

---

16. William quotes Isaiah 28:19, verbatim ("Sola vexatio intellectum dabit auditui") also in the Vita Bern I, iii, 11 (PL 185:233B). Bernard, on the other hand, never quotes it verbatim: Ep 189 (PL 182:254C): "*Ipsa* vexatio *dat* intellectum auditui"; Conv VI, 11 (PL 182:840D): "*Ipsa* vexatio *dat* intellectum"; QH XI, 3 (PL 183:226B): "Ipsa nos erudit experientia, *ipsa* vexatio *dat* intellectum"; Div XII, 1 (PL 183:517B): "Jam si *nec* vexatio intellectum *dederit* auditui"; SC XXXV, 6f (PL 183:965C): "Merito quidem, quod *nec* vexatio *dederit* intellectum auditui"; Ep 202 (PL 182:370D): "*Illarum* [Ecclesiarum] vexatio *det* intellectum auditui"; Csi I, iii, 4 (PL 182:732A): "Vexatio *dat* intellectum auditui, *ait quidam.*" The last two words seem to suggest that Bernard did not know exactly where the quotation was from. (Italics mine.)

17. Bernard, Asspt III, 2 (PL 183:422B): "Putas in domo, in qua Christus suscipitur, vox murmurationis audietur? Felix domus, et beata semper congrega-

lorum et anxietatum nostra-
rum, quibus propter Deum
et fratres morte afficimur
tota die; et *in sudore vultus
nostri* pro *poena peccatorum* nostrorum laborare
compellimur, ... *ne* ... *in
via deficiamus.*
(*Documents inédits,* p. 108,
1. 24—p. 109, 1. 7.)

Med XII:
... Panis ... quem *in poenam
peccati* Adae vescimur *in
sudare vultus nostri.* (PL
180:244B-C.) Ep frat:
Vescamur saltem *secundum
poenam* Adae pane nostro,
si non possumus *in sudore
vultus* nostri. ... (PL 184:
334 D; Davy, p. 119, 11
9-11.)

William was very fond of the expression of Mt 15:32, "*ne-
deficiant in via.*" It is used here in the same context as elsewhere in William's works.[18]

After the above passage another typical instance of William's style occurs, "Quicquid enim *pro puritate veritatis et
veritate puritatis* nos arbitramur facere..." (p. 109, 1. 18), to
which a perfect parallel can be found in his *De contemplando
Deo,* and perhaps nowhere else: "...Perfecte eos conver-
tentem *in puritatem veritatis* tuae, *in veritatem puritatis*
tuae...."[19]

tio est, ubi de Maria Martha conqueritur. Nam Mariae Martham aemulari prorsus
indignum, prorsus illicitum est. Alioquin ubi legis Mariam causantem, quia soror
mea reliquit me solam vacare? Absit, absit, ut qui Deo vacat, ad tumultuosam
aspiret fratrum officialium vitam! "

18. Ceglar, *William of St Thierry,* p. 367.

19. PL 184:375D; Davy, p. 56, 1. 3; Hourlier, §11, 11. 57-58 [*La contemplation de Dieu* (ed. and trans. Jacques Hourlier; *Sources chrétiennes,* 61 bis; 2nd
ed., Paris, 1968)].

There are in the *Reply* many other features, proper to William, like the expressions: (1) *severitatis judicium* (p. 106f), compare Nat am (Davy, p. 106, 1. 20; PL
184:394): "ex veritate et *severitate judiciorum* vultus Dei"; (2) *cum sanguineo
sudore* (p. 110, 1. 30), compare Nat am (Davy, p. 122, 1. 28; PL 184:402B),
"cum sanguineo sudore," Med V (PL 180:219A&B), "in sanguineo sudore" and
"sanguineum sudorem"; (3) "quod *ante nos dictum est*" (p. 110, 1. 10), compare
Contemp (PL 184:378A; Davy, p. 62, 1. 5; Hourlier, §12, 1. 37), "sicut jam ante
nos dictum est"; (4) "*adoramus vestigia* pedum eorum" (p. 110, 1. 15), compare
Spec fid (PL 180:374C), "in omnibus *veneratur et adorat* veritatis sancta *vestigia,*" Aenig (PL 180:416D), "Pie ergo et humiliter in via hac qua ambulamus,
praecedentium Patrum *vestigia venerantes* procedamus"; (5) "semper *movent* et
nunquam se *promovent*" (p. 103, 1. 20), compare Nat am (Davy, p. 110, 1. 31;

The above are only some samples selected at random of Williams's typical usages, but there are many more turns of expression that are completely in his style, for example, "...non patres *conscripti*, sed fratres ...*proscripti*" (p. 103,

---

PL 184:397C), "ad Deum voluntas animum *movet*, amor *promovet*," and (Davy, p. 112, 1. 14; PL 184:397D), "movisset ... promovisset"; Ep frat (Davy, p. 129, 1. 8; p. 132, 1. 13; p. 138, 11. 16-17; PL 184:340A, 341C, 345A), "movet ac promovet," "movemur et promovemur per spem," "movetur ... promoveatur"; (6) "cum desiderium et *conatum* prospicit paupertatis nostrae" (p. 104, 1. 13), "in religionem ordinis nostri vel religionis *conatum*" (p. 106f), compare Nat am (Davy, p. 90, 1. 24; PL 184:388D), "Amor ergo prius habuit *conatum* et aliquem affectum, caritas habet effectum," (p. 128, 1. 22; PL 184:404C) "conatu naturalis ingenii"; In lacu (PL 184:366B), "affectuum et operum conatus"; Spec fid (PL 180:383B, 395D), "ambientis conatu rationis," and "humilis devotio, cujus conatus pietas est"; Aenig (PL 180:423A), "expediendus est intellectus, et verborum conatus erigendus"; (7) "*rationis oculi*" (p. 103, 1. 21), compare Spec fid (PL 180:382B), "oculus humanae rationis"; (8) "*res et spem* saeculi" (p. 105, 1. 16), compare Cant (PL 180:507D, 509A, 536C), "non in spe, sed quasi in re," "sine re ... sine spe," "non ... in flore spei, sed in fructu rei"; (9) "*in sudore vultus nostri*" (p. 109, 1. 5), compare Med IV (PL 180:216C), "in sudore vultus mei"; Spec fid and Aenig (PL 180:397D and 406B), "in sudore vultus sui"; Ep frat (PL 184:334D; Davy, p. 119, 1. 11), "in sudore vultus nostri"; (10) "pro *poena peccatorum* nostrorum (p. 109, 1. 5), compare Spec fid (PL 180:386C and 377A), "*ex* peccato primi hominis, et *poena peccati* ejus," and "ex poena peccati"; Ep frat (Davy, p. 95, 1. 20; PL 184:322D), "ex poena peccati," and (Davy, p. 130, 1. 18; PL 184:340D) "*in* poenam peccati"; Vita Bern §63 (PL 185:262A), "*par poena peccati*"; (11) "Sed *quid dicemus?* " (p. 104, 1. 30), " ... *quid dicemus?* " (p. 106, 1. 36), "Sed *quid dicemus?* " (p. 109, 1. 15), compare Contemp (PL 184:371B; Davy, p. 44, 1. 7; Hourlier, §6, 1. 29), "Quid dicemus ad haec? Quid, inquam, dicemus? "; Nat am (PL 184:388A; Davy, p. 88, 1. 26), "De caritate quid dicemus? "; Ep frat (PL 184:333B), "Quid ad haec dicemus nos ..."; (12) "*Si durius* aliquid *loquimur, ignoscite,* quia laesa caritas *acrius dolere* solet" (p. 104, 1. 18), compare Adv Abl (PL 180:269C), "Si durius hic loquor, ignoscite si durius gemo, ubi gravius doleo"; (13) "in *erroris* devia *impingimus*" (p. 109, 1. 16), compare Sacr altar (PL 180:360C), "notam erroris impingere"; (14) "*respuere* vel *conspuere*" (p. 110, 1. 18), compare Sacr altar (PL 180:360A), "respuendum et conspuendum"; (15) "*exordinatos reordinate*" (p. 110, 1. 24), compare Cant (PL 180:513D), "... in tantum fervet caritas, ... ut saepius videatur *exordinari*, nisi a rege *reordinetur*"; *Brevis commentatio* (PL 184:435A and 436A [PL 184:435A, misprints "ordinata," but MS D (Bruges, ms. lat. 128; fol. 139ᵛ, 1. 21) gives the correct reading, "exordinata"]), "Cumque caritate *exordinata* sibi et Deo vacaret, filiosque negligeret, actumque Dei actui eorum praeponeret, facta est fames verbi Dei .... Audiens haec sponsa, caritatem *reordinavit*." Compare Bernard's Par IV (PL 183:769D), "acies ordinata facta est ... *de*ordinata."

11. 1-2), "exclamare vel declamare" (p. 107, 1. 2), "in reves-
tiendo et divestiendo" (p. 110, 1. 3), "ad exeundum *leniter
et* percutiendum *duriter*" (p. 104f) (compare PL 183:692A,
Bernard, Div 71, 1: Israel...duriter affligiture), "*quaedam
quasi* superflua" (p. 106, 1. 2), "litterata *quadam* aemula-
tione" (p. 109, 1. 30), "severissimo districtionis iudicio" (p.
105, 1. 13), "si *ratio* exposcat *cum caritate*, et *caritas
cum ratione* melius dederit consilium" (p. 110, 1. 28),
"exordinatos reordinate, *non aemula insectatione, sed* amica
et paterna correctione" (p. 110, 1. 26) (compare PL
184:371A, Contemp 7: Desiderat...te amare...non aemula
insectatione, sed pia et devota imitatione), etc. In short, with
the exception of the biblical texts and allusions, and quotations from Matthew's letter, the rest of the *Reply* reveals
William's thought, vocabulary, and style.

In the *Reply* William utilized some thoughts and expressions employed in his previous writings (Contemp, Nat am,
Med XI, Sacr altar, Brev com): "puritas veritatis: veritas
puritatis," "non aemula insectatione, sed...et..." (Contemp), the Godolias passage (Nat am), the peculiar turn given
to the Martha-Mary passage (Med XI), "respuere, conspuere"
(Sacr altar), "exordinari, reordinare" (Brev com). Since the
Reply may be safely dated in 1132, this year can be taken as
the *terminus ante quem* for the above works. Contemp and
Nat am must have been composed within the decade
1122-1132.

Moreover, Déchanet has pointed out[20] that St Paul's
line (I Cor 14:19), freely quoted in the *Reply* (p. 109,
11. 10-11) in defense of reducing the excessive number
of Psalms in the divine office, was later repeated by
William in the *Golden Epistle* (Ep frat I, x, 29, PL 184:
326C; Davy, p. 102, 11. 23-24) with the additional explanation of the same topic (PL 184:326D; Davy, p. 103,
11. 6-8): "...non expedit multitudine psalmorum obruere
intellectum, et exhaurire spiritum vel exstinguere."

20. J.-M. Déchanet, *Guillaume de Saint-Thierrry: l'homme et son oeuvre*
(Bruges, 1942), p. 143.

In the *Reply* there are two quotations from classical poets. As in other instances, William probably became acquainted with them at second hand. The first one (p. 105, 1. 2: "sicut de apibus dicitur et vos *animam in vulnere ponitis*") is a free adaptation of Virgil's *Georgics*, 4, 238:

Adfixae venis, animasque in vulnere ponunt. [21]

The other (p. 107, 1. 1), "Multo clementius Poeta: *simplicitas* inquit, *digna favore fuit*," is from Ovid's *Epistles (Heroides)*, 2, 64. The whole elegiac couplet reads as follows:

Fallere credentem non est operosa puellam
    Gloria: simplicitas digna favore fuit.

The latter quotation by William in the *Reply* is remarkable for several reasons. First, it is the only quotation of Ovid by William. Second, "the poet" for William, at least in this instance, was Ovid, and not Virgil as it always was for St Augustine and his contemporaries. This seems to give support to the suspicion that Willaim may have erroneously thought that the words "insanire libet" he quoted in his treatise *On the Nature of Love* (Nat am 6f; PL 184:384B; Davy, p. 80, 1. 16), were from Ovid, since both passages are alike attributed simply to "the Poet."[22] Third, in this case, by quoting almost a whole pentameter from Ovid, William seems to have acted against his customary attitude in respect to the poet. This could be explained by the fact that it was written in a public letter, in a piece of polemical writing, and not in his own name but in the name of the abbots. It was apparently a matter of custom and style to embellish such documents with words of a poet.[23]

Some eight years before the composition of the *Reply*, Peter the Venerable in his open letter to Bernard in the name of the Cluniacs called the Cistercians pharisees.[24] In the *Apo-*

---

21. Compare St. Ambrose, *Hexaemeron*, V, xxi, 69 (PL 14:235C): "Habent tamen [apes] spicula sua, et inter mella fundunt venenum, si fuerint lacessitae, *animasque ponunt in vulnere* ardore vindictae."

22. Ceglar, *William of St. Thierry*, pp. 302-303.

23. See Bernard, Ep 191 (and 324), and 338 (PL 182:358A, [547B], and 543A).

24. See note 10 above.

logia Bernard registered the epithet[25] and for the rest ignored it. But now with Matthew's letter in the open, with its attribution of phariseeism to William and his fellow abbots, Bernard remarked in kind:

> . . . Nor can distance of place and absence of body altogether separate me from the assembly and the counsels of the righteous, in which not the traditions of men are obstinately upheld or superstitiously observed, but diligent and humble inquiry is made as to what is the good and acceptable and perfect will of God. . . .[26]

Let those depart both from me and from you who call good evil and evil good. If they call the pursuit of righteousness evil, what good thing will be good in their eyes? The Lord once spoke a word, and the Pharisees were scandalized. *Now,* however, *it is not the saying of a word, but silence which scandalizes these new Pharisees* [italics mine].[27]

Discussing the date of Bernard's *Letter 91*, Berlière concluded that the Chapter at Soissons was probably the first of the chapters of the Benedictine abbots of the province of Reims held after the papal approval, in 1136, of yearly chapters.[28] He apparently failed to note that the passages

25. Apo 1 and 10 (PL 182:899B, and 905A-B).
26. Ep 91, 1 (PL182:223A).
27. Ep 91, 4 (PL 182:224A-B): ". . . Unum verbum olim locutus est Dominus, et Pharisaei scandalizati sunt. At *novos nunc Pharisaeos non verbum, sed silentium scandalizat* [italics mine]."
28. "Les chapitres généraux," p. 258. "La lettre de saint Bernard semble faire allusion aux mesures disciplinaires à prendre par les membres du chapitre, et les chapitres ne commencèrent qu'après l'approbation du Saint-Siège donnée en 1135 ou 1136. Il peut donc se faire que le chapitre de Soissons soit le premier des chapitres de la province de Reims, mais rien nous autorise à en placer la date avec Mabillon à l'an 1130." See also, *ibid.,* p. 257, note 2. The letter of Pope Innocent II of November 17, placed by Jaffé (P. Jaffé *et al.* (edd.), *Regesta Pontificum Romanorum ad annum 1198* [2nd ed., Leipzig, 2 vols., 1885-88; reprinted, Graz, 1956], No. 7738) between 1133-1136, could be only of the year 1136, since Hellin, who is mentioned in the letter, in November 1135, was not yet abbot of St Thierry (see Ceglar, *William of Saint Thierry,* p. 146). But there is nothing in Bernard's *Letter 91* that would place it beyond the year 1132. Nor is there justification for Knowles' opinion that "at almost the same moment" two different chapters were held, one in Reims where "the abbots were answering the cardinal-legate," and the other "a similar gathering at Soissons [which] received a most heartening letter from the abbot of Clairvaux" (Knowles, *Cistercians &*

cited above in the letter make perfect sense only if it is dated after Cardinal Matthew's letter to the Benedictine abbots. These passages are a clear reference to Matthew's arguments.[29] Mabillon may have dated the letter about two years too early, but he was apparently correct in calling the Chapter of Soissons, not the first, but "one of the first chapters" of the Black Monks of the province of Reims.[30] The order of events must have been, in all probability, the following: (1) the first Chapter at Reims (October 1131), (2) Matthew's letter to the Benedictine abbots (spring 1132),[31]

Cluniacs, pp. 25-26). It is nowhere said that the abbots wrote their letter from Reims. The chapter of Soissons to which Bernard addressed his *Letter 91,* and the gathering at which the abbots wrote their reply to Matthew, must have been one and the same (see note 30 below).

29. Especially the last sentence: "At novos nunc Pharisaeos non verbum, sed *silentium scandalizat."* The largest part of Matthew's letter (pp. 95-100) had been directed against the abbots' reintroducing the rule of silence in the cloister. He concluded his defense of the Cluniac practice in this regard with a biblical quotation: "Patrum terminos nolite transgredi" (Prov 22:28: "Ne transgrediaris terminos antiquos, quos posuerunt patres tui"), (Berlière, *Documents inédits,* p. 100). Ep 91, 3, is Bernard's answer to this kind of argument (PL 182:223-24): "Recedant a me at a vobis qui dicunt: nolumus esse meliores quam patres nostri. ... Elias ... non dixit se nolle patribus esse meliorem .... Minime pro certo est bonus, qui melior esse non vult."

30. See PL 182:222D, note 274: "Hoc unum est ex primis capitulis generalibus nigrorum, ut vocant, monachorum ex provincia Remensi."

31. *Documents inédits,* I, 92, 11. 6-7: "C'est donc à la fin de 1131 ou dans les premiers mois de 1132 qu'il dut écrire sa lettre aux abbés du chapitre provincial de Reims." Berlière seems to suppose that Matthew did act or could act as cardinal-legate only as long as Pope Innocent II was in France, and that therefore Matthew's letter must have been written before the pope's departure for Italy (on April 10, 1132, Innocent II was in Asti, Piedmont). In the present case, the pope's departure for Italy seems to be rather the *terminus post quem* than the *terminus ante quem* for Matthew's letter. It must have been written and made public toward the end of spring, or in summer of 1132, after he had returned from his diplomatic mission to the Empire (on Easter Sunday, April 10, 1132, he was in Aachen), and settled at Cluny for his convalescence (see Berlière, "Le Cardinal Matthieu d'Albano," *loc. cit.,* pp. 290-91). It is in reference to Matthew's stay with the monastic community of Cluny that the following passage of the *Reply* is to be understood: "Relatum etiam nobis est quae adversum nos scripsistis, coram clericis et quibuslibet monachis in mensa vestra lectitari, et de contumeliis nostris captare vos gratiam eorum et benevolentiam, qui et in hoc se placere vobis arbitrantur, si derogant religioni" (*Documents inédits,* I, 106, 11. 26-29). The Chapter of Soissons was most probably held in autumn 1132, for at their first gathering in autumn 1131, the abbots had decided to meet every year in one of their monasteries. The *Chronicle of Lobbes* says: "Ad confirmandam ... vel *silentii* vel *cete-*

(3) Bernard's *Letter 91*, and the Chapter of Soissons, at which William must have been delegated to write the abbots' *Reply* to Matthew (1132, most probably in the autumn). [32] It is usually assumed that the Chapter of Soissons, to which Bernard addressed *Letter 91*, was convoked and organized by Geoffrey, abbot of St Medard at Soissons. [33] But this could hardly have been the case, since Geoffrey had become bishop of Châlons before October 1131. [34] Odo, his successor at St Medard, received the abbatial blessing from Pope Innocent II himself on September 30, 1131, in Orléans. [35] It is not evident whether Abbot Odo took part in the first chapter at

---

rorum huiusmodi religionis exercitiorum observantiam ... *annuatim abbates in unum collecti ..." (Spicilegium* [Paris, 1732], II, 752; MGH, SS, XXI, 324, 11. 44-50; *Documents inédits*, I, 91). It is clear from the narrative of the Chronicle that at their first chapter in 1131 the abbots decided to meet once every year. Cardinal Matthew's letter must have preceded the second chapter in 1132. From the letter of approval of Pope Innocent (November 17, 1136), it is also clear that the abbots had decided to assemble yearly *in one of the monasteries of the province* (PL 179:253C: "... singulis annis *in uno monasteriorum vestrorum* celebrare conventum communiter decrevistis"), therefore not necessarily in Reims (PL 179:253-54). There is no evidence for the supposition that the second chapter (in 1132) was held in Reims. Bernard's *Letter 91*, which clearly refers to the same chapter, definitely places it at Soissons. Matthew's words at the beginning of his letter, "... abbatibus illis qui condixere *singulis annis Remis convenire* pro monastici ordinis correctione" (*Documents inédits*, I, 94), were written before the second chapter. They confirm the fact that the abbots had decided at their first meeting to assemble yearly, but, concerning the place of the assembly ("Remis"), his designation of Reims is disproved by the letter of Pope Innocent, which says that the abbots decided to gather *in one of the monasteries* of the province. Since the first chapter was held in Reims, Matthew must have erroneously inferred that the subsequent chapters would be likewise held in the same city.

32. In the early 1132, Bernard was on his mission to Aquitaine, and early in 1133 he went to Italy; E. Vacandard, *Vie de saint Bernard, abbé de Clairvaux* (2nd ed., Paris, 1897) I, 323, note 1, and 331, note 2.

33. See Mabillon's note (274) to Ep 91 (PL 182:223D): "Habitum est [hoc concilium] indubie apud Sanctum Medardum sub abbate Gaufrido ...."

34. D'Achery, *Spicilegium*, II, 488-89: "MCXXXI .... Gaufridus, cognominatus Collum-cervi, Abbas Ecclesiae beati Medardi, Episcopus Catalaunensis effectus est, & Odo Abbas successit ...."; and *Teulfi Chronicon Mauriniacense,* II (PL 180:160D-161A): "... Mortis hujus [Philippi] audito nuntio, papa praecordialiter permotus, mittit a latere suo ad consolandum regem venerabiles episcopos, *Gaufridum Catalaunensem* [italics mine], et Mattheum Albanensem .... Initur consilium, ut rex quantocius ad concilium properaret."

35. *Spicilegium*, II, 889: "MCXXXI.... Papa [Innocentius II] ... Odonem Abbatem Ecclesiae beati Medardi ... Aurelianis benedixit pridie Kalendas Octobris."

Reims, which according to Berlière very probably took place during the Council of Reims in late October or early November 1131.[36] If Berlière's dating of the chapter of the Benedictine abbots in Reims is correct, then the Chapter of Soissons, which probably followed it about one year later, must have been held in 1132, while Odo was abbot of St Medard at Soissons.

In the light of these events, one may venture the conjecture that the glowing praise which Peter the Venerable heaped on Geoffrey's reforming zeal may have been an indirect and subtle reproach of William's aims and actions. The reforming activity for which Geoffrey was praised by Peter the Venerable has no reference to the acts of the Chapter of Reims or to the contents of the abbots' *Reply*.[37] Peter knew well who inspired Bernard's *Apologia* and he must also have known who wrote the Benedictine abbots' *Reply* to his bosom friend Matthew. As far as Abbot Peter and Cardinal Matthew were concerned, William of St Thierry was an enemy of the Cluniac ideal for which they stood. For them the Cluniac customs took precedence over the *Rule*,[38] while for William and his adherents the *Rule* took precedence.[39] Their monas-

36. *Documents inédits*, I, 91-92. The Council of Reims opened on October 18, 1131. The Pope remained at Reims until at least November 5. It must have been during the council, or immediately after it while the pope was still at Reims, that the chapter was held. For, according to the *Chronicle of Lobbes*, it was at the beginning of the tenure of Abbot Leonius (in 1131) that with the encouragement and blessing of Pope Innocent II and Archbishop Raynald, the first chapter was held, at which provision was made that the abbots should gather yearly: ". . . Ita ut eorumdem auctoritate pontificum, Romani scilicet atque Remensis, Innocentii papae et Remensis archiepiscopi, constitutum sit et initiatum, ut quicumque unius in observantia et religionis fervore essent consuetudinis, annuatim abbates in unum collecti in se ipsis prius ordinem firmarent, quem postea tenendum traderent subditis."

37. See Peter the Venerable, Ep II, 43 (PL 189:256B; *Bibliotheca Cluniacensis*, col. 781D). See also PL 182:173D and 223D.

38. See Peter the Venerable, Ep I, 28 (PL 189:102-159; *Bibliotheca Cluniacensis*, cols. 657-95), *passim*, and Matthew's letter, *Documents inédits*, I, 98, 11. 11-20, and 101.

39. *Reply* (p. 103, 1. 29-p. 104, 1. 6): "Profitemur nos non in consuetudines Cluniacenses iurasse, sed in legem et regulam Sancti Benedicti . . . approbantes et venerantes omnes ubique consuetudines quae regulae subserviunt familiarius."

tic ideals were quite different. [40] In their two letters, Matthew and William, who differed widely in their interpretation of Benedictine ideals, engaged in open confrontation. In the letters Williams's superiority is evident. One feels almost sorry for the well-meaning, if ill-advised, Cardinal Matthew. The freedom with which William spoke to him in the *Reply* would indicate that they had known each other for many years and that William must have been his senior.

Once it is recognized and accepted that William of St Thierry not only cooperated in the first chapters of the Benedictine abbots of the province of Reims, but was their efficient, though unassuming leader, spokesman, and author of the *Reply*, the minute study of the *Reply* may add new dimensions to our knowledge of William's thought, style, and personality. [41]

40. The affable Abbot Peter managed to remain on speaking terms with Bernard amidst the most bitter disagreements (Ep 166, 1, and 168, 1; PL 182: 326 and 328A-B), but there is no indication that he ever met William or wrote to him. As for Cardinal Matthew of Albano, Knowles's characterization of him is worth repeating: "His criticisms are not those of a lax monk but of one who stood wholeheartedly for the Cluniac system as it was and deplored any infiltration of Cistercian ideas"; M. D. Knowles, *Cistercians & Cluniacs*, p. 24.

41. When provoked, William could be quite fiery: "If we speak rather harshly, forgive us, for when charity is hurt it usually suffers more grievously" (Si durius aliquid loquimur, ignoscite, quia laesa caritas acrius dolere solet) (*Reply*, p. 104, 1. 18).

William must have taken part in the next two chapters, of 1133 and 1134. No mention of, or allusion to any activity of the abbots in connection with the chapter of 1133 has yet been found or noticed. Could it be that Cardinal Matthew used the occasion of the chapter in 1133 to become reconciled with the abbots (either in writing or in person)? Although rough on surface, yet being a good man at heart (compare Peter the Venerable, Ep II, 9 [PL 189:98-99], and Berlière, "Le Cardinal Matthieu d'Albano," *loc. cit.,* pp. 293-94), on second thought Matthew must have realized how imprudently he had acted. His reconciliation with the abbots before his final departure for Italy would be also a diplomatically sound gesture, as he must have realized that he, a papal legate, had opposed an undertaking to which the pope himself had given his encouragement and blessing (see note 36 above). It would be perfectly feasible for Matthew to do so, since he must have left for Italy only some time in November 1133 (his signature does not appear on papal documents before December 20 and 21, 1133 (see Berlière, *ibid.,* p. 294, note 2). But all of this is mere speculation.

As for the chapter of 1134, Sigbert's *Auctarium Aquicinense* (MGH, SS, VI, 395), provides some interesting information on one aspect of the abbots' activity in connection with their yearly chapter in 1134, namely their critical interest in the reputed holiness of Aibert, a monk-recluse:

"1130. Domnus Aibertus ex monacho Crispiniensis coenobii assensu et consensu Lamberti abbatis claret in Gallia reclusus; vir nostris temporibus nulli, aut fere rarissimo comparandus. Hic viginti quatuor annis ab omni pane abstinuit, et totidem ab omni potu, exceptis duobus; quod dictu mirum est . . . ."

"1134. Hoc tempore capella, a domno Aiberto iam pridem cepta, Deo volente et auxiliante est peracta. Ad cuius benedictionem Lietardus Cameracensium episcopus invitatur, et cum magno tripudio eam devote benedixit. Quae per 40 dies ab omnibus pene partibus regni Dei instinctu ita frequentatur, ut vix aut numquam adhuc hominem mortalem huic similem nemo viderit. Quo tempore similiter apud Oscannum ab episcopo Remensi aecclesia consecratur; cui archiepiscopus, episcopi et *abbates comprovintiales* faventes, *multitudinem, domnum Aibertum frequentantem, prohibere ceperunt,* et de eo multa infamando dicere, quae reticere melius putavimus. In tantum enim eorum prevaluit contentio,. ut *causa probationis ad eum mitterent abbatem Sancti Amandi domnum Absalon, et abbatem Sancti Sepulchri* [Cameracencis] *Parvinum,* utrum talis ac tantus esset, qualem fama de eo diffusa aures omnium percellerat. Qui eius sanctitate comperta, per omnia laudantes Deum, ad eos a quibus missi fuerant rediere."

"1135. Obit domnus Aibertus piae memoriae, et nobis perpetuum merorem reliquit absentiae suae, anno incarnationis Domini 1135, inclusionis autem suae 25, die santo paschae [April 7, 1135]."

How greatly his fellow abbots appreciated William's work on behalf of monastic renewal, and how badly they missed his inspiring presence at their annual chapter in autumn 1135, held shortly after William's retirement to Signy, can be seen from the narrative of the *Vita Willelmi* (ed. A. Poncelet; *Mélanges Godefroid Kurth;* Liége, 1908), p. 90, ll. 13-19: " . . . Unde et ipse domnus Willelmus sinceritate ordinis provocatus, solitudinis etiam et spiritualis quietis accensus desiderio, onus et honorem prelationis deseruit et Signiaci habitum sancte illius paupertatis suscepit. *Exiit sermo iste inter fratres et coabbates ipsius;* qui Rainaldo archipresuli tunc Remensi *dampnum proprium ipsorum, commune plurimorum, in eius recessu* allegantes, accepto mandato ut ad regimen sui monasterii remearet, Signiacum festinant precibusque multis ac rationibus, pontificis mandato novissime, reditum persuadere nituntur . . . . [p. 91, l. 6:] Frustratis igitur ab [batum precibus] . . . ." (Italics mine.)

CONDITIONS OF LAND TENURE AND THEIR RELIGIOUS IMPLICATIONS

PHILIP F. GALLAGHER

Brooklyn College of the City University of New York

IN 1134 A GROUP OF BENEDICTINE MONKS left their priory in Normandy because they believed its site too exposed to the influences of the world and sought the wilderness of the Forest of Lyons where they established a nearly inaccessible abbey, hidden amongst the trees and swamps. Clearly pursuing ideals of poverty and solitude, they joined the Order of Cîteaux three years later. They called their abbey Mortemer which in less than five decades was an abbey of some importance, having grown in numbers and property at a fast rate. It was also badly in debt, however, and seems to have lost the purity of commitment to poverty and solitude that characterized its founders.[1] In the paper which follows, I hope to describe the contradiction between certain conditions of land tenure at Mortemer and the maintenance of the ideals of poverty and solitude. The problem was a perennial one for medieval monks generally and most dramatically for the Order of Cîteaux.

The ideals and intentions of the Cistercian Founders can perhaps best be discerned in the *Exordium parvum*, interpreted in the context of the early twelfth-century monastic renewal. Modern historians are in essential agreement on its general meaning and focus attention on chapter fifteen, the

---

1. The source of my material on Mortemer is the abbey's unpublished twelfth-century cartulary (Paris, Bibliothèque Nationale MS lat. 18369) which I am editing for publication. All references to this cartulary are abbreviated: *M*.

so-called *instituta*, where the Founders explained their ideals, their actions, and their motivation:

> Thereupon the Abbot and his brethren. . .rejected what was contrary to the Rule. . . .And since they could not find either in the Rule or in the life of Saint Benedict that this teacher ever possessed churches, altars or offerings, burial places or tithes of other people, or bakeries or mills or farmhouses or serfs,. . .they renounced all of that, saying, where the holy father Benedict teaches that the monk stay aloof from the doings of the world, there he distinctly explains that those things should not have any place in the actions or in the hearts of the monks who, in fleeing the world, ought to live up to the etymology of their name. . . .

Having renounced both ecclesiastical and manorial sources of income, the Founders continued:

> They also wanted to take on landed properties which lay removed from human dwellings. . . . Since it was also known to those holy men that Saint Benedict had built monasteries not in towns or in fortified places or in villages, but in places removed from the traffic of men, they promised to follow the same. . . .It was their desire to serve God devoutly day and night, [that] nothing [should] remain that savored of pride and superfluity or eventually [would] corrupt poverty.[2]

The ultimate aim of this monastic reform was, of course, the maintenance of a life of perfect charity. But two means stand out clearly in the *Exordium parvum*—poverty and solitude. No historian of Cistercian history has thought otherwise. "Everything contrary to real poverty and to a real separation from the world [was] rejected," comments Jean Leclercq. This included sources of both ecclesiastical and manorial revenue *"because all these bring the monks into contact with those who live in the world."*[3] Cluniac monks had accepted

2. *Exordium parvum*, translated by Robert E. Larkin in Louis J. Lekai, *The White Monks: A History of the Cistercian Order* (Okauchee, Wisconsin, 1953), pp. 262-65.

3. Jean Leclercq, "The Intentions of the Founders of the Cistercian Order," in *The Cistercian Spirit: A Symposium* (ed. M. Basil Pennington; CS 3; Spencer, Mass., 1970), p. 94. Emphasis mine.

both of these forms of income. The Cistercian reform of the late eleventh and early twelfth centuries aimed to end these close links with the secular world and return to the sole practice of the *Rule* of Saint Benedict. "They expected to realize this purpose," says Leclercq, "by locating on sites which were truly solitary, and by adopting a form of poverty which included living by their own labor and that of their lay brothers."[4] Writing on the "Motives and Ideals of the Eleventh-Century Monastic Renewal," Louis J. Lekai forcefully points to the connection between poverty and solitude: "The revival of eremitism was closely linked with the new concept of poverty. . . .The hermit not only withdrew from society but lived in total renunciation, in total poverty. . . ."[5] Real poverty and solitude meant drastic changes economically and socially in the monastic relationship with the world. "The implications of such thoughts were plain enough. *Monks must free themselves from the entanglements of the feudal society*."[6] There is no doubt then concerning the intentions of the Founders in this regard: both poverty and solitude were at the core of the Cistercian reform.

Although most historians have recognized the general nature of the Cistercian commitment, few have emphasized the precise

4. Leclercq, "Intentions," pp. 100-101. One finds the same insistence on the notion of poverty and effective separation of the monk from the world in the writings of the leading theorists of the early Cistercians, for example, William of St Thierry and St Bernard. See Patrick Ryan, "The Witness of William of St Thierry to the Spirit and Aims of the Early Cistercians," in *Cistercian Spirit,* pp. 224-53, especially p. 226: "William speaks of the way of life of the Cistercians as one of poverty, simplicity and austerity in an atmosphere of silence and solitude conducive to reading, prayer and contemplation." Bernard of Clairvaux is equally insistent on the role of poverty in Cistercian life. On Bernard, see Leclercq, "Intentions," pp. 111-14.

5. Louis J. Lekai, "Motives and Ideals of Eleventh-Century Monastic Renewal," in *Cistercian Spirit,* p. 37.

6. Lekai, "Motives," p. 40. Emphasis mine. David Knowles, *The Monastic Order in England: A History of its Development from the Times of St Dunstan to the Fourth Lateran Council, 940-1216* (2nd ed., Cambridge, 1963) offers essentially the same analysis of the *Exordium parvum*; see pp. 208-216, esp. pp. 210, 211, and 216. Another classic presentation is Jean-Berthold Mahn, *L'Ordre cistercien et son gouvernement des origines au milieu du XIIIᵉ siècle (1098-1265)* (2nd ed., Paris, 1951), pp. 45-54.

social and economic meaning of that commitment.[7] The monks of Cîteaux aimed at ending monastic contact with secular society. Some means of support was necessary, however, and in the early twelfth century the only possibility conducive to poverty and solitude seemed to be the land. But where was this land to come from? And on what terms? The answers to these questions created problems that were never successfully solved.

The moral dilemma of the monks may be described as follows. To avoid all feudal entanglements and contacts with secular society, an abbey had to receive land in an unconditional manner, that is, with no strings attached. The land had to be received in perpetual free alms with no obligations on the abbey in its regard. But uncultivated land which might be given free of feudal burdens was becoming scarce in the twelfth century as the pressure of population on land grew more intense and cultivated land for the most part was burdened with feudal obligations of many sorts. If the abbey could not get uncultivated, unburdened land, it had no accept land conditionally. In this regard there were at least two possibilities: neither was completely compatible with the intentions of the *Exordium parvum*.

First, an abbey might accept needed land on feudal tenure, agreeing to pay annually either rents or scutage on it, a conditional acceptance of land that bound the abbey in permanent relationship to the feudal society around it. Second, an abbey might accept land that was not given in free alms and yet avoid feudal commitments attached to it or any unseemly litigation over the land by buying out either the donor's right to rent and scutage or the litigant's claim with a substantial initial cash payment. Monastic charters reveal that such pay-

7. An exception to this statement is Bennett D. Hill, *English Cistercian Monasteries and Their Patrons in the Twelfth Century* (Urbana, 1968). What separates this zestfully written book from previous analyses of the Cistercian reform is the author's empirical emphasis on the socio-economic meaning of the term "feudal" and his consistently applied insight into the implications of the *Exordium parvum* vis-à-vis the feudal world. His conclusion that the Cistercian ideal was almost inevitably destined to failure will, no doubt, continue to be disputed.

ments were frequently made under the rubric *de caritate ecclesie*, "out of the love of the church." This second alternative aimed at avoiding land quarrels and the permanent relationship inherent in paying rent and scutage, but it necessitated the availability of surplus cash or the willingness of the abbey to go into debt. It was an attempt to follow the spirit of the *Exordium parvum* but had it own pernicious results, for debts could mount up and create anxiety over finances. Thus neither accepting land on feudal conditions nor paying cash to avoid them were really desirable alternatives, although the former was probably more deleterious to Cistercian goals than the latter.

It is difficult to read the *Exordium parvum* in light of the evolution of the Cistercian Order without feeling that the Founders should have considered terms of land tenure a potential major problem in the achievement and maintenance of both poverty and solitude. Their insistence on these virtues seems to imply a desire to accept land solely on unconditional tenure as the only guarantee of detachment from feudal society. While the Founders were very specific about many practical matters (for example, tithes and other ecclesiastical and manorial revenues), they did not address themselves directly to conditions of land tenure (although ownership of manors and their serfs was prohibited).[8] Tenure of land was a basic social reality, an unavoidable necessity, the source of all material support. Reform could not be synonomous with the rejection of all land; rather, it had to focus on *changes in the conditions* on which land was to be held. The absence of specific legislation in this regard thus suggests that the Founders either took such changes for granted or, on the

8. One finds no prohibitive references in the early documents of the Order to such things as specifically feudal as "land tenure," "rents," "scutage." Nor do the *Exordium parvum* or the *Carta caritatis* forbid the outright purchase of land by cash. Furthermore, most contemporary historians of monasticism (Bennett Hill excepted) have not considered conditions of land tenure central to the problem of maintaining the Cistercian spirit and aims. Neither the intention to avoid land tenure on feudal terms nor the aim of eschewing great expenditures on land are mentioned in the most recent study of the Cistercian reform. See *Cistercian Spirit, passim.*

contrary, considered them to be beyond the realm of possibility. But if they considered the acceptance of land on feudal tenure inevitable, was not their quest for detachment utopian? And if the Founders intended to reject lands burdened with feudal conditions, ought they not to have legislated forcefully on the matter?

The conflict between the ideals of poverty and solitude, on the one hand, and conditions of land tenure, on the other, can be clearly seen by examining the charters of donation provenant from Cistercian abbeys. They are a fountain of information on an abbey's foundation, its endowment, its acquisition of land, and the terms on which that land was held. The charters of the abbey of Mortemer are a case in point; by examining them we can observe specific instances of the manner in which some conditions of land tenure both reestablished ties with the secular world which the *Exordium parvum* sought to end and partially extinguished the spirit of poverty which lay at the heart of Cistercian spirituality.

No doubt some of Mortemer's lands were unconditional gifts. The monks received a charter confirming a gift of land from King Stephen in 1137. All the lands given to the abbey by the king were explicitly declared "exempt from all rent" (*quiete et sine omni redditu*), "free and quit of every custom" (*libera et quiete sine omni consuetudine*). The charter ended with the statement: "and so that all these [possessions] may remain to that church in perpetual alms, free, quit, and forever unattached, I have confirmed them by the strength of the present seal and by the testimony of those [whose names appear] below."[9] It is possible that because these lands came from the king himself they were both free of feudal obligations and unburdened by any demands for payment of annual rent. If so, this donation represents the type sought by the Founders. On the other hand, charters of donation that speak of free alms, exemption from rents, and other payments lead us astray if we assume that the poverty and

9. "Et ut omnia ista libera et quieta et inconcussa illi ecclesie in sempiternum permaneant in elemosinam sempiternam presentis sigilli corroboratione et subscriptorum testimonio confirmavi." *M*, Act No. 1, fol. 13r-v.

solitude of the monks was thereby automatically and adequately protected. A charter's profession that land is being given in free alms, that is, in frankalmoin tenure, can not be taken to mean that there were no conditions attached to the grant; grants in free alms frequently were matched by "gifts" from the abbey to the donor, gifts "which were actually sales or rents in disguise."[10]

Let us look at a twelfth-century donation situation. A baron or vavassor gave a portion of his lands to an abbey. He wished to grant it in frankalmoin, that is, in free alms, quit of all feudal services and rents, but if the land was ultimately held of the king and thus had services connected to it, the baron or vavassor could not alienate both the land and the king's services with it. In such circumstances the abbey could be given the use of the land forever, but in one way or another the service due to the king had to be protected. This could be done by paying scutage to the king or, more commonly, to the immediate donor in lieu of military service. In the twelfth century this expedient was becoming very common among the barons and knights of the Anglo-Norman and Angevin kings. To pay scutage, however, was to recognize one's feudal obligations—for Cistercians to pay scutage was to return to the society they had resolved to abandon.

The charters of donation in the cartulary of Mortemer make it clear that this abbey began receiving lands on conditions of tenure involving scutage and/or rent not too long after its foundation. Many other charters testify that Mortemer frequently purchased land outright and paid cash or kind to avoid either the permanent commitments that rents and scutage entailed or unseemly litigation over land. In the former case, the abbey became feudally obligated to secular society; in the latter, it ran the risk of debt, a gamble Mortemer seems to have lost. We will examine each of these two situations in their turn.

10. In other words, the rubric *in perpetuam elemosinam* does not necessarily mean "unconditional donation." Bennett Hill suggests that "very probably the amount of secular service that a monastery owed to a patron for a grant of land was . . . settled between the benefactor and the monastery in a verbal agreement and not recorded in the charter at all." Hill, *English Cistercian Monasteries*, p. 57.

I. FEUDAL TENURES AT MORTEMER

The abbey of Mortemer received land on conditions of feudal tenure as early as 1146, only ten years after it had joined the Cistercian Order. In that year the vassals of William of Roumare, count of Lincoln and one of the most important barons of the realm, made a large grant of land to Mortemer. The next year William ratified the grant and specified what the abbey had to do in lieu of the services owed on the land.[11] The abbey received the entire land called Bremulia both in alms and for a rent (*in elemosinam simul et ad censum*), namely, for two measures of common grain and one of oats, to be paid yearly to the donors, Odo of Grainvilla and Arnulf Bendengel and their heirs, without any other rent or service or custom (*sine omni alio redditu et servicio vel consuetudine* . . .). In return for making the donation, each of the two donors received 20 pounds of Paris, while their wives, sons, and daughters each got 30 sous of Paris. For recognizing the grant, the lord, Robert of Alisio, from whom the two donors immediately held the land as a fief, received 40 sous of Paris. Moreover, Robert of Alisio agreed to the transfer of land on condition that it be not detrimental to the service which Arnulf owed him (*salvo servicio quod ei Arnulfus debet*). To protect both Robert of Alisio and the monks, it was agreed that if Arnulf could not fulfill his services, Robert could seize the rent that the monks owed Arnulf, but the land itself would remain forever in the hands of the monks.

The next men up the feudal ladder, Nicholaus of Perers and his son Hugh, recognized the transaction on condition that the monks accept three clerics into the abbey as monks, for the good of their souls. And they added a condition in respect to the service that Robert of Alisio owed them, namely, that the transfer be not detrimental to the service owed Nicholaus and Hugh by Robert, but that, if it were, they would take the rent owed by Mortemer to the immediate

11. *M,* Act No. 113, fol. 46r-v.

donors while not touching the land itself. There the com-
plications seem to have ended; Nicholaus and Hugh were
vassals of Count William of Roumare (of whose fief the land
was a part) and William put no further (written) conditions
on the agreement.

The terms of the donation seem to have protected the
monks from losing the land and to have made certain that
they would not owe military service as such. The rent owed
each year was a hidden scutage. The large sum of money (40
pounds) paid to the immediate donors was perhaps the result
of the donors' willingness to sacrifice a larger yearly scutage
for a greater sum in the hand. The significance of the charter
lies in the fact that the abbey was willing by 1146 to accept
previously cultivated lands burdened with feudal services.[12] It
also signals Mortemer's consent to risk future litigation over
possible feudal land disputes. Furthermore, the fact that the
abbey agreed to receive men as monks as part of a land-deal
suggests even more strongly the unwholesome influence of
accepting land on conditions of feudal tenure. The whole
situation represents a considerable deviation from the spirit
of the *Exordium parvum*, a loss of determination to avoid
entanglement with laymen and an almost certain occasion of
future intercourse with them.

By another charter, an important Norman lord, Jocelin
Crispin, ratified a grant to Mortemer of 128 acres of land
around Pomereia "to be possessed forever in free alms, altogether free from every tie of service, custom, or exaction."
Later in the document, the essentially conditional nature of
the grant is revealed when the donor added the phrase *salvo
servicio meo*, that is, the grant should not infringe on the
service owed him. Each year on the feast of St-Remy
(October 1) the monastery was to pay 7 sous of Rouen to the
vavassors and their heirs.[13] It is admittedly difficult to be

---

12. The aggregate of the cartulary's documents on Bremulia shows that the area
was heavily burdened with feudal services, most of its components being fiefs.
Such a circumstance was less likely vis-à-vis uncultivated land. See *M*, Acts No.
113-38, fols. 46r-51r.

13. *M*, Act. No. 16, fols. 28v-29r.

sure what this means, but it is likely that for an annual rent the monastery was purchasing perpetual use of the land and freedom from the feudal service owed on it. In other words, the abbey was paying scutage in disguise.

Other examples of such feudal involvement were very numerous. Mortemer's cartulary reveals that at least twenty-six such arrangements involving land occurred between the foundation in 1137 and the year 1170.[14] The total effect of such involvement on the spirit of solitude and poverty cannot be measured, but it is hard to avoid the conclusion that the effect was cumulative and significant.

II. TENURES BY CASH PAYMENT AT MORTEMER

A second class of transactions involving land is documented by eighty-nine of one hundred seventy-three documents in the abbey's cartulary.[15] Here we find the abbey making payments to donors under the rubric *de caritate ecclesie*, lump sums in either cash or kind paid "in thanks" for the donation. In some cases, Mortemer purchased the use of the land outright by making a "gift" to the donor. In other cases, the abbey paid to avoid future commitments, hoping to put an end both to disputes over land and the obligations attached to it. Such payments were not contrary to the letter of the *Exordium parvum*. The amount of money involved in any one example of these *de caritate ecclesie* payments was usually not large; the danger lay in the fact that the accumulation of such payments could become an important factor (among others, no doubt) in the abbey's overall financial health with the potential to undermine indirectly but no less effectively the spirit of poverty. Let us look at examples of such payments.

A certain Guerard Boudart gave the abbey one half acre of land and 6 denarii of annual rent which a tenant of his

14. See Appendix No. 1: "A Fist of Land Donations to Mortemer Made on Condition of Annual Payment to the Donor and/or Heirs."

15. See Appendix No. 2: "A List of Land Donations to Mortemer Made on the Basis of a *de caritate ecclesie* Payment to the Donor."

paid him for another parcel of land; the tenant then gave the second parcel to Mortemer. But this donation had strings attached: Mortemer paid the tenant 12 sous of Paris, *de caritate ecclesie*. The tenant then surrendered to Mortemer 4 denarii which the abbey owed in annual rent on that land and for this action he received from Mortemer 20 sous and an overgarment.[16] This undated document ends with the note that all of the above were ceded to the abbey "in perpetual free alms, altogether free from every exaction." The document clearly reveals the steps the abbey took to free itself from the rent-paying situation.

Mortemer also made payments to laymen to escape litigation and wrangling over land, which was another threat to the spirit of poverty and solitude. A father and his three sons are said to have given the abbey a field and five other grants and to have "relinquished the claims which they were making on the lands which the brothers held." In return they received from Mortemer a horse worth 100 sous *de caritate ecclesie*. For confirming the agreement the father received 20 sous of Paris and each of his three sons five sous of Paris.[17] Could such disputes have occurred without detrimental effect on the spirit of detachment and poverty?

Some payments were unrelated to the effort to escape feudal obligations. Sometimes the abbey had to pay cash for land that it would then retain on feudal tenure. This could be very costly. One undated charter reveals that Mortemer paid Odo Pance and Baldwin of Ponte 16 and 7 pounds respectively, *de caritate ecclesie*, for two ten-acre donations. In addition the abbey owed the two men annual rents on the land, four and five measures of grain respectively.[18] There were many other donations accepted under condition of *de caritate ecclesie* payments to the donor. Richard of Verclives was paid 4 pounds for land of an unspecified size;[19] Radulf of Plaisseit received 60 sous for one and a half acres and 4

16. *M*, Act No. 47, fol. 34r.
17. *M*, Act No. 43, fol. 33r-v.
18. *M*, Act No. 85, fol. 41r-v.
19. *M*, Act No. 91, fol. 42v.

pounds for one virgate and three acres.[20] Amalric of Turfre-
villa gave one field and received 60 sous of Angers for his
generosity;[21] Hugh of Pleisseio took 103 sous for three acres
and sixteen perches.[22] The abbey paid 15 pounds to Amalric
Thorel for an entire enclosure purchased between 1165 and
1183.[23] Robert Iugluer got 6 pounds of Angers for a vineyard.[24]

The result of all these payments is uncertain but there are
strong indications that they helped to sink Mortemer in debt.
The relative paucity of specific information on expenditures
and the almost entire absence of documentation on income,
coupled with the fact that most of the charters are neither
dated nor arranged in chronological order, makes a precise
assessment of the relationship between land-related expenditures and the abbey's overall financial condition impossible.
But the context enables us to make some judicious observa-
tions. Constant expansion of land tenures surely increased
the abbey's expenditures. Both Abbot Adam (1138-1154)
and Abbot Stephen (1154-1163) are known to have increased
the abbey's holdings.[25] The chronicle says specifically that
Abbot Geoffrey (1164-1174) acquired a great many lands by
both gift and purchase and attributes numerous vineyard
acquisitions to him.[26] The charters of donation reveal that in
aggregate these purchases cost the abbey a significant sum,
whether paid in annual rents and scutages or *de caritate ecclesie*. By the end of Geoffrey's reign, the abbey was in financial

---

20. *M,* Act No. 92, fol. 43r.
21. *M,* Act No. 106, fol. 44v.
22. *M,* Act No. 109, fol. 45r.
23. *M,* Act No. 143, fol. 53r.
24. *M,* Act No. 156, fol. 55r.
25. Regarding Abbot Adam: "In tempore ipsius domus Mortuimaris plurimum
excrevit . . . in acquisitione terrarum. . . .". "Alias quoque plurimas ibidem terras
acquisivit. . . ." "Alie quoque terre a pluribus ibidem sunt ab eodem abbate acquisite
tam dono quam emptione. . . ." *M,* fol. 6v. Regarding Abbot Stephen: " . . . plurimas terras tam dono quam emptione acquisivit." *M,* fol. 8v.
26. Regarding Abbot Geoffrey: "In tempore ipsius domus Mortuimaris excrevit,
nam et terras acquisivit et domos edificavit. . . ." "Alias etiam terras quamplurimas
in Vilcassino tam dono quam emptione ipse abbas acquisivit. . . .". "Vineas, ortos, et
pomeria in valle de Portmort comparavit." *M,* fol. 9v.

trouble. When Abbot Richard de la Chaussée (1174-1179) took over, he found Mortemer up to its neck in debt: *Invenit eam maximis debitis obligatam.*[27]

Details of the situation are effectively hidden by the cryptic quality of the documents, although the chronicler of the abbey alludes to the problem, noting that Abbot Richard attempted to remedy the budgetary imbalance in every possible manner.[28] The unfortunate abbot lasted only five years before being deposed for reasons that are entirely unclear. There is nothing that directly implicates his deposition with the financial problems that he inherited, but one cannot help reflecting that such problems were among those the Founders hoped their abbots would be able to avoid. The *Carta caritatis* of 1119 made it clear that anxiety over finances was to be feared as detrimental to Cistercian ideals: "If any abbot be less zealous about the rule than he ought, or be too much intent upon secular business, . . . he shall be charitably reprimanded in the General Chapter. . . ."[29] Surely the avoidance of anxiety-inducing debt, a debt easily aggravated by frequent land acquisition, was part of the meaning of the Founders' insistence on poverty and effective separation from the world.

The major point of this essay has been that whether or not the Founders specifically legislated against the reception of lands on feudal tenure, whether or not they actually warned against purchase of lands on condition of a *de caritate ecclesie* return to the donor, both types of land reception were eventually inimical to the maintenance of the spirit of poverty and solitude. Both directly and indirectly, the payment of perpetual rents and scutages necessitated frequent and spiritually unhealthy contact with feudal society. And the purchase of lands on a *de caritate ecclesie* condition contributed to financial burdens in no way conducive to the spirit of

27. *M,* fol. 10r.
28. *M,* fol. 10r.
29. *Carta caritatis,* translated by Denis Murphy, SJ in Lekai, *White Monks,* pp. 270-71. See Jean Leclercq's comments on the Founders' intentions in this regard in "Intentions," p. 97.

poverty, for, if anything, debt drew attention to financial affairs by engendering anxiety over them.

It should be noted, however, that in discussing the dangers to poverty and solitude implicit in certain conditions of land tenure, I have avoided speaking of what has often loosely been termed "corruption." There is nothing about this matter which necessitates assigning it to the realm of "corruption." It is more a mater of the fabric of life in a feudal society, a matter of the unavoidable interdependence of many aspects of a society that was so largely grounded in the land. If fault is to be found, perhaps it should be laid on the success of the Cistercian reform in as much as its popularity brought on the expansion which made poverty and solitude so difficult to maintain. One must always take note of the distinction between the individual and his environment: if it was possible for the monk to leave the world, it was not possible for the abbey to do so.

APPENDIX No. 1: A LIST OF LAND DONATIONS TO MORTEMER MADE
ON CONDITION OF ANNUAL PAYMENT TO THE DONOR AND/OR HEIRS

Act No.	Amount of land given (ans—amount not specified)	received by donor annually
16	128 acres	7 s of Rouen
82	1 field	6 nummos of Tours
83	ans	7 s of Rouen
85	20 acres	9 minas of grain
95	ans	3 minas of grain
106	1 field	1 sextarius of grain
108	3 acres	1 mina of grain
112	1 1/2 acres	6 denarii
113	ans (entire area of Bremulia—a large area)	2 modius of common grain 1 modios oats *ad mensuram Andeleio*
114	20 acres	4 minas of grain *ad mensuram de Nongun*
115	ans	1 summam ripe grain *ad mensuram de Nonium*
138	(composition: re:tithes)	6 minas grain *ad mensuram Nogione* 6 minas oats *ad mensuram Nogione* 4 minas grain

Act No.	Amount of land given (ans—amount not specified)	received by donor annually
139	12 arpents of vineyard	20 s
140	1 field	ans for use of winepress plus another unspecified annual assessment
142	ans	rent of winepress plus annual assessment and 6 denarii
143	entire enclosure (ans)	3 s
144	1 vineyard	19 denarii
145	1 vineyard	12 denarii to one party 8 denarii to lords
152	ans	winepress rent plus annual assessment (ans)
153	3 small portions of land	3 denarii
159	1 virgate of vineyard	4 denarii
163	1/3 of 2 acres	6 denarii
165	3 acres	2 s
166	1/2 virgate of vineyard	4 denarii
167	ans	12 denarii
172	1 field	12 denarii

APPENDIX No. 2: A LIST OF LAND DONATIONS TO MORTEMER MADE ON THE BASIS OF A *DE CARITATE ECCLESIE* PAYMENT TO THE DONOR

Act No.	Amount of land given (ans—amount not specified)	received by donor
22	ans, in 2 places	60 s plus 1 piece of land
23	ans, in 3 places	60 s plus 10 s
24	4 fields	12 s Paris and 1 ox
25	3 fields	12 s Paris
26	1 field	13 s and 1 ox
27	ans	23 s
30	a road	1 uncultivated field
32	2 fields	40 s and an unspecified number of greaves of Cordova
34	2 fields	22 s
35	about 7 acres	90 s Paris and 1 horse

Act No.	Amount of land given (ans—amount not specified)	received by donor
37	2 fields (1 long)	13 s
40	3 fields	horse worth 60 s
42	1 field	22 s Paris and 1 sextarius of wheat
43	1 field and 9 plots	horses worth 100 s and 20 s Paris
44	2 fields	43 s and shoes worth 18 pennies
45	8 acres	60 s (?) (amount not certain)
47	1 acre	32 s plus an overgarment
62	1 field	30 s Paris
66	2 fields	8 s plus field in exchange
67	(claim relinquished)	10 s
70	oats (ans)	12 s
76	1 field	4 pounds
77	1 field	40 s
79	30 perches	8 s
81	2 acres	56 s
85	20 acres	23 pounds
86	10 acres	40 s
89	4 acres	26 s
90	1 field	30 s
91	ans	4 pounds
92	1 virgate and 4 1/2 acres	4 pounds, 60 s
95	ans	10 s
96	(claim relinquished)	12 s Paris
98	2 fields	36 s Paris
99	2 acres	24 s
100	4 acres	30 s
101	1 virgate, 4 acres	53 s
102	2 acres	24 s Beauvais
103	2 acres	24 s Paris
105	1 field	16 s
106	1 field	60 s Angers
107	3 acres	53 s
108	3 acres	120 s
109	16 perches, 3 acres	103 s
112	1 1/2 acres	45 s
113	ans (entire area, large)	40 pounds Paris, 40 s Paris
114	20 acres	300 s, 25 s. Chartres

Act No.	Amount of land given (ans—amount not specified)	received by donor annually
115	ans	20 s Paris
116	1 field	60 s Paris
117	3 acres	16 s
118	4 acres and another ans	22 s
119	2 acres	10 s
120	3 acres	20 s Paris
121	1 1/2 acres	10 s
122	14 acres and 2 gardens	80 s
124	3 acres	21 s Paris
125	3 1/2 acres	19 s Paris
126	2 acres	15 s Paris
127	1 field	10 s
128	2 acres	32 s
129	ans	10 s
130	1/2 virgate, 5 acres	33 s
132	6 acres	36 s
133	ans	30 s
134	about 23 acres (?)	30 s, 6 denarii, 2 minas oats
135	2 fields	20 s Paris
143	ans (entire enclosure)	15 pounds
145	1 vineyard	50 s plus 20 s to heirs
146	1 vineyard	70 s
147	2 vineyards	57 s
148	1 vineyard	69 s
149	1 vineyard	79 s
150	1 vineyard	110 s
151	1 virgate of vineyard	30 s. This transaction is actually called a sale.
153	3 small pieces of land	4 s
154	ans	14 s Angers
156	1 vineyard	6 pounds Angers
158	ans	30 s Angers
161	1 arpent of land	30 s
162	2 acres	15 s
163	1/3 of 2 acres	15 s
164	(claim relinquished)	10 s
165	3 acres	60 s
167	ans	40 s Angers
169	2 fields	75 s
170	1 virgate	20 s
173	ans (vineyard and fields)	1 horse

CISTERCIAN AIDS TO STUDY IN THE THIRTEENTH CENTURY *

RICHARD H. ROUSE

University of California, Los Angeles

IT IS GENERALLY AGREED, I think, that medieval Europeans had a genius for creating tools to help them in their tasks.[1] This genius was not limited to the creation of agricultural and mechanical implements or to the harnessing of power, but it also manifested itself in the area of medieval thought and letters in the creation and development of a host of technical aids to study, among them the verbal concordance, the subject index, and the location list of books. This aspect of medieval technology, what one might term the technology of thought, has not, as yet, received particular attention from either historians of medieval technology or historians of medieval thought.[2]

* This paper is part of a study of thirteenth and fourteenth Century aids to preaching, in particular the *Manipulus Florum* of Thomas of Ireland, which my wife and I have in progress. Research for this study has been supported by grants from the American Philosophical Society and the American Council of Learned Societies.

1. See in particular the following articles by Lynn T. White, Jr.: "The Medieval Roots of Modern Technology and Science," *Perspectives in Medieval History* (ed. E. F. Drew and F. S. Lear; Chicago, 1963), pp. 19-34; "What Accelerated Technological Progress in the Western Middle Ages?" *Scientific Change* (ed. A. C. Crombie; New York, 1963), pp. 272-91; and "The Changing Middle Ages," *The Knowledge Explosion: Liberation and Limitation* (ed. F. Sweeney; New York, 1966), pp. 161-80.

2. The following provide some introduction to the problem as a whole via the analysis of specific tools: M. Grabmann, "Hilfsmittel des Thomasstudiums aus alter Zeit," *Mittelalterliches Geistesleben* (Munich, 1936), II, 424-89; *idem, Methoden und Hilfsmittel des Aristotelesstudiums im Mittelalter (Sitzungsberichte der Bayerischen Akademie der Wisenschaften*, Phil.-hist. Abt., 5; Munich, 1939); J. de Ghellinck, "*Originale* et *originalia*," *Archivum Latinitatis Medii Aevi*, 14 (1939), 95-105; D. A. Callus, "The 'Tabulae super originalia patrum' of Robert Kilwardby OP," *Studia Mediaevalia in honorem admodum reverendi patris*

The late twelfth and early thirteenth century witnessed a basic change in the attitude of scholars toward inherited written authority. This change has been characterized by M.-D. Chenu as the evangelical return to the original sources and the faith-inspired search for appropriate tools.[3] In the words of R. W. Hunt, the main effort of theologians in the twelfth century had been directed towards the organization of inherited material in systematic form. In the thirteenth century there was a return to the sources. Students were eager to go behind the mosaic of patristic texts brought together in the Gloss on the Bible and in the *Sentences* of Peter Lombard, and to search out the *originalia patrum*.[4] To help them in this search they created a variety of tools—verbal concordances, subject indexes, alphabetically arranged compendia, and location lists of books.

It is difficult to impress upon the non-specialist the truly revolutionary nature of this change; the whole complex of aids to searching—indexes, alphabetical arrangement, the numbering of pages, for example—is so thoroughly, and yet so prosaically, a part of our lives that we cannot imagine a world that did without them. Two aspects of this change are particularly interesting: first, it has an identifiable and almost explosive beginning, in the opening years of the thirteenth century. The practice of indexing did not evolve over centuries, through a gentle progression of cultural mutations; it out-and-out began. The rapid development of indexing forms is visible and measurable in terms of geography and chronology. Subject indexes to Aristotle's *Ethics* are available by 1250, to Gregory's *Moralia* by 1260 or 1270, to Gratians's

Raymondi Josephi Martin (Bruges, 1948), pp. 243-70; *idem,* "New Manuscripts of Kilwardby's *Tabulae super originalia patrum,*" *Dominican Studies,* 2 (1949), 38-45; *idem,* "The Contribution to the Study of the Fathers made by the Thirteenth-Century Oxford Schools," *Journal of Ecclesiastical History,* 5 (1954), 139-48; R. W. Hunt, "Manuscripts containing the Indexing Symbols of Robert Grosseteste," *The Bodleian Library Record,* 4 (1953), 241-55. A. D. von den Brincken, "Tabula Alphabetica: von den Anfängen alphabetischer Registerarbeiten zu Geschichtswerken," in *Festschrift für Hermann Heimpel* II (Güttingen, 1972), pp. 900-923.

3. M.-D. Chenu, *Introduction à l'étude de Saint Thomas d'Aquin* (Université de Montréal, *Publications de l'Institut d'études médiévales,* 11; Montréal, 1950), pp. 40-41.

4. Hunt, "Indexing Symbols," pp. 249-50.

Decretum, the Lombard's *Sentences*, and the corpus of St Augustine by 1280. By the end of the century virtually every major work was equipped with an apparatus by means of which it could be searched. Second, the invention and use of these tools appear to have been unique to Western intellectual development: devices similar to these were not known in the Greek, Oriental, Arabic, or Hebrew intellectual experience —to my knowledge.

The development of aids to study, where it has been examined, is normally associated, as the quotations from Chenu and Hunt indicate, with the schools and the mendicants. This is an understandable assumption, given the facts that many thirteenth-century aids to study were produced by mendicant schoolmen, and that the friars stemmed from an evangelical spirit. However, a search for, and an examination of, the earliest aids to study, particularly subject indexes, shows that one must consider the origins of the subject index—or the desire to get at material—in broader terms. I want first to illustrate this by examining early-thirteenth-century aids to study in three Cistercian houses, Clairvaux, Villers-en-Brabant, and Ter Duinen in Bruges; and second, I want to illustrate, with one specific example, how these tools tie directly to those produced in the university at the end of the century.

The first devices which were specifically created to help one perform another task, in the period under examination, were the alphabetical collections of *distinctiones*.[5] These emerged in the last decades of the twelfth century in Cistercian and school circles and were employed in scriptural exegesis and the composition of sermons. The collection of interest here is Warner of Rochefort's *Angelus*.[6] Warner, abbot of

5. Regarding the development and use of collections of *distinctiones* see P. S. Moore, *The Works of Peter of Poitiers (Publications in Mediaeval Studies;* Notre Dame, 1936), pp. 78-96; A. Wilmart, "Un répertoire d'exégèse composé en Angleterre vers le début du XIIIe siècle," *Mémorial Lagrange* (Paris, 1940), pp. 307-346, especially the list of collections in the appendix; and B. Smalley, *The Study of the Bible in the Middle Ages* (Oxford, 1952), pp. 246-49.

6. The *Angelus* is printed in PL 112:849-1088 under the name of Rabanus Maurus. Regarding its authorship see A. Wilmart, "Les Allégories sur l'écriture attribuées à Raban Maur," *Revue Bénédictine,* 32 (1920), 47-56. Concerning

Auberive, became the ninth abbot of Clairvaux in 1186. In 1193 he was named bishop of Langres. He resigned the office in 1198 to retire to Clairvaux where he died after 1216. The *Angelus* is a vast biblical dictionary in twenty-three books, containing roughly 900 words in first letter alphabetical order from *Angelus* to *Zona.* For each word one finds listed various figurative meanings, each meaning being supplied with a biblical quotation and a terse explanation of the symbolism.[7] Wilmart knew of twenty manuscripts of the work of which six came from Clairvaux itself, two of which, Troyes MSS 32 and 392 (formerly Clairvaux M. 2 and 3), were bequeathed by Warner himself.

Far more sophisticated tools were to be produced in the first half of the thirteenth century. Cistercian writers at Clairvaux and its daughter-house, Villers in Brabant, devised a mature means of indexing *florilegia* sometime before 1246. Let us examine the Clairvaux *florilegia* first. Two indexed *florilegia,* the *Liber exceptionum ex libris viginti trium auctorum* and *Flores Bernardi,* were compiled at Clairvaux, from Clairvaux books, during the first third of the thirteenth century, probably by William of Montague.[8] William was prior of Clairvaux, then abbot of La Ferté, and in 1227 became abbot of Cîteaux. At some time late in life (after 1239) he resigned the abbacy and retired to spend his final years as a

---

Warner see: C. Baeumker, *Contra Amaurianas (Beiträge zur Geschichte der Philosophie des Mittelalters,* 24; Münster, 1926), and N. M. Häring, "The Liberal Arts in the Sermons of Garnier of Rochefort," *Mediaeval Studies,* 30 (1968), 47-77.

7. These meanings appear under the first heading: "Angel means Christ, or the Holy Spirit—as in the Gospel of John: 'An angel descended into the pool and stirred up the water, and whoever first went down into the pool after the motion of the water was healed'; thus, Christ came to the Jews, so that by stirring up that people through faith in his Passion, the whole body of the faithful would be healed. Or: thus, the Holy Spirit, descending into the baptismal font and making it fruitful, cleanses the faithful. *Angel* means John the Baptist . . . as the prophet said: 'Behold I send my angel, and he shall prepare the way before me'; thus, John preceded the Lord to make ready his pathway. *Angel* means 'an evil spirit' . . . . *Angels* means 'heavenly spirits'. . . . *Angel* means 'a priest'. . . ."

8. See the biographical notice by Petit-Radel in *Histoire littéraire de la France,* 18 (1835), 338-46. "Guillaume, abbé de Cîteaux," the subject of a notice by Daunou in the same volume (pp. 149-52), is of course the same William of Montague.

monk at Clairvaux where he died in 1245 or 1246. It was probably in these later years that he worked on the two *florilegia*.[9] The *Liber exceptionum* survives in eight manuscripts, of which the oldest is Troyes MS 186 (formerly Clairvaux L. 50). The *Flores Bernardi* survives in two manuscripts, of which the older is Troyes 497 (formerly Clairvaux H. 49). The two manuscripts were written and decorated by the same scribe of the first half of the thirteenth century and in all likelihood represent fair copies of William's works.

Each *florilegium* is a collection of 5000-6000 extracts arranged in the order of the books from which they were taken, provided with reference symbols, and equipped with an extensive alphabetical index. The reference system and the index are the items of interest for us. Montague divided his *florilegia* into numbered "distinctions," and each *distinctio* was subdivided by letters of the alphabet. The divisions in both cases are arbitrary and bear little relation to divisions in the text of the *florilegium*. The indexes occupy about 23-25 folios each, contain ca. 2,300 subjects with up to eighty or ninety references each. The reference provides *distinctio*, letter) and lemma, for example, "Abducere: XIX. A. *Magni*." In the case of both books, and particularly for the *Liber exceptionum*, we can identify the very books which Montague used in compiling his *florilegium*. The great folio "edition" of the works of St. Augustine and other fathers in ten (or more) volumes, which apparently formed the nucleus of many twelfth-century Cistercian libraries (the Clairvaux set is now Troyes MS. 40 in 10 parts) was the starting point.[10] In

9. The attribution to William is based on the knowledge of the fifteenth-century librarian of Clairvaux who added the ex-libris, "Liber sancte Marie Clarevallis quem compilavit frater Guillermus de Monte Acuto monachus Clarevallis. Ora pro eo Lector," in Troyes MSS 186 and 705.

10. Regarding the twelfth-century library of Clairvaux and this edition of the Fathers see A. Wilmart, "L'ancienne bibliothèque de Clairvaux," *Collectanea Ordinis Cisterciensium Reformatorum*, 11 (1949), 101-127, 301-319, reprinted from *Mémoires de la Société Académique de l'Aube*, 3rd ser., 54 (1917), 125-90, J. de Ghellinck, "Une édition ou une collection médiévals des opera omnia de Saint Augustin," *Liber Floridus: Mittellateinische Studien P. Lehmann* (St Ottilien, 1950), pp. 63-82, and W. M. Green, "Mediaeval Rescenions of St Augustine," *Speculum*, 29 (1954), 531-34. The edition of the catalogue of 1472 being prepared by André Vernet is now well advanced.

some of these manuscripts, the folio volumes of St. Augustine, for example, we find what are probably physical vestiges of William's work. Passages which reappear in the *Liber exceptionum* are designated with a *Nota*, later to be copied out by William or a scribe.

This method of indexing was also applied at Clairvaux to the Scriptures. An extensive set of extracts from the Old and New Testaments was made in the mid-thirteenth century; it survives in two manuscripts, of which the older is Troyes 1037 (formerly Clairvaux A. 61). The extracts run in the order of the Scriptures, and are supplied with a marginal reference system consisting of sequences of letters of the alphabet (Aaa, Aab, Aac...Aba, etc.) and a large index of approximately 1000 topics, occupying 43 folios. While the *Liber exceptionum* and the Villers book were influential outside their places of origin, I have not found other examples of indexed biblical *florilegia*.

Turning now to Villers in Brabant, we find a similar example of an indexed *florilegium* in the *Flores paradysii*.[11] This work survives in three distinct states, each of which is represented by a single manuscript. The text was compiled at Villers and developed there in the first half of the thirteenth century. We have found no way of determining whether it was older or younger than the *Liber exceptionum*, but I would suggest that it was older if only because it is more primitive. In each, the extracts flow in the order of the books from which they were taken. The earliest of the three versions, *Flores paradysii A* (now Brussels, Bibliothèque Royale MS 4785-93; Van den Gheyn 970), was written after 1216 and probably before 1230. It bears an artificial reference system, in which each opening of the book is designated by letters of the alphabet (Aa, Ab, Ac...etc.), and each extract in the opening by a letter of the alphabet. The index of 450 subjects refers to opening and *sententia*, for example, Ac.g. Version B of the *Flores paradysii* (Brussels, Bibliothèque Royale MS 20030-32; Van den Gheyn 1508) is greatly en-

11. Villers was founded from Clairvaux in 1146. Regarding its library see H. Schuermans, "Bibliothèque de l'Abbaye de Villers," *Société archéologique de l'arrondissement de Nivelles*, 6 (1898), 193-236.

glarged. Three concentric series of the alphabet replace the sequence of lettered openings, and the index grows to almost 1000 subjects. The *Flores paradysii* got to Paris by 1260 or 1270, by which time it was found at the Sorbonne in a third version, *Flores paradysii C* (Paris B.N. MS lat. 15982). Fortunately the author of *Flores paradysii B* supplied it with a prologue in which he explained the nature and the purpose of the work and how to use the index. His book, he says, "filled with the choicest sentences, offers grace to its readers as if it were filled with the finest flowers of paradise." Through them a knowledge of truth is attained, permitting one to recognize good and shun evil, to fear the Lord and turn from the mortality of this world. Wishing to leave something for posterity, the author has collected sentences from the Fathers (and the ancients, I would add) which, like the flowers of paradise, will not wilt but will change their admirers for the better. Here one finds compactly all that one might find in the great books of many libraries. The second part of the prologue describes the purpose and mechanics of the index. The compiler says that the topics among the extracts which are most important for sermon-making are listed alphabetically with references to their location; and he gives a detailed description of the reference system on which the index depends, complete with exhortations to the faint-hearted. The instructions are clear and precise, and display a sympathy for man's horror of the complicated.

These books from Villers and Clairvaux are a striking merger of a traditional form, the *florilegium*, with a wholly new and original tool, the alphabetic subject index.

The problems of gaining access to material was also clearly in the minds of the Cistercians of Ter Duinen and its daughterhouse Ter Doest on the outskirts of Bruges. They developed their own devices for indexing. Lieftinck has shown that the scriptorium of Ter Duinen,[12] which served both

---

12. G. I. Lieftinck, *De Librijen en scriptoria der Westvlaamse Cisterciën-serabdijen Ter Duinen en Ter Doest in de 12ᵉ en 13ᵉ eeuw ... (Mededlingen van de koninklijke Vlaamse Academie voor Wetenschappen, Letteren en Schone Kunsten van België*, Klasse der Letteren, 15, n. 2; Brussels, 1953). The surviving books of Ter Duinen and Ter Doest are for the most part in the Municipal Library of Bruges.

houses, devised a method of foliation composed of letters
and dots: a through z, followed by dot-a through dot-z, followed by a-dot through z-dot, double-dot-a, and so on
through seventeen different sequences of the alphabet. In
spite of its clumsiness, this system of foliation was method-
ically applied to all products of this scriptorium in the first
half of the thirteenth century. Lieftinck suggests that the
dotted letter system was used because the monks still lacked
a numeral system with a decimal base. At least five manuscripts from these houses have short subject indexes using
letter and dot to indicate page, followed by one of the first
seven letters of the alphabet, A-G, to indicate the relative
vertical location on the page; this latter element was borrowed from the reference system of the St. Jacques concordance to the Bible. By sheer luck, a device, or key,
employed by the users of these indexes has survived. It is an
eight-inch strip of parchment, serving as a book marker,
which bears a key or reminder to the sequence of alphabets:
"Ut memoriter teneatur alphabetum taliter ordinatur: a .a a.
:a . . . ." On the other side are a set of letters A-G spaced out
vertically; the strip could be laid against the edge of a text by
a reader to help him find his reference. Attached to the head
of the strip was a rotatable parchment disk, marked I II III
IV, for the columns of an opening, which the reader could set
to mark the column where he had stopped reading.[13] While
such disks, and the A-G reference system, are known elsewhere, the system of foliation involving letters and dots is
peculiar to Ter Duinen—a unique local response to a common
need.[14]

13. Regarding this and similar devices see J. Destrez, "L'outillage des copistes
du xiiie et du xive siècle," *Aus der Geisteswelt des Mittelalters (Beiträge zur
Geschichte der Philosophie und Theologie des Mittelalters, Texte und Unter-
suchungen,* suppl. 3, pt. 1 (Münster, 1935), pp. 19-34, P. Lehmann, "Blätter,
Seiten, Spalten, Zeilen," in his *Erforschung des Mittelalters,* 3 (Stuttgart, 1960), p.
55, and A. de la Mare, *Catalogue of the Collection of Medieval Manuscripts
Bequested to the Bodleian Library Oxford by James P. R. Lyell* (Oxford, 1971),
p. 181 and plate XXXIa.

14. Tools also develop around important works; a nice example of a text being
provided with an apparatus and tools to enhance its use is provided by J.
Leclercq, "La littérature provoquée par les sermons sur les Cantiques," *Recueil
d'études sur Saint Bernard et ses écrits* (Rome, 1962), I, 175-90, first printed in

What conclusions can we draw about these tools? *First*: they are the product of a common desire to get at material, embodying a concept of utility, of sheer practical usefulness. They are meant to be used—as the homely word "tool" implies and as the manuscripts reiterate: "Ad utilitatem predicandi...," "...utilem et salutarem scientiam apprehenderis." The makers and users of these devices were practical workmen.[15] *Second*: the makers of these tools devised a number of new techniques, or adapted old techniques to new situations: (1) Of primary importance is the acceptance of alphabetical order.[16] A knowledge of complete alphabetization is nothing new to Europe in 1220, but the medieval world was disposed to arrange materials logically; to put extracts concerning *Angelus* before those concerning *Deus* simply because the alphabet required it would have seemed absurd. With surprising suddenness however the idea occurred, and spread, that alphabetization of key-words be applied to the task of making bodies of literature searchable on a massive number of topics. (2) Of equal importance is the invention of a system of reference by which portions of the text may be specified. Here we have seen letters used, both in margins to designate portions of the text, and at the head of the page to mark physical units of the codex—namely, the openings. Each of these practices will give way to foliation with Arabic numerals in the course of the century. It is, in fact, this necessity for foliation which accounts, I think, for the earliest examples of widespread employment of Arabic numerals in the West in the thirteenth century.[17] *Third*: These tools are associated with the writing and preaching of sermons, whether in the monastery, the town, or the school. They are clearly a product of the expansion of the role of

---

Revue Bénédictine, 64 (1954), 208-222. For the application of another system of numeration which appears in several Cistercian manuscripts among others see, B. Bischoff, "Die sogenannten 'greichischen' und 'chaldäischen' Zahlzeichen des abendländischen Mittelalters," *Mittelalterliche Studien,* 1 (Stuttgart, 1966), 67-73.

15. It would, I think, be useful to explore in this context the concept of utility and its application.

16. See Lloyd W. Daly, *Contributions to a History of Alphabetization in Antiquity and the Middle Ages* (Collection Latomus, 90; Brussels, 1967).

17. See Paul Lehmann, "Blätter, Seiten, Spalten, Zeilen," pp. 1-59.

preaching in the life of the Church; by constant interaction, they are both products of and prerequisites to the development of the scholastic sermon.[18]

The roads between Clairvaux, Villers, Bruges, and Paris were well traveled in the thirteenth century. Parisian indexing forms were used in Bruges. The *Liber exceptionum* appeared in two copies at the Sorbonne, another Parisian copy is now in Tortosa, and at least three copies reached England, where one went to Rochester, another eventually to Oxford, and a third to Worcester.[19] The *Flores paradysii* also made its way to the Sorbonne in Paris. These tools were used at the schools, and both influenced the structure of, and provided material for, new compendia. A good example by which to illustrate this is the *Manipulus florum*, a popular collection of some 6000 extracts, ranged under 265 alphabetized topics (abstinencia-Christus) compiled by Thomas of Ireland for use by preachers; written at the Sorbonne and finished in 1306, it survives in 200 manuscripts and went through 50 printed editions.[20] The structure of the *Manipulus* was shaped by the *Liber exceptionum* and the *Flores paradysii*. Thomas simply by-passed the subject index and instead entered his extracts under 265 subject headings which he put in alphabetical, or index, order. He also borrowed from his Cistercian predecessors the practice of designating each extract by means of a letter of the alphabet in the margin, so that it could be refer-

18. The literature on late-twelfth- and early-thirteenth-century preaching is ably reported and discussed by P. B. Roberts, *Studies in the Sermons of Stephen Langton* (Pontifical Institute of Mediaeval Studies, *Studies and Texts*, 16; Toronto, 1968).

19. Paris, BN MSS lat. 2115 (s. xiii-xiv; Paris, Nicholas de Sancto Marcello), and 15983 (s. xiii; Sorbonne, used by Thomas Hibernicus); Tortosa, Biblioteca del Cabildo (s. xiii; Paris); London, BM MS Royal 7 B.xiii (s. xiii ex.; Rochester); Oxford, Trinity College MS 41 s. xiii; Trinity Coll., Thomas Pope); Worcester Cathedral MS. f 51 (s. xiv; Worcester); Klosterneuburg, Stiftsbibliothek MS 3331 (s. xv; Klosterneuburg).

20. The *Manipulus florum* is best cited from the manuscript which Thomas gave to the Sorbonne, BN lat. 15986, or from the *editio princeps*, Piacenza 1483. Regarding Thomas see the biographical notice by B. Hauréau, *Histoire littéraire*, 30 (1888), 398-408, and R. H. Rouse, "The List of Authorities Appended to the *Manipulus florum*," *Archives d'histoire doctrinale et littéraire du Moyen Age*, 32 (1965), 243-50. I have a monograph in progress on the *Manipulus*—its sources, structure, and influence.

red to individually in a system of cross-references. Equally important, Thomas took perhaps two-thirds of the extracts in the *Manipulus florum* directly from the Sorbonne copies of the *Liber exceptionum* and the *Flores paradysii*. What we see in the *Manipulus* hence does not reflect what was being read in Paris or at the Sorbonne in 1306, but rather what was in vogue at Clairvaux and Villers in 1216-1246. What successive generations of users of the *Manipulus* were quoting ultimately derived from and was determined by the Cistercian world of the twelfth century. Hence, for example, in Christine de Pisan's *Epître d'Othéa*, c. 16, "Othea" holds up the bad example of Narcissus and observes, "Origin says in the homilies, 'How can Earth and Ashes pride themselves, and how dare Man rise up in arrogance, when he considers what he shall become and how frail the vessel in which he is contained?' "[21] Christine borrowed this quotation from the fourteenth-century *Chapelet des Vertus* (under *Orgueil*);[22] the writer of the *Chapelet* took the quotation from the *Manipulus florum*, under the heading *Superbia*; Thomas of Ireland took it from the *Liber exceptionum*, whose compiler William of Montague took the passage from the Clairvaux manuscript of Origin's *Homilies on Ezechiel* (now Troyes MS 95 s. xii, formerly Clairvaux F19). Christine de Pisan's use of Origen in the early fifteenth century is thus tied in a general sense to the twelfth-century revival of Origen in Cistercian houses,[23] and in specific to the thirteenth-century enterprise

21. Homily 9, PG 13: 734. The *Epître* has not been edited. Besides the works cited in this and the following note, see also G. Mombello, "Per un'edizione critica dell' 'Epistre Othea' di Christine de Pizan," *Studi francesi*, 24 (1964), 407-417 and 25 (1965), 1-12. Christine's use of the *Manipulus* was first noted by P.G.C. Campbell, *L'Epître d'Othéa: Etude sur les sources de Christine de Pisan* (Paris, 1924), pp. 160-69. Campbell also knew of the existence of the *Flores paradysii* but did not recognize it as the ultimate source of certain of Christine's passages. See also C. F. Bühler's edition of the English translation of the *Epître* by Stephen Scrope (*Early English Text Society*, 264; London, 1970), the notes to which are extensive.

22. Regarding the *Chapelet*, see C. F. Buhler, "The *Fleurs de toutes vertus* and Christine de Pisan's *L'Epître d'Othéa*," PMLA, 62 (1947), 32-44; *idem*, "The *Fleurs de toutes vertus*," PMLA, 64 (1949), 600-601; and the notes to his edition of Scrope.

23. See J. Leclercq, *The Love of Learning and the Desire for God* (trans. C. Misrahi; New York, 1961), pp. 118-22.

of Cistercian indexing and its passage to the university. A similar chain of relationships can be demonstrated for virtually any author who used the *Manipulus florum*, for example, William of Pagula, the Augustinian John Schoonhoven of Rooskloster, or the compiler of *Lumen anime B*, Godfrey of Vorau, or the Elizabethan writer, Thomas Lodge. For, as Petrarch noted when he accused a certain Frenchman (Jean de Hesdin) of having only a handful of extracts, "unum manipulum florum, opus vere gallicum," the *Manipulus* was a well known substitute for a first-hand knowledge of a whole work.[24] It determined, as did its predecessors, the *Flores paradysii* and the *Liber exceptionum*, the limits of what an author quoted.

To return now to the question raised at the beginning of this note regarding the origins of aids to study. The period 1170-1250 witnessed a strong and widely felt need to get at material, material to be used in a rapidly growing number of sermons. This need produced a variety of individual responses in numerous widely separated locales, among them Cistercian houses in northern Europe, the Dominicans at St Jacques, and the Franciscans at Grey Friars in Oxford. While the mendicant orders and the University would dominate the production of aids to study in the course of the thirteenth and fourteenth centuries, the beginnings of these devices can be seen emerging in Cistercian circles as traditional monastic forms were adapted to meet new and different demands.

24. See E. Cocchia (ed.), "Magistri Iohannis de Hysdinio Invectiva contra Fr. Petrarcham et Fr. Petrarchae contra cuiusdam Galli calumnias apologia," *Atti dell'Reale Accademia di Archeologia, Lettere e Belle Arti.* ns. 7 (1920), 91-202; and P. de Nolhac, *Petrarch et l'Humanisme*, II (Paris, 1907), pp. 303-312. The incident is also noted by B. L. Ullman, "Some Aspects of the Origins of Italian Humanism," in his *Studies in the Italian Renaissance* (Rome, 1955), p. 34.

THE ECONOMIC ADMINISTRATION OF A MONASTIC DOMAIN BY THE CISTERCIANS OF POBLET, 1150-1276

LAWRENCE J. MC CRANK

Whitman College

ACONSIDERABLE AMOUNT OF MATERIAL, both valuable diplomatic collections and studies, concerning the monastic domains of the medieval Iberian kingdoms has been produced in recent years.[1] However, the study of the economic activity of the Cistercians south of the Pyrenees has been largely neglected. Medievalists, hispanists, and church historians still rely on the useful but dated, general, romantic, and frequently inaccurate survey of Spanish monasticism by Justo Pérez de Urbel.[2] The general histories of the Cistercian Order simply ignore the fact that the White Monks had any important sub-Pyrenean houses and the standard works in Spanish history too often do no more than allude to the major contributions of the Order to the reconquest, resettlement, and church reforms of the Christian kingdoms and repeat the usual text-book descriptions of the normative Cistercian economic program.[3] It was not until 1964 and 1966, with the studies of Maur Cocheril, that there

1. For example, see José Angel García de Cortazar y Ruiz de Aquirre, *El dominio del monasterio de San Millán de la Cogolla (siglos X a XIII)* (Salamanca, 1969), and Salustiano Moreta Velayos, *El monasterio de San Pedro de Cardeña: historia de un dominio monástico Castellano (902-1338)* (Salamanca, 1971).

2. Justo Pérez de Urbel. *Los monjes españoles en la Edad Media* (Madrid, 1933-1934); idem, *El monasterio en la vida española de la Edad Media* (Barcelona, 1942).

3. Especially useful for general reference are Louis J. Lekai, *The White Monks* (Okauchee, Wisconsin, 1953), republished in French as *Les moines blancs, histoire de l'ordre cistercien* (Paris, 1957); and J. de la Croix Bouton, *Histoire de l'ordre de Cîteaux* (Westmalle, 1959).

appeared an adequate survey of the expansion of the Cistercians in Spain which made the much-quoted but unreliable work of L. Janauschek obsolete.[4] Consequently it is still too early to expect an adequate synthesis and study of the role played by the Cistercians in the reconquest of any of the Spanish kingdoms.[5]

4. Maur Cocheril, *Etudes sur le Monachisme en Espagne et au Portugal* (Paris, 1966); *idem,* "La tradición monástica et monaquismo en España," *Revue d'Histoire Ecclésiastique,* 54 (1959), 125-28; *idem,* "L'atlas de l'ordre Cistercien," *Cîteaux: Commentarii Cistercienses,* XVII (1966), 119-44; *idem.* "L'implantation des Abbayes Cisterciens dans la Péninsule Ibérique," *Anuario de estudios medievales,* I (1964), 217-87. The last article is especially important because it updates the general work of Leopold Janauschek, *Originum Cisterciensum in quo praemissis congregationem domiciliis adjectisque tabulis chronologico-genealogicis veterum abbatiarum a monachis habitatarum* (Vienna, 1877; reprinted by A. Hälder, Ridgewood, N. J., 1964). Janauschek's erros often seem to be transmission of erroneous data from Gaspar Jongelincex, *Fundationis Monasterium Regnorum Hispaniae,* Liber VI, *Notitia abbatiarum Ordinis Cisterciensis per orbem universum* (Cologne, 1640). Cocheril also points out numerous errors in Angel Manrique's standard but dated reference work, *Cisterciensium seu verius ecclesiasticorum Annalium a conditio Cistercio . . .* (Lyons, 1642-1656) in his analysis "Les *Annales* de Fr. Angel Manrique et la chronologie des abbayes cisterciennes," *Studia Monástica,* 6 (1964), 145-83.

5. This essay is part of a comprehensive study which I have undertaken concerning the Cistercians of the Corona de Aragón prior to 1276. I am now working with the unedited documents of the Archivo Histórico Nacional (AHN) of Madrid; however, the material related here is the result of a preliminary investigation into the edited cartulary of Poblet: J. Pons i Marquès (ed.), *Cartulari de Poblet: Edificio del Manuscrit de Tarragona* (Barcelona, 1938). The statistical data in the *Cartulario maior,* of Poblet is so plentiful that there is the possibility of using a quantitative approach to the economic history of the medieval Aragonese, Catalan, and Valencian Cistercian houses, as I demonstrated in a paper read before the Cistercian Studies Conference at the Sixth Conference of Medieval Studies at Western Michigan University, Kalamazoo, Michigan, on May 5, 1971, published as "The Frontier of the Spanish Reconquest and the Land Acquisitions of the Cistercians of Poblet, 1150-1276," *Essays in History,* XV (University of Virginia, 1969-1971), 48-76, and in *Analecta Cisterciensia* (Jan.-June 1973), 57-78. The AHN collection contains 2,754 *carpetas* of parchments, about twenty documents per *carpeta,* from the 1040s to 1833. Of the approximately 55,000 charters in this cartulary, 172 date between 970 and 1150, prior to Poblet's foundation. Another 1,980 date between 1150 and 1209, the year of the last documents edited from the manuscript of Tarragona. Of the 358 edited charters, 119 are not duplicated in the *Cartulario maior,* twenty are undated, and 219 are copies. There are 2,860 parchments dating from 1209 and 1276, all unedited. Likewise, the documentation for Santes Creus is rich; 397 charters of its cartulary have already been edited by Federico Udina Martorell (ed.), *El "Llibre Blanch" de Santes Creus: Cartulario del siglo XII* (Barcelona, 1947). 153 of these,

There is presently considerable interest in the history of the two most important and influential houses of Cataluña, both here and in Spain, and several fine special studies have appeared in recent years. Scholars have hitherto relied on the chronicle of Poblet, begun in 1746 by Jaime Finestres y de Monsalvo,[6] and the work begun in the 1920s by Joaquín Guitert y Fontseré.[7] Most important for the medieval period are the contributions of E. Fort y Cogul, J. Vives Miret, Manuel Riu, and P. Serramalera on Santes Creus, the contributors to the *Miscellanea Populetana* of Poblet,[8] the excellent dissertation of Jaime Santacana Tort which is currently being published by the Consejo Superior de Investigaciones Científicas of Barcelona,[9] and the forthcoming three-volume history of Poblet by Augustín Altisent.[10]

The great bulk of the collection of charters housed in the

dating between 925 and 1197, are duplicated in the AHN collection, 244 are not, and the AHN contains 835 more unpublished charters which date between 1197 and 1276. This makes a total of over 6,500 unworked Cistercian charters for Cataluña Nueva, and these can be supplemented by AHN charters relating to Poblet's neighboring houses of Vallbona, Bellpuig de Avellanes, Bonrepós, and Scala Dei, and the exceptionally fine edition of charters for the same area by José María Font Ríus, *Cartas de población y franquicia de Cataluña* (Madrid, Barcelona, 2 vols., 1969). The total collection numbers over seven thousand, averaging fifty-five documents per year before 1276, and constitutes one of the richest sources in medieval history and an invaluable record of the social and economic development of the Spanish frontiers.

6. Jaime Finestres y de Monsalvo, *Historia del real monasterio de Poblet* (Barcelona, 1746; reprinted 1947-1955), I-VI, especially vol. II for the period between 1150 and 1276.

7. Joaquín Guitert y Fonteré, *Poblet, guía y notas históricas y artísticas del monasterio: leyendas y tradiciones* (Barcelona, 1921); *idem, Poblet, Colección de curiosidades, leyendas, y tradiciones* (San Baudillo del Llobregat, 1937); and *idem, Compendio de la guía notas históricas, leyendas y tradiciones del Real Monasterio de Ntra. Sra. de Poblet* (Barcelona, 1922). Guitert y Fontseré was also a pioneer in the studies concerning Santes Creus: *Guía del Real Monasterio de Santes Creus: Descripción, fundación y destrucción del monasterio, privilegios, leyendas, tradiciones, y curiosidades* (Barcelona, 1927).

8. *Miscellanea Populetana*, I, *Scriptorium Populeti* (Espluga de Francolí, 1966); and note the various publications of the Archivo bibliográfico de Santes Creus, especially the *Boletín de Santes Creus*, I and II (Santes Creus, 1954-1959, 1960-1964) and the *I Colloqui d'Història del monaquisme català* (Santes Creus, 1966), I and II.

Archivo Histórico Nacional of Madrid which relate to Poblet's monastic domain between 1150 and 1276, from its foundation until the death of its greatest patron and last king of the eastern Reconquista, Jaime I, testifies to the influence of this monastic establishment in the business of reconquest and reconstruction behind the frontier.[11] In fact, the use of ecclesiastical institutions to control and develop the land of the frontier after the armies moved further southward was very characteristic of the Reconquista of the Houses of Barcelona and Urgel. Most of the eleventh-century frontier of Cataluña Nueva was carved into five twelfth-century ec-

9. The work of Jaime Santacana Tort is based on his unpublished licenciate and doctoral theses: *Los orígenes del dominio territorial de Poblet, 1151-1166* (University of Barcelona, 1961); *idem, El monasterio de Poblet: Estudio histórico y diplomático, 1151-1181* (University of Barcelona, 1966). I wish to thank Professor Emilio Sáez of the Instituto de Historia Medieval de España, the director of these studies, for allowing me to peruse portions of the galley proofs during my stay in Barcelona this past year.

10. Father Agustín Altisent also worked under Professor Sáez at the University of Barcelona, and his dissertation, like the studies of Santacana Tort, contains a valuable appendix of edited charters from the AHN. In addition to his general history which is in progress, Altisent has a study in press which is especially important for several considerations in this paper: *Les granges de Poblet al segle XV: Assaig d'història agrària d'unes granges cistercenques catalanes* (Barcelona, 1972) pp. 11-19. This study is based largely on a register of 1415 compiled for Abbot Joan Martínez de Mengucho. Some preliminary material concerning Poblet's barony in the 1400s has already been made available by Father Altisent in his "L'estructura econòmica del monestir de Poblet, el 1460," *Miscellània històrica catalana: Homenatge al P. Jaume Finestres, historiador de Poblet (d. 1769)* (Poblet, 1970), pp. 267-332.

11. Nearly seventy per cent of the charters referred to in note 5 relate to Poblet between 1150 and 1276. Most of these treat the history of Cataluña Nueva in the post-frontier stage of development and colonization. The term "frontier," like its Latin root, *frons,* means a forehead, an exterior, or a front. Late Latin used the term *frontaria* technically as a surveyor's term meaning a boundary of a section of surveyed land, Poblet was a "frontier monastery" in the sense that the initial development of her domain, before the 1170s, involved carving up the land retaken from the Moors, resettlement, and the perils of warfare and defense. However, after the 1170s the military frontier moved past the Ebro into Valencia, and Poblet rapidly lost her frontier character. The major part of this study treats Poblet in the post-frontier era, one of land redistribution, continued rather than initial development, and furthered resettlement. See the *Thesaurus linguae latinae* (Leipzig, 1926), VI, cols. 1360, 1363, and 1365.

clesiastical baronies. That of the archbishop of Tarragona, which encompassed the fertile Campo de Tarragona and the city, was founded first, in 1118.[12] The other four were monastic domains: those of the Cistercian monasteries of Poblet and Santes Creus, the Premonstratensian abbey of Bellpuig de Avellanes, and the Carthusian house of Scala Dei. The issue here is, what institutions did Poblet's monks use in the second phase of frontier activity, development and settlement, in Cataluña Nueva while the battle zone was pushed into the Kingdom of Valencia in the 1170s?

The obvious answer would be the grange, the institution so characteristic of Cistercian exploitation in other parts of Europe. However, many of the older generalizations about the Cistercian economic program and its conception of a grange system, usually based on studies of the communities in England and France, or on the legalistic treatments of the Order's statutes, may not be applicable to Poblet and her Iberian sisters. In the area behind the frontier of the Reconquista, where land was extensive, labor scarce, and settlers were in demand, the normal economy of the Cistercian plan may have been more theoretical than real. Some tentative conclusions, based on my preliminary investigation of Poblet's economic activities before 1276, may serve to question some current misconceptions about the administrative use of granges in the medieval Cistercian enterprise.

It is generally asserted that although the Cistercian reform was originally a scheme for spiritual renewal, a major con-

---

12. The standard authority on the reconquest and restoration of Tarragona is Emilio Morera y Llauradó, *Tarragona cristiana: Historia del arzobispado de Tarragona y del territorio de su provincia* (Tarragona, 1897). A useful but unoriginal introduction to the background of the reconquest of these areas is the series of short essays by Josep Iglésies, *La restauració de Tarragona (Episodis de la Història,* XLV, directed by Ferran Soldevila; Barcelona, 1963); *La Reconquesta a les valls de l'Anoia i el Gaió (Episodis de la Història,* XL; Barcelona, 1963); and *La Conquesta de Tortosa (Episodis de la Història,* XX; Barcelona, 1961). For the general context, see Ferran Soldevila, *Història de Catalunya* (Barcelona, 1934-1935; 2nd ed., 1962), I; and Percy E. Schramm, Joan-F. Cabestany i Fort, and Enric Bagué i Garriga, *Els primers comtes-reis (Biografies Catalanes sèrie històrica,* IV; Barcelona, 1960, reprinted 1963).

sequence of the Order's popularity and phenomenal expansion in the twelfth century was a largescale improvement of Western Europe's agrarian economy.[13] The Order's prosperity is usually attributed to two important, though not entirely original, innovations at Cîteaux: (1) the use of isolated centers for land exploitation, granges, for the support of the abbey, and (2) the integration of a lay brotherhood, the *conversi*, into the Order. The Order expanded partially because Cistercian settlements were acts of colonization, and the reputation of the White Monks' ability to convert wasteland into prosperous domains was one of the basic motives for Count Ramón Berenguer IV's invitation of 1149 to the community of Fontfroide to send a colony of monks to Cataluña.[14] It is also thought that as the Order expanded geometrically rather than arithmetically, the Cistercians relied more heavily on *conversi* labor and the choir monks specialized in administration and the *Opus Dei*, in spite of this apparent breach of the original ideal of not living by the sweat of other men. Out of this tendency came systematization of economic policies, one of which was, as Dom David Knowles calls it, the "converse-and-grange" system.[15]

Whereas the regional meaning of *granja* varied, the Cistercians meant more precisely a "self-contained farm" worked by *conversi*.[16] Each grange was managed by a senior

13. Lekai, *White Monks,* pp. 209-210.

14. James Westfall Thompson, *Economic and Social History of the Middle Ages, 300-1300* (New York, 1928), pp. 609, 611. The generalization that the Cistercians were active colonizers refers to their activity in northern Europe, but it also applies to Spain and Portugal. Pérez de Urbel, *El monasterio,* p. 68: "Aquel programa de trabajo [the Cistercian], muy sugestivo en todas partes, se presentaba en los estados cristianos de España como un remedio salvador." See also, Cocheril, *Etudes,* pp. 342-43; *idem, Anuario,* p. 233. For other examples of the Count's eagerness to settle this region, see Antonio Palau y Dulcet, *Guía de la Conca de Barberá* (Barcelona, 1932), pp. xvi, 2.

15. David Knowles, *From Pachomius to Ignatius: A Study in the Constitutional History of the Religious Orders* (Oxford, 1966), pp. 29-30.

16. E. Hoffmann, *Das Konverseninstitut des Cisterzienserordens in seinem Ursprung und seiner Organisation* (Freiburg, 1905), pp. 83-84, suggests that the etymology of *grangia* is connected with *granum,* corn or grain, and that the original meaning may have been any building used for grain storage. The

conversus, or sometimes by a monk, called a *rector grangiae*, who supervised from four to ten laborers.[17] Each rector was held responsible to the abbey's cellarer, who was always a monk, or to his subordinate, the *grangiarus*, who was often the highest ranking *conversus*. The cellarer, of course, was the chief temporal officer of the community and was responsible directly to the abbot.[18] He was usually able, as the sole financial administrator of the abbey, to co-ordinate planting, harvesting, payments of revenue in kind, marketing, and parcelling out of land in the best interest of the monastery. Consequently, although the Cistercians used the same farming techniques as others, it is generally thought that they were able to surpass the capacity of the ordinary manorial estate because of the simple, direct, and efficient administration of the monastic domain.[19] Businesslike management and centralized control of the monastic enterprise are the hallmarks of economic success of the Cistercians.[20]

Each grange was supposedly a permanent establishment, a dwelling for a group of laborers varying from a dozen or

secondary literature concerning the grange system in northern Europe, especially in England, is voluminous and the major studies cannot be cited here. For the best bibliography, consult the series of R. A. Donkin, *Documentation Cistercienne*, I (Rochefort, Belgium, 1969) and continuing.

17. B. H. Slicher von Bath, *The Agrarian History of Western Europe, A.D. 500-1850* (trans. O. Ordish; London, 1963), p. 154.

18. The General Chapter prohibited Cistercian abbots from letting anyone other than their cellarers administer monastic lands, especially granges. P. Guignard (ed.), *Les monuments primitifs de la Règle Cistercienne publiés d'après les manuscrits de l'abbaye de Cîteaux* (Dijon, 1878), *Instituta*, lxviii, p. 269, and lxxvii, p. 274.

19. Lekai, *White Monks*, pp. 210-11; Cocheril, *Etudes*, p. 334: "Cette administration intelligente qui faisait des Cisterciens les seuls agronomes competents au moyen âge incitait les souverains à leur donner de noveaux domains."

20. Archdale King, *Cîteaux and Her Elder Daughters* (London, 1954), p. 342. Slicher von Bath, *Agrarian History*, pp. 153-54, maintains that Cistercian granges were not model farms for neighboring laymen "nor was there any sign of innovation in farming technique," but that "what was new was the businesslike management and centralized control" of the Cistercian system. For an opposing view, see Robert Delatouche, "Elites intellectuelles et agriculture au Moyen Age," *Recueil d'études sociales à la mémoire de F. Le Play* (Paris, 1956), pp. 147-57.

more during harvest or shearing season to only a pair of *conversi* in the winter months. The location and number of granges per house varied throughout Europe, depending on regional terrain and size of the domains, but usually there were no more than twelve granges for each abbey.

Ideally, as shown by R. W. Roehl in 1968, the Cistercian plan called for special spatial relationships between the granges and the abbey, and between the arrangement of one domain and another.[21] The "triangulation patterns" which Roehl depicts involve the following requirements: (1) abbeys were to be approximately ten leagues or fifty miles from each other, (2) a monastery's granges were to form a ring around the abbey with a radius of four leagues or twenty miles, a likely estimate for a round-trip journey of "one day's travel," and (3) the granges of one monastery were to be *circa* two leagues or ten miles from the nearest grange of the neighboring house.[22] In practice, however, grange sites were chosen not according to theoretical spatial relationships, but governed by several common sense considerations such as the locations of owned property, the site's proximity to roads and trails, the availability of high ground suitable for construction, the abundance of water or facilities for its acquisi-

21. I wish to thank Professor Richard W. Roehl for permission to cite his unpublished doctoral dissertation *Plan and Reality in a Medieval Monastic Economy: The Cistercians* (University of California, 1968). A condensed version of this study, with the same title, is in *Studies in Medieval and Renaissance History*, 9 (1972), 83-113. Subsequent references will be to the dissertation, a study which was conceived in response to his mentor, Professor Carlo M. Cipolla, who suggested the possibilities of analyzing the Cistercian directives as a "planned" economy. See Carlo M. Cipolla, "Questioni aperte sul sistema economico dell'alto medio evo," *Rivista Storica Italiana*, LXIII, no. 1 (1959), 95-99, cited by Roehl, "Plan," p. 26, note 1.

22. Roehl, "Plan," Appendix I: "Cistercian Theoretical Spatial Relationships," pp. 111-12. The second and third distances are based on the *Instituta*, v and xxxii, Guignard, *Monuments*, pp. 250-51 and 258, the former being a maximum of "non tamen ultra dietam" and the later being a minimum stipulation that "grangiae autem diversarum abbatiarum distent inter se ad minus duabus leugis." The first is based on statutes passed in 1134, an addition to the original legislation which gave the minimal separation of two houses as "decem leucis Burgundiae." *Statuta*, I, 33-34.

tion, and a reasonable security from attack or destruction.[23] The ideal layout included housing for the workers, storage areas for tools and surplus produce, a repair shop which might include a forge, and some kind of shelter for the domesticated animals. Areas immediately adjacent to the building site were turned into gardens, outlying areas were farmed, and the peripheral lands might be used for grazing.

Poblet established five granges within the Huerto de Poblet, the land given to the Cistercians by Count Ramón Berenguer IV in the original donation of 1149: Mitjana, Riudeabella, Castellfullit, Milmanda, and La Pena.[24] Of these, Mitjana was the oldest and closest to the abbey. It had been the site of the primitive hermitage of San Salvador before serving as the temporary home of Poblet's community until the abbey's construction was completed.[25]

Perhaps the second oldest grange was Milmanda, a castle located less than two miles north of the abbey near the marshy springs which give birth to the Río Milans. Because of its proximity and ample housing, it was often visited by Poblet's abbots and visiting dignitaries and may have been used as a summer house more than as a real grange. However, after 1254 Milmanda had its own mill, built with money donated to Poblet by the rector of the church of Arbeca. The monks first started using the castle as a grange after 1173 when Bernardo de Graneña defined the boundaries of an *honor* near the old castle which he had given to the monastery in 1164.[26] Milmanda grew in importance because it lay on the northern border of the Huerto de Poblet, in a com-

23. These general considerations are conveniently listed in "Granja," *Enciclopedia Universal Ilustrada* (Barcelona, 1921), XXVI, 1087.

24. Cocheril, *Anuario*, pp. 279-80, citing manuscript 4, Joaquín Guitert i Fontseré (ed.), *Collecío de manuscrits inèdits de Monjes del Monestir de Santa Maria de Poblet* (Barcelona, 1948), p. 76. This manuscript is a study by Pere Fortuny entitled "Dels Pobles, Terms, Privats, Granjas, y demás cosas es Sr. le RR. Mr. de Poblet." Toponymical problems were resolved by the *Diccionari nomenclàtor de pobles i poblats de Catalunya* (Barcelona, 1936; 2nd ed., 1964); Enric Moreu-Rey, *Els noms de lloc: Introduccío a la toponímia* (Barcelona, 1965); and Francisco Carreras y Candi (ed.), *Geografía de Catalunya* (Barcelona, 1910), I-VI.

25. Fontseré, *El real monasterio de Poblet* (Barcelona, 1929), p. 93.

26. *Ibid.*; Finestres, *Historia*, p. 86.

manding position immediately across the river from the road
between Espluga de Francolí and Vimbodí, and because in
1184 and 1198 Poblet received additional land donations
along the Río Milans.[27]

Riudeabella, located some two and one-half miles from the
abbey, in the direction of Prades, was first used for animal
husbandry because of the surrounding highlands, but later,
after 1220, when the inexhaustible supply of water from the
springs of Narola was diverted into the fields by a system of
canals built by Guillén de Montoliu, the grange's land was
cultivated.[28] Further away still was the grange of Castellfullit,
which, as its name implies, was formerly a defense tower in
the Huerto de Poblet's southern highlands which faced the
Muslim rebel-infected mountains of Prades. The grange was
especially important in providing the abbey with construction materials and firewood, and for grazing sheep in the
small *puertos* of the Sierra de Prades after Alfonso II finally
quelled the last Muslim rebellion near Poblet in 1172. The
Huerto's fifth grange, La Pena, was also a converted site which
was used for grazing, gathering wood, and as a retreat center.[29]

Cérvoles (Sorboles) was characteristic of those granges
which were developed outside of the Huerto de Poblet. The
beginnings of land development in this area date to May 26,
1157, while fighting continued in the surrounding hills.
Count Ramón Berenguer IV donated the site of Cérvoles,
irrigation rights, and permission to build a chapel there, to a
hermit named Ramón and his brother, Oton, both of Vallbona. The Count also promised the hermit six pair of sheep
annually so that Ramón de Vallbona could convert the wasteland of Cérvoles into productive grazing lands. However,
because of irrigation from the Río Sed (Seth), Cérvoles from
its origin could support both agricultural and pastoral pursuits.[30] The hermit agreed to follow the Benedictine *Rule* and

27. Finestres, *Historia,* p. 117; *Cartulari,* no. 77, p. 43; no. 63, pp. 34-35.
28. Fontseré, *Real monasterio,* p. 94; Finestres, *Historia,* p. 213.
29. Fontseré, *Real monasterio,* pp. 94-95.
30. Finestres, *Historia,* p. 73; *Cartulari,* no. 346, p. 212.

to settle there, but he initially had no connection with Poblet. On June 24, 1161, Berenguer de Campairal gave Poblet his land, some of which had already been plowed, within the *termini* of Cérvoles.[31] Two years later the noble Guillén de Cervera donated the site known as "Pobla de Cérvoles" to Poblet and defined the monastery's holdings as the area bounded by the Río Sed, the Sierra de Flina, the public road from the Torre de Lena to the river, and the highlands in which the Sed had its source.[32] Poblet's property around Cérvoles was as large in area as the Huerto de Poblet itself, encompassing about 2,500 acres. The donation of 1163 ultimately brought Poblet's claims into conflict with those of Ramón de Vallbona.

On April 1, 1171, Poblet secured the hermit's lands by agreeing to supply the recluse and his one disciple, Bernardo, with twelve measures of wheat, a tunic, a cowl and a scapular, two pairs of sandals, and an annual supply of oil as long as he lived.[33] In addition, the Cistercians moved Ramón from their lands at Cérvoles to Vallbona where they built him a chapel according to his specifications. Evidently the old man had enough of the rugged frontier around Cérvoles and the unruly Muslims of Prades, and the monks of Poblet were eager to occupy his lands even though the transaction may have violated the dictates of their Order; their motive was clearly consolidation in order to make the grange at Cérvoles into an autonomous holding. It is uncertain what happened to the "vill" or "pobla" of Cérvoles, but it seems unlikely that Poblet destroyed it, as other houses did with similar settlements, especially in England.[34] In addition to being the

31. *Cartulari,* no. 154, pp. 89-90.
32. Finestres, *Historia,* p. 73; Fontseré, *Real monasterio,* p. 124; *Cartulari,* no. 157, pp. 91-92.
33. Fontseré, *Real monasterio,* p. 125; *Cartulari,* no. 340, pp. 208-209. This arrangement was confirmed in 1206: *Cartulari,* no. 327, pp. 199-200. King Pedro II met Abbot Pedro IV de Curtacans at Montblanch and designated Poblet as his burial place (he was actually buried at Sigena, next to his mother Sancha in 1213), and the king then forfeited the Crown's rights to Cérvoles while confirming Guillén de Cervera's donation of 1163. See Finestres, *Historia,* p. 199.
34. This was a charge leveled against the Cistercians throughout Europe, but especially in England. A vehemently anti-Catholic historian, George G. Coulton,

beginning of Cérvoles as an important grange, this transaction was the origin of Vallbona de las Monjas, which eventually became a Cistercian nunnery dependent upon Poblet.[35]

Poblet continued to expand and consolidate her holdings around Cérvoles. In 1179, the Cistercians bought an *honor* from Ramón Potellas for forty-three *sueldos*; in 1192 the monastery successfully defended its claims to more land,[36] and in 1201 the grange's boundaries were expanded further by the donation of another *honor*, near Riudeset on the Río Sed, by Hermesinda de Zaguardia.[37] Charters of confirmation from 1183, 1220, 1255, and 1272 all cite Cérvoles, indicating that it served as a grange for more than a century. It is difficult to ascertain the grange's value, although one transaction does indicate the wealth Cérvoles contributed to Poblet's coffers. After the provincial council of Tarragona in 1180, Abbot Hugón met with Esteban de San Martín, bishop of Huesca and a former abbot of Poblet, and with Pedro de Paris, bishop of Pamplona. On October 29, Poblet agreed to lend her grange at Cérvoles to the bishops until their death, after which it was to revert to the control of the cellarer. The bishops agreed not to alienate any of the grange's property, devalue its holdings, or decrease its boundaries in any way. The grange had for the bishops' use twelve yoke of oxen,

has made the most of these accusations, but his work is often soundly based on the sources. See his *Five Centuries of Religion* (Cambridge, England, 4 vols., 1923-1950), especially II, 97-98 and appendix 34, p. 512. For a more balanced treatment concerning English granges, see T.A.M. Bishop, "Monastic Granges in Yorkshire," *English Historical Review*, II, no. 202 (April, 1936), 193-214, especially pp. 212-13; and R. A. Donkin, "The Cistercian Order in Medieval England, Some Conclusions," *Institute of British Geographers: Transactions and Papers*, 33 (December, 1963), 181-98, especially p. 186. See also the standard authority on the English Cistercians, David Knowles, *The Monastic Order in England* (Cambridge, England, 1940), p. 352.

35. The hermitage was later converted into a convent which, although dependent upon Poblet, competed with the abbey for land acquisitions, notably in the case of Montesquiu. Doña Isabella, the Mother Superior of the convent, won a suit against Poblet over the lands of that castle on January 29, 1238. See Finestres, *Historia*, pp. 314-15; Fontseré, *Real monasterio*, p. 144.

36. Finestres, *Historia*, p. 134; *Cartulari*, no. 152, pp. 88-89; no. 148, p. 86. Consolidation around grange sites was a common practice. See the model study of a Franch grange by C. Higounet, *La Grange de Vaulerent: Structure et exploitation d'un territoire cistercien de la plaine de France, XIIe-XVe siècle* (Paris, 1965).

37. Finestres, *Historia*, p. 184; Fontseré, *Real monasterio*, p. 124; *Cartulari*, no. 153, p. 89.

one hundred and fifty female goats, forty-seven sheep and lambs, one ass, two mules, and three horses. This cursory inventory would indicate that the greater share of the grange's land was already under cultivation. Indeed, the bishops paid Poblet an annual rent of five hundred measures of wheat and barley from the harvests, and under a four-year lease or commendation their debt of four hundred gold pieces to the monastery was cut in half.[38] The substantial income which a grange like Cérvoles brought Poblet allowed the monastery to consolidate her holdings with new purchases, to continually invest in land elsewhere, and to assign her *conversi* to other, less well-developed granges. The reason and motivation for such a transaction are clear: it resulted in the mutual benefit of both the bishops and the Cistercians. However, the act was a direct violation of the Order's statutes, constituting a denial of the original ideal of self-cultivation of all monastic property. The General Chapter did not approve such transactions until 1208, and the specific leasing of granges such as Poblet's commendation of 1180 was not approved until 1220.[39] After 1224, the Order considered such maneuvers to be permissible whenever they were expedient, but Poblet was operating in a manner far more flexible than was the Order as a whole.[40]

Whereas Poblet worked for nearly two decades in developing Cérvoles, other granges were donated fully developed and

---

38. *Cartulari,* no. 159, p. 93; no. 160, p. 94. The date of the second charter is uncertain. It may have been issued by either Abbot Esteban III Droc (1181-1185) or Abbot Esteban IV (1188-1190). See Finestres, *Historia,* p. 76, p. 90.

39. "De terris qui minus utile fuerint aut sic remotae quod utiliter excoli non possint, sic dispensat Capitulum generale, ut liceat iis qui tales habuerint dare ad medietatem vel aliter prout poterunt competentur." *Statuta,* I, 346 (1208). The importance of this modification has been stressed by Hoffman and others. *Statuta,* I, 463 (1220) is equally important: "De grangiis et terris utilibus colonis ad tempus concedendis, permittitur abbatibus ut cum consilio seniorum suorum, patrum abbatum vel visitorum, si patrum haberi non possit copia faciant super hoc quod iussum fuerit faciendum."

40. *Statuta,* II, 31 (1224): "Indulgetur abbatibus Ordinis nostri auctoritate Capituli generalis, qui sibi crediderint expedire, dare saecularibus terras, vineas et etiam grangias, et alias possessiones ad excolendum dum consensu et voluntate contentus sui et patris abbatis, vel visitatoris, facta tamen prius de decimus compositione assensu et auctoritate episcopi diocesani."

the Cistercians chose not to increase their size. Doldellops, for example, was a joint donation made in 1155 by Count Ramón Berenguer IV, Prince Robert of Tarragona, and Archbishop Bernardo Tort, which included a mill and ten sheep on its lands.[41] Seemingly there was room for expansion, but Poblet never increased her holdings here, nor did the monks seek new acquisitions in the Campo de Tarragona, the archiepiscopal domain.

It is uncertain how many granges Poblet operated in the outlying areas of her vast domain. Most of her more distant granges were established after 1200 when Poblet's lands were already scattered over most of Cataluña Nueva. In 1183, King Alfonso II placed the abbey under his royal protection, and in an attempt to specify what possessions came under this privilege, his charter enumerated the granges of Poblet as being seven in all: Doldellops, Cérvoles, Avingaña, Torre de Ferran, Rocavert, Barbens, and Torredá.[42] If one counts the five granges within the Huerto de Poblet, which were not named, the total reaches the canonical number of twelve. On May 5, 1220, Pope Honorius III, reiterating the penalties for violating Poblet's Apostolic Protection which was granted by Innocent III in 1201, cited seventeen granges in a list which included the five granges of the Huerto, deleted Avingaña, and added to the six granges named in 1183 those of Cudoz, Teillar, Fumada, Torre de Bernardo de Estopaño, Viverol, and Figuera.[43] When on December 22, 1255, Pope Alexander IV confirmed this privilege and all of the graces conferred on Poblet by the papacy, he listed twenty granges as operative, adding those of Media (which could be an alternate listing for Mitjana which is dropped from the enumeration), Montbellet, Orchea, Molasserrada, and Orta, while excluding Rocavert and Cudoz and reinstating Avingaña to the list.[44] A fourth document confuses the issue further. In 1272, King Jaime I

41. Finestres, *Historia,* p. 60; Fontseré, *Real monasterio,* p. 123; *Cartulari,* no. 246, p. 149.
42. Finestres, *Historia,* pp. 70, 116, 361; Fontseré, *Real monasterio,* p. 128; *Cartulari,* no. 33, pp. 14-15.
43. Finestres, *Historia,* p. 220; Fontseré, *Real monasterio,* p. 135.

dispatched a letter from Valencia which confirmed Poblet's ownership of fourteen granges, a tally which only partially agrees with the other three. It added the grange at Manresana and one on the Río Apis, and deleted the names of ten previously cited granges.[45] In all, twenty-five different granges were cited for the years between 1183 and 1272.

What can be deduced from a comparison of these lists? It seems unlikely that the discrepancies are the results of mere scribal error. Two of the variations provide a possible explanation as well as some information about the flexibility of Poblet's converse-and-grange system. First, the grange at Avingaña was listed in 1183 and 1255, but in 1272 the reference was to the "possessions" of Poblet at Avingaña, without any specification that the Cistercians still operated a grange there. Second, the grange at Montbellet, cited in 1255, was listed as a *mas* in 1272. Given the nature of a cartulary, it is impossible to ascertain conclusively whether Poblet sold her grange property at those sites. This is unlikely, however, because the monastery at various times added "rights and possessions" to the tower of Avingaña which was originally given to the community in 1151 by Geraldo de Jorba.[46] The documents seem to pertain to the same property, but the classification changes. Why?

First, contrary to the general opinion, derived from the *Exordium parvum* itself, that Cistercian granges were sites chosen and first developed by the monks and their *conversi* in totally unproductive lands, the majority of Poblet's granges were converted sites, founded and partially developed in the first stage of the Reconquista's frontier activity by a

44. Finestres, *Historia*, III, 49-50.

45. *Ibid.*, pp. 303-305. The following list gives the locations of the grange sites, the date of the first acquisitions in that area, and the type of property which was first acquired. The numbers within parentheses refer to the confirmations in chronological order: (1) the confirmation of Alfonso II in 1183, (2) the confirmation bull of Honorius III in 1220, (3) the confirmation bull of Alexander IV in 1255, and (4) the confirmation charter of Jaime I in 1272.

Locations:	Date and type of first acquisitions:	Confirmation documents:
Doldellops	1155, mill	1,2,3,4
Cérvoles (Sorboles)	1157, vill	1,2,3,4
Avingaña (Serós)	1151, tower	1,3,4 (property)
Ferran	1176, tower	1,2,3,4

donor who later became Poblet's benefactor. At least five of Poblet's granges were originally defense towers or small castles which became obsolete after Alfonso II re-assumed the offensive in 1172 and pushed the frontier's battle lines toward Valencia.[47] Two were originally hermitages which may date prior to Poblet's foundation, one was a mill, and one originated as the result of the acquisition of village rights.[48] Moreover, because most of Poblet's land donations date after 1170, nearly two-thirds of the monastery's acquisitions had been owned by other landlords who presumably had undertaken some land development in the twenty to thirty years when they had possession of the property. In short, Poblet's granges were not really new developments, but they were institutions which continued the development and settlement of the land behind the real frontier.

Rocavert	1171, grange	1,2
Barbens	1181, grange	1,2,3,4
Torredá	1183, grange	1,2,3,4
Milmanda	1173, mas	2,3,4
Cudoz, Vall de	1182, mas	2
Riudeabella	1220, grange (Huerto, 1150)	2,3
Teillar	1220, grange	2,3,4?
Castellfullit	1220, castle (Huerto, 1150)	2,3,4
Mitjana	1220, hermitage (pre-1151)	2
La Pena	1220, hermitage (pre-1151)	2,3,4
Fumada (Nueva)	1213, grange	2,3,4
Torre de B. Estopaño	1220, tower	2,3
Viverol	1194, mas	2,3,4
Media	1255, grange	3,4
Montbellet	1255, mas?	3,4 (mas?)
Orchea, Torre d'	1203, tower	3
Molaserrada	1255, grange	3
Orta (Horta)	1255, grange	3
Río Apis	1272, grange	4
Manresana	1186, tower	4

46. Finestres, *Historia*, II, 50-51; Fontseré, *Real monasterio*, p. 120.

47. The towers of Avingaña, Ferran, Manresana, and Bernardo de Estopaño, and the castles of Castellfullit and Orchea, were all part of the defenses of the old eleventh-century frontier.

48. R. A. Donkin has demonstrated that the English Cistercian houses were established within existing patterns of rural settlement, although their original sites tended toward marginal lands. Thus, it was not always true that Cistercian

Secondly, Poblet's granges were not necessarily permanent establishments. Grange sites could be rotated. If towers and castles could serve as granges, they could be converted back into mere towers or changed into any kind of farmhouse. Some of these converted sites which were used for farming fell under the generic label of *masies*, a term which originated in the Carolingian *mansi.*[49] However, the Catalan *mas*, the farmhouse, and *masia*, the farm itself, of the twelfth and thirteenth centuries were not the same as the older *mansi*. The terms *mas* and *granja* were not mutually exclusive, as the case of Montbellet demonstrates. Most of the *masies* which were built during the first wave of Christian occupation in Cataluña Nueva had some constructions for defense, and, like the *masies* of Cataluña Vieja, they met all of the requirements of a well-equipped grange and served the very same purpose.

---

settlements were located centrally within wastelands. The units of previously established holdings such as *masies*, towers, mills, hermitages, and vills, which were incorporated into Polblet's grange system, suggest that the monastery also adjusted to local pre-existing patterns of settlement. See R. A. Donkin, "The English Cistercians and Assarting, c. 1128-1350," *Analecta Sacri Ordinis Cisterciensis*, 20, nos. 1-2 (January-June, 1964), 49-75.

49. It seems preferable to use the Catalán term *mas* and its variant forms than to confuse the issue with the use of *mansus* and *mansi*, the terminology of the documents. The singular *mas* (plural, *masos*) refers to the farmhouse itself, a mansion; the term *masia* (plural *masies*) refers to the homestead, that is, the *mas* plus the land which is subject to it and all related buildings, corrals, and mills. The Catalán term, derived from the Latin *mansus*, meant the amount of land needed to support an extended family and it usually referred to a farm on the open range, a "casa de campo de descanso." See Antoni Marís Alcover, (ed.), *Diccionari Català-Valencià-Balear* (Barcelona, 1969), VII, 276. A reasonable estimate for the average size of the *masies* in medieval Cataluña Nueva might be from four to six hundred acres; no doubt they were smaller in Cataluña Vieja and other areas which were more densely settled than the area of the eleventh-century frontier. For general information on the Catalán *masies*, see the standard work of Eduardo de Hinojosa, *El régimen señorial y la cuestión agraria en Cataluña durante la Edad Media* (Madrid, 1905), especially p. 42. The older standard authority on the *mas*, with special emphasis on the architectural features of the *masos*, is Josep Puig i Cadalfalch, *La casa catalana (Primer congrés d'història de la Corona d'Aragó de 1908*, I (Barcelona, 1913). This should be supplemented by the studies of Joaquim Camp i Arboix, *La Masia Catalana* (Barcelona, 1959); *idem*, "Agrarisme medieval català," *Història de l'agricultura catalana* (Barcelona, 1969), pp. 41-58, especially "El mas feudal," pp. 50-54. The differences between the later *masies* and the Carolingian *mansi* are clearly evident. See the brief comments of Robert Latouche, *The Birth of Western Economy: Economic Aspects of the Dark Ages* (trans. E. M. Wilkenson; New York, 1966), pp. 73-96; and F. L. Ganshof, "Manorial Organization in the Seventh, Eighth, and Ninth Centuries," *Transactions of the Royal Historical Society*, 4th series, 31 (1949), 45.

A *mas* was a large farmhouse, usually with ample housing for an extended family, surrounding sheds, barns, corrals, granaries, vineyards, and sometimes forges, situated around an open courtyard with their windowless back walls forming a fort-like enclosure. At least nine of the twenty-five holdings which were called granges at one time were cited by other documents as being towers or *masies*. Since Poblet acquired sixty-five *masies* before 1276, there was ample opportunity to interchange *masies* for granges.

The criterion for the classification of granges and *masies* is not clear, except that the Cistercians generally meant that a grange was worked by *conversi*. However, this did not deter Alfonso II from labeling Cérvoles as a grange in 1183 when between 1180 and 1184 this site was not under the monastery's direct administration. There is little doubt that the key issue in the administrative classification was Poblet's inability to obtain an adequate labor supply to administer all of her domain directly. A grange the size of Cérvoles required even more than the customary number of *conversi*, and Poblet operated more than the usual number of granges. While the Order was still expanding, in the mid-twelfth century when Poblet was founded, some of the Cistercian houses had an estimated two or three *conversi* for every choir monk.[50] Poblet governed a domain as vast as any of the great houses, an estimated 55,000 acres by 1276, but the size of her community never approached the numbers of the great houses in France.[51] Unfortunately no accurate count of the choir

---

50. The number of *conversi* in any community at any given time is usually unknown, and estimates for many of the leading houses vary, with a ration of 3: 2 and 3: 1 of *conversi* to choir monks. But this standard ratio has been questioned recently, and more than likely scholars have hitherto overestimated the number of *conversi* for the great houses. Some of the more often quoted estimates follow: Clairvaux in 1150, approximately three hundred *conversi*; Pontigny in 1157, *circa* three hundred; and Morimund at her apogée, about five hundred *conversi* and a ratio of 1: 1. The largest ratio commonly cited is 500: 140 for Rievaulx in 1165. See Lekai, *White Monks*, p. 232; King, *Cîteaux*, p. 155; K. Hallinger, "Woher kommen die Laienbrüder?" *Analecta Sacri Ordinis Cisterciensis*, 12, nos. 1-2 (January-June, 1956), 1-104; and note the skepticism of Roehl, "Plan," pp. 36-37, note 43.

51. McCrank, *Essays*, pp. 67, and 76, note 54; this estimate is based on the number of vills, granges, and *masies* controlled by Poblet before 1276 and the approximate acreage of the Huerto de Poblet and the grange of Cérvoles.

monks at Poblet exists, to say nothing of the *conversi*. Finestres names one hundred and fifty-five monks who entered the Order before 1250, but his count is incomplete.[52] He lists only those monks mentioned in his chronicle; most of these were named because they belonged to the local nobility. Although the size of Poblet's community is conjectural, a conservative estimate, based on the size of the dormitories at Poblet, the number of granges cited, and the prestige of the monastery, shows that the community averaged about seventy-five monks.[53] Given the modest size of the inner community, as compared to some French communities, Poblet would have averaged no more than a hundred *conversi*. At any rate, the ratio of *conversi* to choir monks at Poblet was certainly not sufficient to meet the demands the monastery placed on its limited labor supply. This would have discouraged the operation of all twenty-five granges simultaneously.

A third characteristic of Poblet's grange system needs emphasis: the locations of the granges were in no way arranged according to the ideal spatial relationship described in the Order's statutes. Some of Poblet's granges were much farther off than the suggested distance of "one day's travel." Torredá, for example, near Balaguer, is over forty-five miles from Poblet even by a crow's flight. The two routes used in the twelfth century placed it considerably farther: via Tárrega the grange was forty-seven miles from Poblet: via Lérida

52. Thirty-three monks entered Poblet between 1151 and 1200, in addition to the original colony of twelve monks from Fontfroide; twenty-nine members took their vows between 1151 and 1251 (dates for them are unknown), and ninety-nine monks entered Poblet between 1200 and 1250. Consequently, the community could not have been much larger than forty members before 1200, and by 1250 the average size perhaps increased to seventy-five choir monks and certainly to no more than a hundred. See the listing of Finestres, *Historia*, pp. 26-29.

53. In 1316, Poblet's community numbered ninety-two choir monks and only thirty-five *conversi*, indicating that the ratio of *conversi* to monks was the inverse of what is currently estimated for most of the French and English houses. See Fontseré, *Real monasterio,* pp. 156-58. Cocheril, *Etudes,* p. 146: "Nous ne possedons pas de statistiques pour les monastères ibériques, mais il semble qu'en Espagne comme au Portugal, dans les abbayes fondeés à partir de la seconde moitié du XIIe siècle, le nombre des convers fut moins élevé que dans d'autres pais. Les monastères adoptèrent le système de fermage pour cultiver leurs vastes domaines. . . ."

fifty-one miles. Barbens, Manresana, and Rocavert were also beyond the prescribed distance of twenty miles.[54] This is not too surprising because both Poblet and Santes Creus pastured their sheep far north of Puigcerdá, up into the *puertos* of the Pyrenees, over one hundred and twenty miles north of Poblet.[55] Moreover, the neighboring houses of Bonrepós, Scala Dei, Santes Creus, Vallbona, and Bellpuig were all within a thirty mile radius of Poblet instead of the ideal fifty. This is understandable because most of these foundations and their initial possessions resulted from patronage. The Cistercians could hardly expect to receive only those lands which met the theoretical spatial requirements of their economic program.[56] In fact, theory dictated Poblet's grange organization much less than did the circumstances of the monastery's early frontier life.

Total flexibility was needed to control a domain as vast and topographically varied as that of Poblet. The development of a flexible grange system by Poblet was paralleled by an equally non-doctrinaire approach to the labor problems

54. The "ideal spatial relationships" which I am here accepting as the norm are those described by Roehl, "Plan," p. 42 and Appendix I, pp. 111-12. As Roehl admits, the distances involved are estimates, and other scholars have differed considerably. However, Roehl's methodology is sound and the dimensions which he adopts in diagraming the relationships seem reasonable. He concludes that Cistercian abbeys were to be at least fifty miles apart, that their granges should have been approximately twenty miles out from the abbey and no closer than ten miles from each other. According to his calculations, the ideal grange would farm the land within a five mile radius. Although Roehl does not consider area, the pattern he pictures infers that a grange should encompass about eighty square miles or 512 acres. This estimate agrees with that made by Henri Pirenne in 1947, which· was accepted by Louis J. Lekai, *White Monks*, pp. 222-23 and McCrank, *Essays*, p. 76, note 54. See Henri Pirenne, *Economic and Social History of Medieval Europe* (London, 1947), pp. 68-70.

55. Manuel Riu, *Formación de las zonas de pastos veraniegos del monasterio de Santes Creus en el Pirineo durante el siglo XII (Archivo bibliográfico de Santes Creus;* Santes Creus, 1962), especially the map of the pastures in the Pyrenees inserted between pp. 10 and 11. Poblet mostly used the *puertos* of Peguera and Lanós. Finestres, *Historia,* II, 347, claimed that, in 1240, *conversi* herded Poblet's sheep as far south as Játiva on the Valencian frontier.

56. Roehl, "Plan," p. 55: "The conclusion is unavoidable that the pattern of a monastery's landed possessions which was the product of the donation mechanism, could have conformed to the special requirements of the Cistercian economic program only by coincidence; for such conformance to have resulted regularly, for many abbeys, can only be considered an improbability of high degree."

which faced the community. As previously noted, Poblet never had enough *conversi* to operate the number of the granges the monastery possessed, and the distance involved in managing the domain complicated matters more. In addition to actual farm work, various other demands were made of Poblet's *conversi,* such as marketing surplus goods and foodstuffs at distances up to a four days' journey or about eighty miles from the abbey.[57] Although statistics for the Iberian houses are unavailable, the numerical strength of the *conversi* in other parts of Europe began to decline in the thirteenth century.[58] This trend made the difficult transition to a monetary economy even more painful for many monasteries. Monastic lands, and certainly those developed as grange sites, could not be left unworked and unproductive after years of *conversi* labor and in the face of increased financial pressure to adjust to the new economic trends. What were the alternatives open to the Cistercians of Poblet?

The monastery tried to solve its labor problems by converting its landed wealth into produce and fluid capital. Although the Order prohibited serf labor, slave labor was permissible, and Poblet welcomed the donations of slaves.[59] In 1175, Ramón de Moncada gave Poblet a slave, Mofeirez Avinmelic, along with his property, and, in 1191, Count Armengol VIII of Urgel gave another, a Saracen named Aytona.[60] King Alfonso II presented Poblet with Juan Ferrer and his property in Gerona, to further the work on Poblet's chapel in that city, and Jaime I's testament of 1272 confirms that the Cistercians still owned slaves in Gerona.[61] In her prime, in 1316, Poblet owned no fewer than sixty-three

57. The sale of surplus goods was approved by the General Chapter in 1157; *Statuta,* I, 64. In 1194, however, the Chapter tried to limit the commercial activities of its houses. See Canivez, *Statuta,* I, 171.

58. See J. S. Donnelly, *The Decline of the Medieval Cistercian Lay Brotherhood* (New York, 1949); Cocheril, *Etudes,* p. 146.

59. Robert S. Smith, "Spain: Agrarian Life of the Middle Ages," *The Cambridge Economic History* (edd. J. H. Clapham and Eileen Powers; New York, 1941), I, 346.

60. Finestres, *Historia,* II, 133; *Cartulari,* no. 213, p. 127.

61. *Cartulari,* no. 293, pp. 187-88 and no. 294, p. 189; Finestres, *Historia,* II, 127 and III, 303-305.

slaves.[62] Slaves were certainly an asset to Poblet, but it is unknown how their labor was used. There is no indication that slavery ever provided Poblet with the number of workers needed to supplement her shortage of *conversi*.

Hired help played only an auxiliary role during harvests in the normal Cistercian economy, but it increased in importance with the decline of the lay brotherhood after 1300. There are no records which indicate the extent to which Poblet may have resorted to hired labor. The Iberian houses were younger than those of France and during the thirteenth century they were still in a growth stage which required reinvestment of surplus capital into land. Poblet, after 1190, began to rely more and more on purchases to compensate for the decreased number of donations the monks received.[63] Moreover, it is questionable whether or not a sufficient labor force existed in underdeveloped Cataluña Nueva where, even if sufficient currency existed, an overall shortage of manpower was created by the constant drain of settlers toward the frontier in northern Valencia. To work large estates with hired labor would have required a "large rural proletariat which did not and could not exist" in the areas which were newly occupied during the Reconquista.[64]

One viable source of help was the migration of lay settlers into the frontier regions from Cataluña Vieja. Consequently the Cistercians of Poblet, like the other great landlords and for the same reasons, gradually went "from a regime of direct exploitation to one of leases and rents."[65] The hazy distinction between granges and *masies* in Poblet's documents reflects this trend, and the case of Cérvoles suggests that

62. Fontseré, *Real monasterio*, pp. 156-58.
63. McCrank, *Essays*, pp. 66-68.
64. Marc Bloch, *French Rural Society, an Essay on its Basic Characteristics* (trans. J. Sondheimer; Berkeley, California, 1966), p. 95, where this generalization is applied to most of Western Europe.
65. David Knowles, *Monastic Order*, I, 126, in reference to the English Cistercians: "In the later centuries, however, when *conversi* became less numerous, it was not only necessary to employ hired labor, but also to lease some of the monastic property to seculars." The Cistercians of Poblet may have preceded the English in turning to seculars to solve their economic problems.

Poblet began to use the alternatives of rents and leases before most of the Order did. The reclassification of granges into *masies* may have been comensurate with the monastery's putting their distant granges under the direction of laymen, *mercenarios*, who were loosely affiliated with the Order. The General Chapter acquiesced in their use in 1224 for regular monastic lands, but it was not until 1261 that commendation of granges to laymen was approved.[66] These laymen took no vows nor did they have a voice in the community's government, but because they dwelt on monastic property and leased their plots from the cellarer, it is commonly assumed that they were integrated into the Order as *familiares*. Supposedly they had a membership slightly inferior in status than that of the *conversi*.[67] There is little evidence, in Poblet's case, that the Cistercians considered these laymen as a tertiary grouping within the Order. The affiliation of Poblet's *mercenarios* consisted of contractural business arrangements with men who were legally free and who had the right to move whenever the terms of their contracts were fulfilled or whenever a proposed contract dissatisfied them.

---

66. "Cum pro diversis casibus seu necessitatibus frequenter contingere soleat quod abbates grangias in manibus saecularium cum anno censu sive aliis modis committant. . . ." *Statuta*, II, 477 (1261).

67. Note that the original guidelines for Cistercian administration did provide for the hiring of laymen to supplement a house's *conversi* labor during harvest seasons. The use of laymen, therefore, may be seen as a natural extension of the clauses in the *Exordium parvum* (issued circa 1120), as noted by Roehl, "Plan," p. 15. The *Exordium parvum*, for example, in describing the position of the *conversus* within the Order, distinguised between *conversi* and *mercenarios*: ". . . Tumque diffinierunt se conversis laicos barbaros licentia monachatu, ut suscepturos, eosque in vita et morte, excepto monachatu, ut semetipsos tractaturos, et homines, etiam mercenarios; quia sine adminiculo istorum non intelligebant se plenarie die sive nocte praecepta Regulae posse servare. . . ." *Exordium Parvum, seu Antiquiores Ordinis Cisterciensis Constitutiones* (Paris, 1664; reprinted by H. Sejalon; Solemnes, 1892), p. 63. See the comments of Knowles, *Monastic Order*, I, 349; Donnelly, *Decline*, p. 4; and Hoffmann, *Konverseninstitut*, pp. 90-92. Cocheril, *Anuario*, p. 226, cites MS. 31 Laibach, f. 24, "De conversis VIII": "Per conversos agenda sunt exercita apud grangias et per mercenarios, quos utique conversos episcoporum licentia tamquam necessario et coadiutores nostri sub cura nostra sicut et monachos suscipimus fratres, et participes nostrorum tam spiritualium quam temporalium bonorum eque monachos habemus. . . ." Cocheril, *Etudes*, p. 334, concludes that ". . . l'exploitation à l'écart des grandes voies de communication, possidant son propre personnel, religieux ou laîc. . . ."

In practice, however, *mercenarios* seldom moved because they were often in arrears of rent, and their debts reduced their lot to something comparable to that of a serf.[68]

But the affiliation which is so often taken to be characteristic of the leases used by Cistercians was really an option to affiliate at some later time. That is, the community often promised to consider the *mercenario* for membership as a *conversus* after the expiration of his contract. One lease, dated March 15, 1176, includes the following mutual pledge which illustrates the close affinity of the *mercenario* and the *conversus*:

> Moreover, we [the abbot, prior, cellarer, and the brothers of Poblet] receive you [the *mercenario*] in life and in death into the prayers and benefits of the Cistercian Order and into the monastery of Poblet. And I [the *mercenario*] give myself to the Lord God, and to the monastery of Saint Mary of Poblet as a brother if I renounce the secular life. . . .[69]

Note that the affiliation on the part of the monastery involved little more than including the *mercenario*'s name in their prayers. The *mercenario* became part of their prayer confraternity, but his current status, that of a freeman, remained unaltered. The *mercenario*'s affiliation was possible in the future when it would require his leaving the secular world. Rearrangement of the terms and the status of the *mercenario* depended totally on the very significant "if" within the option clause. If he became so indebted to the monastery that he could not move, that was affiliation of a different kind. In 1316, the accounting of Poblet credited the monastery with 8806 *sueldos barceloneses* and eight *denarii* as accounts receivable in unpaid rents from the preceding year

---

68. Thompson, *Economic and Social History*, II, 619.
69. *Cartulari*, no. 172, p. 102: "Insuper recipimus te in vita et in morte in orationibus et beneficiis ordinis cisterciensis et monasterii Populeti. Et ego Petrus Pilus de Apela dono meipsum Domino Deo et monasterio Sancte Marie Populeti pro fratre si seculo renunciavero. . . ." It is doubtful that "pro fratre" means a choir monk; if read literally as "brother" the meaning is obviously *conversus*. The term *beneficiis* may apply to the use of the monastery's land as a benefice.

alone! [70] Consequently, there is little doubt that the latter kind of "affiliation" did exist. However, more important than the recruitment of members, these leases were an economic expedient, first to solve the monastery's labor problems, and secondly to collect revenue. [71]

Although the practice of renting monastic lands was contrary in spirit to the original ideal, already in 1155, on March 13, Abbot Grimbaldo leased the monastery's *honor* at Cherta, which Poblet had received six years before from Ramón Berenguer IV, to Bertrand de Tolosa (Toulouse) for a *censo* or annual rent of six jars of oil which was to be paid every Christmastide. [72] Thereafter the practice of renting more distant possessions became common and more profitable, and the rents began to be collected in both currency and percentages of harvests from the estates.

70. Fontseré, *Real monasterio,* pp. 156-58. Judging from a survey of the leases edited in Poblet's cartulary, the rents averaged ten to fifteen *morabatinos* per year for the better holdings. The *morabatino* was based on the Almoravide *dinar,* and in 1157 one *morabatino* was worth six *sueldos* of Barcelona (the old *solidi*), the most commonly used coin in the area. Thus, it would appear that there were nearly 125 and 150 *mercenarios* who were in debt to Poblet in 1316. There is no way of knowing how many *mercenarios* had paid their *censos,* hence the total number of laymen renting monastic lands from Poblet cannot be ascertained. For the exchange value of currencies, see José Balari y Jovany, *Orígenes históricos de Cataluña* (Barcelona, 1899; reprinted, 1964), II, 700-702. The standard numismatic source is Joaquín Botet i Siso, *Les monedes catalanes* (Barcelona, 1908), I-III; supplemented by Alois Heiss, *Descripción general de las monedas hispano-cristianas* (Zaragoza, 1865-1869; reprinted 1963); and O. Gil Farrés, *Historia de la moneda española* (Madrid, 1959).

71. Finestres, *Historia,* II, 412-14: "Un documento de Poblet habla en 1222 de los hombres rústicos y trabajadores, del monasterio, pero y en 1186 tenía tierras que cultivaban los monjes directamente 'con sus propias manos,' y otras en manos de colonos y 'capredmassos.' " Note that the type of commendation practiced by Poblet resembled the old *aprisiones* which the Carolingians and early counts had used in establishing the Marca Hispánica and repopulating the Plains of Vich and Bages. However, whereas the *aprisio* grants implied a "quasi-ownership" by the second party and it was customary for the renter to acquire "full allodial ownership" after thirty years, Poblet made sure that all of the land which was leased reverted to the monastery so that church lands would never become allods of laymen. Moreover, Poblet's leases lack clauses enforcing the older *aprisio* duties of purveyance and corvée labor and they do not reduce the *mercenarios* to vassalage. See the comments of Archibald E. Lewis, *The Development of Southern French and Catalan Society, 718-1050* (Austin, 1965), pp. 68, 70-74, 79-80, 272-74, 390-95.

72. *Cartulari,* no. 202, p. 121; Finestres, *Historia,* II, 60.

Not only did Poblet obtain revenue and the services of lay administration and labor by renting plots and estates, but the monks began systematically to obtain rents from the houses the monastery owned, building sites, and even from application fees paid by those who sought rental privileges. These rents, however, were a form of profiteering quite different from Poblet's use of leases to supplement her *conversi* and slave labor. They were first and foremost a means of collecting revenue, which grew out of the monastery's initial attempts to use rents to solve her labor crisis. Rents varied according to the value of the property when it was leased. If it were developed, the rent could be as much as half of the annual profits as when, on November 2, 1184, Abbot Esteban leased several *masies* to Juan de Cascari.[73] If the land were undeveloped, the rents were less but they were still substantial. When a certain glass-blower named Guillén was established on Pobet's newly plowed fields near Font d'Arola on July 19, 1189, he agreed to pay the monks two-fifths of his future annual produce.[74] Sometimes the rent was a set amount, usually paid in kind, rather than shares. Abbot Pedro, for example, on May 24, 1200, leased a *masia* to Ramón de Mercadal for ten loads of wine and twelve bushels of wheat which were to be delivered every Feast of St Michael.[75]

Privileges were leased as well as land. On February 3, 1203, Poblet gave her fishing rights which had been granted by Count Hugón de Ampurias in 1171, to Ponce Sapas for part of his yearly catch.[76] This was a real labor-saving arrangement and the monastery was especially prone to get laymen to take over her mills for the same reason. On December 30, 1202, Abbot Pedro gave Hermesinda de Rubio and her son, Pedro, control over the monastery's *dominicatura* at Guardia del Prats which included extensive vineyards and Poblet's mills on the Río Anguera. The lease stipulated that Poblet receive an annual rent of fifteen *sueldos*, a token payment to make

73. *Cartulari*, no. 297, pp. 180-81.
74. Palau y Dulcet, *Conca*, p. 110; *Cartulari*, no. 49, p. 25.
75. *Cartulari*, no. 165, pp. 98-99.
76. *Cartulari*, no. 290, pp. 176-77; no. 291, p. 177.

the monastery's proprietorship obvious. The real profit was in Poblet's collection of one-fourth of the revenue of the mills.[77] Lay managers could not alienate any of the monastic property and they often promised to improve their holding at their own expense. There was usually a rent differential between those mills which needed repairs and those which were operational, but Poblet's cellarer saved his valuable man-hours and profits which otherwise would have been spent on construction. On March 31, 1204, for example, Poblet leased her mills at Rocacorba to Bernardo de Montoliu for one-fifth of their annual profits on the condition that he build there two shops for dealing in grain sales and wool. Poblet retained one-fourth of the tithes collected from the mills and the right to have her wheat milled there without charge.[78]

While Poblet's *conversi* worked for the direct support of the abbey, *mercenarios* were used to open up new lands to which the monastery had rights. On September 27, 1171, Poblet leased twenty-one *honors* to residents of Vimbodí after the bailiff of that village completed a survey of the monastery's undeveloped lands near Montagudell.[79] The laymen were to plow new ground, improve the land, and enjoy its immediate benefits, but Poblet retained dominion over the land, title to individual farmsteads, all sales rights, and collected all the tithes and first fruits from the farms once they had been developed. The laymen were to be able to keep their *honors* until death, but the condition that they could not will their property to any heirs was strictly enforced. On the death of the first recipient, the land reverted to the monastery, and the abbot and cellarer could then, if they desired, contract another lease which, because the land was now developed, called for higher rents. Again, in 1183, Abbot Esteban leased two tracts of land near Vallcaire to a certain Bartolomo for one-third of the annual produce on the

77. *Cartulari*, no. 242, pp. 146-47.
78. *Cartulari*, no. 249, pp. 150-51.
79. *Cartulari*, no. 330, pp. 210-12.

condition that the tenant plant vineyards and olive groves, among other things, to increase the value of the land.[80]

The duration of leases varied from contract to contract. Some stipulated a given time, such as when, in 1194, Abbot Pedro leased the large *mas* of Bas to Pedro de Castanyera for six years. The *censo* was moderate, ten *morabatinos,* but the renter agreed to build some houses, at his own expense, on the outlying *honor* and to plant vineyards and trees.[81] In view of these commitments and the relatively short duration of the lease, the terms clearly favored Poblet. Other leases, for even shorter periods, were less favorable, but they were advantageous whenever severe labor shortages plagued the monastery. On May 16, 1183, Poblet leased three *masies* near Pegiana to Pedro de Berga and Bernardo Carcardo for a single season's harvest in return for a nominal rent of one hundred *sueldos.*[82] On November 7 of that year the same *masies* were leased again, this time to Arnaldo de Pegiana for eight years. Without the immediate problem of labor shortages during harvest confronting Poblet, the cellarer could ask for better terms than those arranged in May. Arnaldo agreed to pay Poblet an initial hundred *sueldos* and one-half of his annual income thereafter.[83] Opportunity seemed to be the only guide in ascertaining which property was to be leased, the amount of the *censo*, the duration of the contract, and how many benefit clauses were included in the transaction.

The *mas* of Bas was never converted into a grange, but was an important holding which Poblet continually leased to laymen, possibly because of its location near the confluence of the Río Ciurana and the Ebro, some thirty miles from Poblet in the badlands north of Tortosa. One of these contracts, dated March 15, 1176, illustrates the benefits Poblet reaped by resorting to rents. Abbot Hugón leased the *mas* to Pedro Peldabella for fourteen *morabatinos* annually, a high

80. *Cartulari,* no. 208, p. 124.
81. *Cartulari,* no. 176, pp. 105-106.
82. *Cartulari,* no. 324, p. 198.
83. *Cartulari,* no. 323, pp. 197-98.

censo compared with the revenue Poblet received from three *masies* at Pegiana. The contract was to be for Pedro's lifetime in return for rents and services. Included in the terms was Pedro's acceptance as a "brother" if he ever renounced the secular life. If this happened, Poblet would gain, for it was customary for someone with landed wealth to donate part of it to the community upon his entrance into the Order. The clauses of the contract were specific if he chose to decline membership:

> . . .if, however, I should take a wife, I relinquish and give to the monastery of Poblet, for the health of my soul, after my death, half of all my possessions wherever they be. If indeed I should die and do not have a wife or legitimate children, I relinquish all of my property to Saint Mary of Poblet.[84]

Poblet's real payoff came later. While the *mas* of Bas had an administrator, its lands were worked and its buildings were maintained. In short, the monastery's property perhaps doubled or tripled in value without the labor of *conversi* and without any further investment by the community. Sometime after 1191, Pedro decided to marry and in May of that year he relinquished his rights to the *mas* and also to the vineyards which he had been working in the vicinity of Garcia.[85] Poblet lost a *conversus*, but the monks gained fifteen years of labor which had improved their holdings at Bas plus 210 *morabatinos* in rents, an amount which most likely was more than the original value of the *mas*. Perhaps Pedro accumulated enough savings to go into business for himself by 1191. If he built himself a *mas* and invested in land of his own, Poblet was entitled to half of it when he died. Indeed, the lease of 1176 proved to be very profitable for the monastery. Moreover, even though the terms of the

---

84. *Cartulari,* nos. 170-76, pp. 101-106, all concern the monastery's *mas* at Bas. Note especially no. 172, p. 102: ". . . Si autem vero uxorem, duxero, dimitto et dono monasterii Populeti pro salute anime mee, post mortem mean, medietatem de omnibus rebus meis ubicumque sint. Si vero obiero non habens uxorem neque legitimos infantes, omnia mea dimitto Sancte Marie Populeti."

85. *Cartulari,* no. 171, p. 102.

contract were so clearly favorable to the Cistercians, Poblet had little difficulty in finding a new tenant. On December 28, 1192, Poblet contracted a similar agreement with R. Alfeu for the same *mas*.[86] The lease again stipulated that the tenant must improve the property while he managed it: within the ten years that the lease allowed Alfeu to live at Bas, with moderate rents, he had to build new houses, expand the acreage of the orchards at Bas, and extend his hospitality to Poblet's traveling members. If the lease were to be renewed in 1202 until Alfeu's death, the *mas* was to return to the monastery together with its increments and one-third of all the possessions Alfeu acquired. Consequently the lease contract became a third method of acquisition, in addition to donation and purchase. Moreover, it is obvious that the monastery exploited her land, but the exploitation of labor was equally thorough, whether that of *conversi* or laymen. What the religious vow could not accomplish, the business contract did. There was no need to add a third kind of membership to the Order.

Poblet's grange system, used simultaneously with leases in order to obtain rents and labor, proved to be an efficient, workable means of supporting the community, increasing profits, and developing and expanding the monastic domain. The flexibility with which granges and leases were used indicates the high degree to which Poblet adjusted to her environment in undeveloped Cataluña Nueva, even if this meant violating the Order's constitution twenty to thirty years before her practices were approved by the Chapter General. In terms of the Cistercian Order itself, the economic history of Poblet before 1276 supports the general thesis which R. W. Roehl applied to the Cistercian houses of Saxony: "the length of this period [the period of meaningful adherence to the original plan] appears to be a decreasing function of the macrocosmic chronology, i.e., the farther removed is the date of a given abbey's foundation from 1098 [the date of Cîteaux' foundation], the more rapidly diverges that monas-

86. *Cartulari*, no. 124, pp. 103-104; no. 125, pp. 104-105.

tery's economy from the norm of the plan."[87] Whereas Cîteaux itself had followed the Order's economic directives in the spirit of a strict observance for a half-century, Poblet adhered to the Order's plan for less than one generation before undertaking significant modifications to cope with the economic realities of what had been just a few years before a bitterly contested frontier. However disparaging this may seem to the spirituality and austerity of the Cistercian ideal, in terms of the frontier of the Reconquista, in the development and resettlement of the vast area behind the battle zones, Poblet's administration was eminently successful. Her use of granges was simple and direct, and Poblet's resorting to *mercenarios* to aid her *conversi*, and to leases and rents for revenue, used pre-existant units of administration in an equally simple and utilitarian manner. The result was that Cistercian administration encouraged both churchmen and laymen to cooperate in developing Cataluña Nueva. Count Ramón Berenguer IV had acted wisely in visualizing the colonization effects of a Cistercian enterprise. The economic program of Poblet succeeded in making the monastery self-sufficient and debt-free and produced surplus capital which not only allowed for, but necessitated, reinvestment in lands closer to the frontiers of northern Valencia. The monastic establishment thereby played a crucial role in developing and holding the lands retaken from the Muslims in the Reconquista.

87. Roehl, "Plan," p. 91.

THE CISTERCIAN PILGRIMAGE TO JERUSALEM IN GUILLAUME DE DEGUILVILLE'S *PELERINAGE DE LA VIE HUMAINE*

JOSEPH M. KEENAN

Wadhams Hall Seminary-College

THE LITERARY MOTIF OF THE SYMBOLIC pilgrimage, we are constantly reminded, was ubiquitous in the fourteenth century. The dreamer in *Piers Plowman* saw pilgrimages attempted but not completed; Walter Hilton compared the choices and hazards of the Christian life to the problems confronting the English traveller to Jerusalem. The aggrieved father of the *Pearl* received a vision of the New Jerusalem after a long walk through a dream-like but clearly defined countryside; and Chaucer-the-Pilgrim, who did not seem quite sure what the pilgrimage to Canterbury really meant, heard a humble but dedicated parson compare it to the glorious pilgrimage to Jerusalem celestial.[1]

The most elaborate development of the motif, however, came not from Chaucer, the *Pearl*-Poet, Hilton, or Langland, but from a relatively obscure Cistercian monk of the Abbey of Chaalis, Guillaume de Deguilville, who wrote the *Pelerinage de la Vie Humaine* in 1330, a second version in 1355, and two other long poems as sequals, the *Pelerinage de l'Ame* (1335) and the *Pelerinage de Jesu Christ* (1358).[2] Almost

---

1. On pilgrimage in Hilton and Langland, see Elizabeth Zeeman, "Piers Plowman and the Pilgrimage to Truth," *Essays and Studies*, XI (1958), 1-16; on Chaucer, see Edmund Reiss, "The Pilgrimage Narrative in the *Canterbury Tales*," *Studies in Philology*, LXVII (1970), 295-305. A broad cultural approach is in Gerhart Ladner, "Homo Viator: Medieval Ideas on Alienation and Order," *Speculum*, 42 (1967), 233-59.

2. J. J. Sturzinger edited the first recension of the *Pelerinage de la Vie Humaine* for the Roxburghe Club in 1893—all line references in my text are to this edition

totally ignored by modern scholars and critics, the *Pélerinage de la Vie Humaine* was in its time and for centuries after an enormously influential work. Surviving in more manuscripts than the *Canterbury Tales*, it was translated into practically every European language during the fourteenth and fifteenth centuries. Chaucer turned a part of it into English as the "A.B.C. of the Virgin" before beginning the tales, and John Lydgate translated the entire second recension. It was the source of at least one French morality play, Spenser knew it, and Bunyan may have read a version while preparing *Pilgrim's Progress*.[3] Outside of St. Bernard, Guillaume de Deguilville is probably history's most popular Cistercian poet, although his present reputation is very low in respect to both quantity of studies and estimations of his ability.

In spite of deeper appreciation for the complexity of medieval allegory in recent years, especially of that based on biblical and religious imagery, modern criticism's attacks on the *Pélerinage* assume that Guillaume wrote solely in the tradition of the *Roman de la Rose,* what Dante called the "allegory of the poets," in which there is no literal, narrative base. To this way of thinking, the *Pélerinage* has no real plot beneath its arrangement of abstract concepts and is in fact a massive internal debate, a disembodied *psychomachia*, and a boring poem.[4]

My purpose here is not to defend the quality of Guillaume's poetry, but to challenge the assumption upon which negative judgments have been made. Medieval readers found the *Pélerinage* interesting not merely as an extended sermon but as narrative poetry that could be visualized concretely as actual, physical experience. To them there was indeed a

---

—and the other two poems in 1895 and 1897. The Old French second recension has never been edited, although John Lydgate's translation was edited by F. J. Furnivall for the Early English Text Society in 1899. The only full-length study is Edmond Faral, *Guillaume de Deguieville, Môine de Chaalis* in *Histoire Littéraire de la France* (Paris, 1952), XXXIX, 1-132.

3. For Deguilville's popularity and influence, see Rosamond Tuve, *Allegorical Imagery* (Princeton, 1966), pp. 145-218.

4. See especially C. S. Lewis, *The Allegory of Love* (Oxford, 1954), p. 268; and D. Pearsall, *John Lydgate* (Charlottesville, 1970), p. 176.

"doubleness" to the allegory, the literal level rooted in the experience of pilgrims to the earthly Jerusalem spread by word of mouth and written up in many *Itineraria,* or pilgrim-texts, during Guillaume's time and for centuries before. To pilgrims and crusaders, the voyage to Jerusalem symbolized progress to salvation, or at least an attempt at it: their journey was physical but their pilgrimage was spiritual. Whether the inherent symbolism may be properly called "typological" or "allegorical" is not considered here. But if it were allegorical, it was fundamentally so in the manner of what Dante called the "allegory of the theologians." [5] Jerusalem from the time of the earliest Scriptures was a type or allegory, as well as a literal city, and travel there obtained the same sort of spiritual significance. During the Second Crusade, this notion became a fundamental part of the world-picture of St. Bernard and his Cistercian followers. It is my contention that Guillaume, an extremely well-read Cistercian, but bound by his vow of stability and living during a time of high but mostly disappointed hopes for yet another crusade, wrote an *Itinerarium,* or pilgrim-text of an interiorized pilgrimage, based literally on common experiences of pilgrims to the Holy Land and symbolically on what had become an important part of the Cistercian heritage. [6]

The movement of the *Pélerinage de la Vie Humaine* is familiar to the reader of *Pilgrim's Progress.* The narrator—a

5. Good discussions of allegory, typology, and literature are in A. C. Charity, *Events and Their Afterlife: The Dialectics of Christian Typology in the Bible and Dante* (Cambridge, 1966); Robert Hollander, *Allegory in Dante's Commedia* (Princeton, 1969); and Judson B. Allen, *The Friar as Critic: Literary Attitudes in the Later Middle Ages* (Nashville, 1971). I do not, of course, use "allegory" in the limited sense of the exegetes, implying that the *Pélerinage* is about Christ and the Church, but in the sense Dante used it: real experience from which spiritual truth is obtained. Dante used the pilgrimage in Exodus as his example; see *Opere di Dante* (ed. Società Dantesca Italiana; Florence, 1921), pp. 438-39.

6. S. Galpin, "On the Sources of Guillaume de Deguilville's *Pélerinage de l'Ame,*" *PMLA,* 18 (1910), 275-308, shows that, although an omnivorous reader, Guillaume had not read Dante. The only detailed study of the relation of pilgrim writings to medieval literature is John G. Demaray, "Pilgrim Text Models for Dante's Purgatorio," *Studies in Philology,* LXVI (1969), 1-24. Pilgrim experience was spread orally, often in sermons; see G. Owst, *Preaching in Medieval England* (Cambridge, 1933), pp. 56, 61, 199.

monk at Chaalis, Deguilville himself but also an "Everyman" figure—describes a dream-vision he had, one night long before, of the Heavenly Jerusalem in the Apocalypse. Still dreaming, he is inspired to make a pilgrimage there. The first book of the poem (11. 1-5067) concerns his preparation: he must find a guide, plan a route, consult with "travel experts," and gather equipment. The guide is Grace Dieu, a "bel pucele" who brings him to her house, or the Church, to be baptized, receive instructions on the sacraments, and hear advice from various personifications, like Dame Nature, Dame Raison, Penitence, and Charite. Realistically, the advice is often conflicting, but Pélerin is soon fitted out with a script and burdon, representing Faith and Hope, and even a set of armor (allegorized according to St. Paul) for emergencies.

The second and third books (11. 5067-9054; 9055-11,406) describe the first part of Pélerin's journey, to "la mer de cest monde." His first obstacle is Rude Entendement, a churlish sort who dislikes pilgrims of any kind. Next is Orgueil (pride), Envie, Ypocrisie, and Detraction. In the beginning of the third book, he descends "le val parfont et avaloie," where lurk murderers and vicious beasts like Avarice, Symonie, Gloutonnie, and Venus. Arriving at "la mer de cest monde," he finds a ship called Religioun that sets out for the Heavenly Jerusalem. There are great storms, however, and more than once it is forced to land in strange countries. After surviving one last storm and a mutiny on the ship, Pélerin nears the end of his journey. Just as he is about to land, he dies. The narrator awakes and joins the other monks in the chapel for matins.

There are three important facets of the imaginative genesis of Deguilville's poem that should be looked at quite separately from the "allegory of the poets" and the tradition of the *Roman de la Rose*. The first is the typology of Jerusalem in Scripture and exegetical commentary. The second is the symbolism inherent in pilgrim-texts and pilgrim traditions that Guillaume most certainly knew. And the third is in the writings of St Bernard and other Cistercian authors, who, especially during the Second Crusade, attempted to resolve the active pursuit of pilgrimage to the Holy Land with contemplative pursuit of the Heavenly Jerusalem.

As early as the Psalms, Jerusalem had a figurative sense to the Jews, and, by the time of the Second Isaiah, hope for rebuilding the destroyed city lay in a transformation that would be supernatural and apocalyptic, not earthly. St Paul spoke of Jerusalem as the "mother of us all," calling his phrase *allegoria*, not *typos*, thus fixing that slippery term "allegory" in ambiguity. Throughout the Patristic period, Jerusalem in Scripture was interpreted in various ways. To St Augustine the physical city was significant only because it was a figure for the Celestial City and City of God. In the *Glossa ordinaria*, Jerusalem literally is a city pilgrims go to, allegorically the Church, tropologically the Christian soul, and anagogically the Heavenly City. Alain de l'Isle viewed it as a type of the Blessed Mother, and one perhaps overenthusiastic Franciscan regarded the Heavenly Jerusalem in the Apocalypse of St John as predictive of the coming of the friars to England.[7]

Regardless of specific designation, the symbolic significance of the Holy City was paramount. And pilgrims who went there saw the sites and their own journies through the eyeglasses of Scripture and liturgy. The scholarly and skeptical Arculf, friend of Adamnan, swore the column in the center of the city cast no shadow (and this after a full day's observation) because the Psalms said it was the center of the earth.[8] The *Hoediporicon* of Willibald, an Englishman, is really a spiritual autobiography. As a young monk at Waldheim, he decided he should "despise and renounce all the perishing things of this world, and forsake, not only the temporal riches of earthly property, but also his country, his parents

7. A convenient tracing of the Jerusalem type is in Johan Chydenius, "The Typological Problem in Dante," *Societas Scientiarum Fennica: Commetationes Humanarum*, XXV (1958), 1-159. On St. Paul, see Harry Wolson, *The Philosophy of the Church Fathers* (Cambridge, Mass., 1956), I, 24; on the friar, M. Rhodes-James, *The Apocalypse in Art* (London, 1957), p. 64.

8. Adamnan, *De locis sanctis* (ed. D. Meehan; Dublin, 1958), p. 42.

and kindred and attempt to seek another land by pilgrimage. . . ."⁹ Willibald's voyage to Jerusalem was motivated not simply by devotion, scholarship, or curiosity; he was following a mysterious destiny, and his theme was the constant intervention of Divine Providence in his journey—which would later make him the "Apostle to the Bavarians" and a canonized saint. Other pilgrims described their land journey from Egypt to Jerusalem as an imitation of the journey of the ancient Jews out of the desert. Speaking of the stops made by pilgrims in the desert, Fetellus said: "Through them the true Hebrew who hastens to pass from earth to heaven must run his race, and, leaving Egypt of the world, must enter the land of promise, the heavenly fatherland."¹⁰ Because of this typological view, pilgrimage became a liturgical gesture: the earthly journey to the actual city was inextricably bound up with spiritual travel.¹¹

Looked at in this light, perhaps, crusading ideology becomes more understandable. If Jerusalem is lost, the Heavenly Jerusalem is lost; if Jerusalem is won, the prophecies are fulfilled. Baldwin of Dol made this clear in his exultation over the coming victory against the Moslems in the First Crusade:

> How blessed are the stones which crowned you, Stephen, the first martyr! How happy, O John the Baptist, the waters of the Jordan which served you in baptizing the Saviour! The children of Israel, who were led out of Egypt, and who prefigured you in the crossing of the Red Sea, have taken that land by their arms, with Jesus as leader; they have driven out the Jebusites and other inhabitants

9. Willibald, *Hodoeporicon* (trans. T. Brownlow; *Palestine Pilgrim Text Society*; London, 1895), p. 6.

10. Fetellus, *Description of Jerusalem and the Holy Land* (trans. J. R. Macpherson, Palestine Pilgrim Text Society; London, 1892), p. 14.

11. See Hugo of St Victor, PL 176:727. Also, Yves Marie-Joseph Congar, "Eglise et Cité de Dieu chez quelques auteurs cistercians," *Mélanges offerts à Etienne Gilson* (Toronto, 1959), pp. 173-202; A. Bredero, "Jérusalem dans l'Occident Médieval," *Mélanges offerts à René Crozet* (ed. P. Gallois; Poitiers, 1966), I, 259-71.

and have themselves inhabited earthly Jerusalem, the image of the celestial Jerusalem.[12]

St Bernard both elaborated on and deepened all of these ideas in his writings concerning Jerusalem and the Second Crusade. The crusade, like pilgrimage, was to Bernard a personal and liturgical gesture towards salvation. In his letter to the English people, probably written in the summer of 1146, he said of that year: "Now is the acceptable time, now is the day of abundant salvation."[13] The time is unique in world history because

> The earth is shaken because the Lord of heaven is losing his land, the land in which he appeared to men, in which he lived amongst men for more than thirty years; the land made glorious by his miracles, holy by his blood; the land in which the flowers of his revelation first blossomed. And now, for our sins, the enemy of the Cross has begun to lift his sacrilegious head there, and to devastate with the sword that blessed land, that land of promise. Alas, if there should be none to withstand him, he will soon invade the very city of the living God, overturn the arsenal of our redemption, and defile the holy places which have been adorned by the blood of the immaculate lamb. They have cast their greedy eyes especially on the holy sanctuaries of our Christian religion, and they long particularly to violate that couch on which, for our sakes, the Lord of our life fell asleep in death.

"The enemy of the Cross," evil personified, has caused all this because of our sins. God could, of course, rectify the

---

12. *The First Crusade: The Account of Eye-Witnesses and Participants* (trans. A. C. Krey; Gloucester, Mass., 1958), p. 35. Also see Guibert of Nogent's report of Urban II's speech at the Council of Claremont, pp. 31-32. On the spiritual Jerusalem in the Crusades, see P. Alphodery, "La Christianité et l'idée de croisade," in L'Evolution de l'humanité, XXXVIII (Paris, 1959), II, 109-110.

13. Bernard of Clairvaux, *The Letters of Bernard of Clairvaux* (trans. Bruno Scott James; Chicago, 1953), p. 461. On pilgrimage and Jerusalem in the Second Crusade, see Giles Constable, "The Second Crusade as Seen by Contemporaries," *Traditio*, IX (1935), 213-80; and E. Williams, "Cîteaux et la seconde croisade," *Revue d'histoire ecclésiastique*, 49 (1954), 116-51.

situation by sending down legions of angels or by merely saying a word. But he does not because he is testing individual Christian men:

> ...But I tell you that God is trying you. "He looks down from heaven at the race of men, to find one soul that reflects, and makes God its aim," one soul that sorrows for him. For God has pity on his people and on those who have grievously fallen away and has prepared for them a means of salvation.

And so the crusade was fundamentally an exercise in personal penance as well as a historical fulfillment of prophecy: "I call that generation blessed that can seize an opportunity of such rich indulgence as this, blessed to be alive in this year of jubilee. The bessing is spread throughout the whole world, and all the world is flocking to receive this badge of immortality."

In each of the ten letter, he wrote concerning the Holy Land, Bernard's sense of the typology of Jersusalem was strong. The Jews were not to be persecuted during the crusade because:

> Ask anyone who knows the Sacred Scriptures what he finds foretold of the Jews in the psalm. "Not for their destruction do I pray," it says. The Jews are for us the living words of Scripture, for they remind us always of what our Lord suffered. They are dispersed all over the world so that by expiating their crime they may everywhere be the living witnesses of our redemption.[14]

Bernard had a practical reason for giving such advice: there had been several massacres and pogroms of the Jews by enthusiasts in the Rhineland, and he hoped to prevent more. But his method of argument suggests the Jews have value within the framework of biblical prophecy and typology. Like pilgrimage, the crusade was a heavenly sign by which men personally as well as communally would act out the central facts of salvation history. Bernard's followers termed

---

14. Bernard, *Letters*, p. 462. On the Jews, see A. J. Luddy, *Life and Teaching of St. Bernard* (Dublin, 1937), pp. 530-32.

its members *peregrini* or *peregrinantes*, and as "voluntary exiles who have willingly accepted poverty"[15]

So also, Bernard regularly viewed his Cistercian monks as pilgrims to and actual citizens of the Heavenly Jerusalem. In a letter to Alexander, bishop of Lincoln, referring to one of the bishop's canons who had started out on an actual pilgrimage to Jerusalem only to join Bernard's monastery instead; he defended the young man's decision by affirming that the monastic vocation is a "higher" pilgrimage than the earthly journey:

> I write to tell you that your Philip has found a short cut to Jerusalem and has arrived there very quickly. He crossed "the vast ocean stretching wide on every hand" with a favorable wind in a very short time, and he has now cast anchor on the shores for which he was making.[16]

What is striking is that Philip's pilgrimage was complete when he entered Clairvaux. Considering Augustine's terminology, the monastery was not simply a "peregrinating" part of the City of God in aspiration but rather a direct correspondent to the Heavenly City. The monk, even on earth, was a citizen, like the angels and saints of St. Augustine, of the Heavenly part of the City of God:

> Even now he stands in the courts of Jerusalem and "of whom he had heard good tidings in Ephrata, he has found in the woodland plains, and gladly reverences in the place where he has halted in his journey." He has entered the holy city and has chosen his heritage with them of whom it has been deservedly said: "You are no longer exiles or aliens; the saints are your fellow citizens, you belong to God's household." His going and coming is in their company and he has become one of them, glorifying God and saying with them: "We find our true home in heaven."

Alluding to St Paul, Bernard distinguished between the two cities:

> He is no longer an inquisitive onlooker, but a devout inhabitant and an enrolled citizen of Jerusalem; but not of the

---

15. Constable, "Second Crusade," p. 237.
16. Bernard, *Letters*, p. 91; PL 182:169.

earthly Jerusalem to which Mount Sinai in Arabia is joined, and which is in bondage with her children, but of that free Jerusalem which is above and the mother of us all.

In Bernard's mystical theology, the purpose of monastic contemplation was to approximate as closely as possible on earth the condition man's soul would have in heaven after death. Man belongs to earth by virtue of his body but to heaven by virtue of his soul. Therefore, on entering the monastery he must "leave his body at the door" and live a life strictly of the soul's perceptions. Cistercian life was to be an image and a foretaste of life in paradise, a heaven on earth. This concept goes a long way to explain Cistercian asceticism—its motive was not simply self-mortification—and Bernard's suspicion, often exaggerated by his critics, of graphic arts and literature. If the monk is already a citizen of the Heavenly City, he is like the angels who inhabit it; hence he must train himself to approximate angelic intelligence. He will eschew physical things except when they have transcendental significance. His own life will be a mirror of heavenly life in the same way that the monastery is an image of the Heavenly Jerusalem:

And this, if you want to know, is Clairvaux. She is the Jerusalem united to the one in heaven by wholehearted devotion, by conformity of life, and by a certain spiritual affinity. Here, so Philip promises himself, will be his rest forever ever.[17]

This idea of the monastery is no doubt the reason why Bernard often referred to his houses as *paradisus claustralis* and why they had names like *Locus Caeli* and *Nova Jerusalem*.

All of this, of course, precludes actual pilgrimage and participation in the Crusade for the consistent and conscientious monk. And in attempting to resolve the two contrary impulses, Bernard laid the groundwork for Deguilville's later allegory:

17. Congar, "Eglise et Cité," pp. 174-81. Also, Thomas Merton, *The Waters of Siloe* (New York, 1949), pp. 300-351; and Claude Peifer, *Monastic Spirituality* (New York, 1966), pp. 441-50. On Bernard, see the sermons in PL 183:259 and 663; and E. Gilson, *The Mystical Theology of St. Bernard* (New York, 1940), pp. 330-35. On names, see Fréderic Van Der Meer, *Atlas de l'ordre cistercien* (Paris, 1965).

It is the vocation of a monk to seek not the earthly but the heavenly Jerusalem, and he will do this not by setting out on his feet but by progressing in his dispositions.[18]

The *De laude novae militiae*, written for the Knights Templars who were to protect Jerusalem, further developed the idea by paralleling the crusading knight and pilgrim with the monk, each engaged in a kind of war or pilgrimage. The new soldiers were to be

> A new kind, I say, of knighthood, untried in the world; where the double conflict is fought out equally and indefatigably, opposing flesh and blood as well as spiritual evils in heaven. And so where physical enemies of the body are resisted by a single man I do not deem it marvelous nor do I think it exceptional. But when war with vices and demons is declared by strength of spirit, this is not extraordinary though I will say it is laudable, as when the entire world is contested by monks.[19]

He was quite plain that the physical city of Jerusalem was important mostly because of its higher significations but that the physical and spiritual were closely related: one is the image of the other:

> Do you see that this crowded new militia approves the witness of old, and that the courage which we have heard of we will also see in the city of the Lord? As long as, of course, the literal interpretation does not prejudice spiritual understanding, providing indeed we hope in eternity; whatever it means at this time, we will use such words of the prophets; lest through that which we know and learn that which we believe vanishes and the lack of faith diminishes its hope, so may the present witness be the driving out of the future. In most respects, the temporal glory of the earthly city does not destroy the goodness of heaven but builds it up; if, however, we do not hesitate in the least to maintain the form of her who is in heaven and our mother.[20]

18. Bernard, *Letters*, p. 503; PL 182:612.
19. Tpl I, 1, PL 182:921.
20. Tpl III, 6, PL 182:925.

This relationship between physical and spiritual, rooted in both biblical typology and common experience, would very easily develop into literary allegory. Bernard's "war with vices and demons. . .declared by strength of spirit" would be portrayed in Guillaume's poem as a series of encounters with strange beasts and evil people. To Bernard, "that knight is truly fearless, and on all sides secure, who, just as the body puts on armour, has his spirit put on the breastplate of faith." Pélerin, we remember, removes his armor because it is heavy and almost suffers defeat on his road to Jerusalem.[21]

In an unusual way, the structure of *De laude* supports the fact that Bernard treated the Crusade as a pilgrimage and the pilgrimage as an interior journey of the soul. Faced with the need to draw up a stringent rule for the new order of soldiers and also an attractive bit of polemic to recruit them, he seems to have chosen the form of a Jerusalem pilgrim-text to fit both purposes. Only the first four chapters dealt directly with the knights themselves, how they were to act, dress, and how they were distinguished from secular soldiers. They were, in fact, as much like monks as knights.[22] The last nine chapters gave what might be called the reason for their conduct: each was a meditation on one of the sites, or stations, of Scripture in the Holy Land. They seem to have been arranged in the order that pilgrims would have visited them: the Temple (the center of attraction in Jerusalem) was first; then Bethlehem, Nazareth, the Mount of Olives and the Valley of Josaphat, the River Jordan, Calvary, the Holy Sepulchre, Bethpage, and Bethany. The meditations also may be of the sort that appealed to actual pilgrims. The Holy Sepulchre was the occasion for a meditation on death, and Bethpage for a discussion of confession and Penance. Here Bernard approached allegory: at Bethany, for example, one entered the dwelling (*castellum*) of Mary and Martha, which he called

21. Tpl I, 1, PL 182:922. On the iconography of Pélerin's armor, see Tuve, *Allegorical Imagery*, p. 166.
22. Tpl IV, 8, PL 182:927.

"the house of obedience."[23] Physical locations along the pilgrim route were associated with sacraments, bibilical events, and states of mind, much as they would be in the *Pélerinage*. To Bernard, pilgrimage and crusade were as much allegorical and typological as physical.

Aside from the fourteenth-century's attachment to allegorical literature, there are many reasons why Deguilville would feel comfortable with a similar style of thought and be inclined to write the sort of poems he did. A new crusade was in the wind, although the French were generally suspicious of the idea. And during his time there was a sudden revitilization of pilgrim traffic, with a resultant increase in the popularity of pilgrim-texts.[24] That these texts inspired creative, or fictional, literature is evident from Guillaume's contemporary "Sir John Mandeville," who claims to write his *Travels* because all people are terribly interested in what it is like to go to Jerusalem.[25] Many of the pilgrim-texts were probably written for monks, nuns, and friars who could not go on pilgrimage either because of their vow of stability or the absence of money or time. These people would make their pilgrimages mentally—as St Bernard said "not by setting out on his feet but by progressing by his dispositions"—in much the same way as Catholics have made the Stations of the Cross. As a Cistercian, Deguilville was one of these.[26] He had

23. Tpl XIII, 31, PL 182:939. Etheria of Aquitaine described how the pilgrims would stop to meditate, "for we always especially desired that when we came to any place the corresponding passage from the book should be read"; St. Sylvia of Aquitaine, *Pilgrimage* (trans. T. Bernard; *Palestine Pilgrim Text Society;* London, 1896), p. 15. For a history of these stations, see Lina Eckenstein, *A History of Sinai* (London, 1921).
24. In 1334, King Philip met with Pope John XXII, the king of Cyprus, and a representative of the Knights Hospitallers to organize a new action, but he abandoned the idea to turn his attention toward England. At the same time, compromises had been reached with the Moslems which allowed for traffic by pilgrims but not armies. See Aziz S. Atiya, *The Crusade in the Later Middle Ages* (London, 1938), pp. 95 f., 155 f.
25. *Mandeville's Travels* (ed. M. C. Seymour; Oxford, 1967), p. 3.
26. To illustrate the relation vicarious pilgrimage had to the devotion of the Stations of the Cross, Herbert Thurston (*The Stations of the Cross* [London, 1906],

read St Bernard and other Cistercian authors who dealt with
the symbolic Jerusalem and was aware that the Knights
Templars, Bernard's ideal men outside the monastery walls,
were being disbanded, charged with, among other things,
failure to keep faith with the ideal of protecting the Holy
Land.[27]

And so in the *Pélerinage* he wrote about a pilgrimage made
with dispositions, not feet. It is an allegory but one rooted in
those realities of pilgrim travel suggestive of spiritual journey-
ing. For example, the division into four books follows the
usual pilgrim-text's order of development: description of
motivation and preparation; leaving familiar territory (usually
southern France); passage through strange lands observing
wonders and countering assorted threats (Italy and the Mediterranean coast); and the fearful ocean crossing from Venice
to Jaffa or Alexandria.[28] Modern critics find the episode at
the House of Grace Dieu, in which allegorically Pélerin enters
the Church and is initiated into the sacraments, most distaste-
ful because it apparently has no literal level. But the medieval
reader, familiar with pilgrim procedures, would recognize the
entire scene as reflective of special liturgies celebrated for
Jerusalem pilgrims in their home dioceses before their departure. A table is set up for a meal, the Eucharistic banquet;
there is a substantial encounter with Dame Penance, readings
from Scripture, a homily, and finally the eating of bread and

---

pp. 16-19) relates a story from a Cistercian chronicle of a lay-sister in the
fourteenth century who was torn between stability and an earlier vow to make a
pilgrimage to Jerusalem. Her confessor advised her to make a spiritual pilgrimage
in her convent, and for a full year she passed from altar to altar and shrine to
shrine, identifying them with the stations of the Holy Land. As the year ended she
died, hands uplifted to the Blessed Sacrament. The day after her death a pilgrim
newly returned from Jerusalem called at the convent asking for her, saying that
she left him suddenly after spending the year on pilgrimage with him in the holy
places.

27. What Cistercian attitudes towards the dissolution of the Templars were is
unknown, but the monks must have been interested. On the dissolution, see Edith
Simon, *The Piebald Standard* (Boston, 1959).

28. A good example is *Itinerarium Symonis Semeonis ab Hybernia ad Terram
Sanctam* (ed. Mario Esposito; Dublin, 1960). The greater part of most pilgrim-
texts, of course, was given over to description of the holy sites.

drinking of wine, followed by the presentation to Pélerin of his coveted scrip and staff. Dame Charity reads Christ's "Testament of Peace," an allusion to the Sign of Peace after the *Agnus Dei*.[29] Similarly, Pélerin's allegorical Baptism—he must swim a stream, assisted by a "sergen,"—has its prototype in ceremonies for Jerusalem pilgrims that symbolized their second baptism as they set upon their journey. As itineraries became regularized, they included a ritual bath in the River Jordan, not only in imitation of Christ's baptism but as a symbol of purification before entering the Holy City.[30] Guillaume's portrayal of Moses, who in traditional biblical typology was a figure of bishops and heads of churches, further establishes the pilgrim liturgy as the literal level of the allegory. He is pictured conventionally as Moses with horns on his head, but he acts as the chief celebrant of the liturgy who distributed bread and ointment for the pilgrims' scrips. Pélerin notes that like a bishop he is the only one who performs Confirmation and Holy Orders while his "sergens Dieu" witness marriages and distribute the Eucharist. Contemporary readers recognized this double identity: manuscripts of the *Pélerinage* illustrate his horns as the *cornua* of the episcopal mitre, showing him as a local bishop rather than the biblical figure.[31]

Pélerin's motive for entering the House of Grace Dieu is to receive a scrip and staff, common implements of pilgrimage but treated allegorically by Deguilville as the virtues of Faith and Hope. Here again there is a literal referent easily lost to the modern reader. The fact that Pélerin's staff, or *bourdon*, features two knobs representing Jesus and the Virgin respectively should not lead us to think it is not a real pilgrim-staff. Sometimes such staffs were designed elaborately, with knobs shaped as musical instruments like the one belonging to

29. See *The Sarum Missal in English* (trans. F. E. Warren; London, 1913), II, 166, 169-71, 222; and *Le Pontifical Romain au Moyen Age*, III, *Le Pontifical de Guillaume Durand* (ed. Michel Andrieu; Vatican, 1940), p. 543 f.

30. Bredero, "Jérusalem," p. 265 f. MS illustrations portray Pélerin as an adult pilgrim, not a child (see Tuve, *Allegorical Imagery*, p. 157).

31. Tuve, *Allegorical Imagery*, pp. 159, 161.

Chaucer's Summoner.[32] The scrip was used by pilgrims to carry bread but no doubt became more symbolic than practical as pilgrimages became better organized. Because of bread's association with the Eucharist, this outward sign of the pilgrim's purpose would easily be emblematic to the allegorical imagination (conversant with Romans 1:17) of Faith. At the culminating part of the pilgrim-liturgy, listed by Durandus of Mende as "De benedictione baculi et pere seu scarpelle peregrinorum," the actual objects are handled as allegories and types. Prayers are said that compare the staff to Aaron's rod, calling it a *signum* of one's defenses against evil, and the bread put in the scrip to the manna given the Israelites in the desert and to the spiritual food needed by all Christians.[33]

As the pilgrims receive the final blessing, the celebrant prays that during their journey they be protected *"contra hostes visibiles et invisibiles et contra omnes diabolicas et humanas insidias."* Much of the remainder of the *Pélerinage* deals with these struggles—allegorically, to be sure, but based on experiences of pilgrims. In Book II the first major confrontation is with Rude Entendement, allegorically a crude natural reason that reads Scripture without an educated background but on the literal level, a sort of person very visible and human to pilgrims harassed by petty bureaucrats and toll collectors. Largely because of the conduct of pilgrims who saw themselves as crusaders rather than humble exiles, authorities in both European and eastern countries were suspicious and often wanted to see a "certificate of pilgrimage" from the pilgrim's king, vouching for the pilgrim's motives and piety. After a long but futile debate, in which Rude Entendement's colloquial language and legalistic thinking suggest a real bureaucrat rather than a "mere abstraction," Lady Reason, Pélerin's lawyer, presents such a certificate and arrests him for violat-

---

32. "General Prologue," 1. 673 in *The Complete Works of Chaucer* (ed. F. N. Robinson; Cambridge, Mass., 1933), p. 23. Also J. J. Jusserand, *English Wayfaring Life in the Middle Ages* (New York, 1939), p. 385.

33. *Le Pontifical de Guillaume Durand*, pp. 544-45.

ing "the safe-conduct of pilgrims."[34] Often real pilgrims were less fortunate and, like Willibald, landed in jail.

Less human but more colorful are the monsters Pélerin meets in Book II, allegorically the Seven Deadly Sins and other dark tendencies of human nature, but literally what pilgrims expected to see and what listeners to their tales wanted to hear about. From the time of the supposed letter from Fermes to the Emperor Hadrian, the East was considered to be a region populated by curious beasts. They were elaborately illustrated on maps, like the Hereford *Mappamundi*, and gradually became absorbed into travel literature, especially in the fourteenth century.[35] The imaginative transformation of these monsters into allegory is easy to envision. The entire beastiary tradition was symbolically oriented, and the odd creatures of Daniel, Ezechiel, and the Apocalypse received constant allegorical scrutiny by exegetes. Further, because the personal spiritual failures of pilgrim-crusaders were commonly accepted as the main cause of Christianity's failure to reach Jerusalem in any permanent way, the obstacles in the pilgrim's path would naturally, in the manner of St Bernard, take on the symbolic significance of sin. Mandeville specifically blamed "*pryde, covetyse,* and *envye* which han so enflaumed the hertes of lordes of the worlds" for his age's failure to launch a successful crusade and claims it was gold and silver (Avarice) that murdered the Christians whose bodies lie in the Valley Perilous.[36] That Deguilville's Envie should be a water-snake with eyes ex-

---

34. On such arrests, see Sidney Heath, *In the Steps of the Pilgrims* (Essex, n. d.), p. 132. On dangers from officials, see Jusserand, *English Wayfaring Life*, pp. 361-62; Atiya, *The Crusade in the Later Middle Ages*, p. 156.

35. On maps, monsters, and travel literature, see J. K. Wright, *The Geographical Lore in the Time of the Crusades* (New York, 1925), esp. pp. 65-70, 121-26; Rudolf Wittkower, "The Marvels of the East: A Study in the History of Monsters," *Journal of the Warburg and Courtauld Institutes*, 5 (1942), 159-97. The classic examples in travel literature are Odoric in Sir Henry Yule, *Cathay and the Way Thither* (London, 1913), II, esp. p. 176; and *Mandeville's Travels*, esp. pp. 206-210.

36. *Mandeville's Travels*, pp. 2-3, 205. See also Odoric in *Cathay and the Way Thither*, II, 266.

tended on long antennae results from the synthesis of monster lore in travel literature with the allegorical vision of pilgrimage.

So also Pélerin's progression from one spot to another, each occupied by a concrete figuration of sin or state of mind, closely parallels the meditations of pilgrims who travelled from Cairo (Babylon), across the Sinai Desert to Mount Sinai and Jerusalem in the path of the Exodus. By the twelfth century, stops along the way had become standardized into "stations" with allegorical associations derived from folk etymologies and from biblical events. Fetellus said that "in Arabia the Lord detained the people of Israel for forty years at forty-two stations."[37] In the tour they were arranged to reflect the spiritual progress of the pilgrims from a state of sin to, upon approaching Jerusalem, order and grace. Before Mount Sinai they included "bitterness" (number 5), "hatred" (8), "discontent" (10), and "the graves of lust" (13); towards Jerusalem there was "Christ" (19), "miracle" (21), and "revelation" (42).[38] The relation Guillaume constructed between actual pilgrims and his allegorical character (himself or everyman) was the same pilgrims felt they shared with the ancient Israelites. Geography itself became symbolic. When Symeon Semeonis set out on the continent, "traversing steep mountains, deep valleys, thick forests, and areas filled with evil ones," and plunged into the great African desert in imitation of the Israelites, "like sheep among wolves," he was aware that his journey was both a physical and spiritual one and that the problems and near disasters he would face were imagistic of the moral struggles of all Christian men and antitypes of the experiences of the Jews.[39] Similarly, when Pélerin descends into a "val parfont et avolie" in Book III and meets his most fully drawn enemy, Avarice, we should be

---

37. Fetellus, *Description of Jerusalem and the Holy Land,* p. 14. See also Pseudo-Bede in *A Holy Land Account* (trans. A. Stewart; *Palestine Pilgrim Text Society*; London, 1894), p. 41 f.

38. Demaray, "Pilgrim Text Models," claims these stations find their way into the *Divine Comedy.*

39. *Itinerarium Symonis Semeonis,* pp. 34-35, 98-99.

reminded of the Valley of Hinnom, just outside Jerusalem and a regular part of the pilgrim itinerary. Mandeville's Valley Perilous, perhaps coincidentally also the den of the same vice, was no doubt based on the same location.[40]

There are other examples of correspondence between the allegorical experience Guillaume presented and actual pilgrim travel. Pélerin is tossed from island to island just as pilgrims were forced to land in strange places in the Mediterranean.[41] He boards the Ship of Religion, choosing the Cistercian "castle" as his residence, and is tied to his bunk by Lady Obedience in the same way pilgrims were tied down at bedtime during storms.[42] He visits monasteries and argues theology just as pilgrims did in the East.[43] He does not, of course, give us a detailed description of Jerusalem, which forms the greater part of most pilgrim-texts: the vision of the Heavenly Jerusalem at the beginning of the poem is the implicit culmination of the narrator's experience. The dreamer awakes to the morning bell calling him and the other monks to chapel, presumably to continue his interior pilgrimage in the Cistercian house of Chaalis.

To say that Deguilville's *Pélerinage* was indebted only to Cistercian thinking would be quite wrong. He cited the *Roman de la Rose* as stimulation to writing—although he quarreled with it constantly[44]—and the debates between his allegorical figures indicate a strong interest in scholasticism, although this was probably encouraged by proximity of the Cistercian college at nearby Paris.[45] Certainly there is a good deal of the "allegory of the poets" in the poem, but its

40. On background of the Valley of Hinnom, see J. L. McKenzie, *Dictionary of the Bible* (Milwaukee, 1965), pp. 299-300.

41. For example, Willibald, *Hodoeporicon*, pp. 11-12. See Atiya, *The Crusade in the Later Middle Ages,* p. 168, for a variety of cases.

42. For example, William Wey, *Itinerarium* (London, 1857), n.p.

43. For example, *Itinerarium Symonis Semeonis,* pp. 48-59; Mandeville's debate with the Sultan in *Mandeville's Travels,* pp. 94-97; and throughout Bernard the Wise, *How the City of Jerusalem is Situated* (London, 1893). It is no coincidence that Pélerin meets personified Heresy on the shores of the Mediterranean.

44. Lewis, *Allegory of Love,* pp. 364-71, describes the differences.

45. Louis J. Lekai, *The White Monks* (Okauchee, Wisconsin, 1953), pp. 54-64, 187-208.

fundamental structure was based on the pilgrimage to Jerusalem as it was understood by St Bernard, which is a matter of the "allegory of the theologians."

The recovery of these lost literal referents may help rehabilitate Deguilville's dismal modern reputation and give us some indication of why he was so popular and influential in his time. For when the Parson utters the final benediction on the pilgrimage to Canterbury—

> And Jhesu, for his grace, wit me sende
> To shewe yow the wey, in this viage,
> Of thilke parfit glorious pilgrymage
> That highte Jerusalem celestial. . . .[46]

Chaucer was, I think, indicating his indebtedness to Guillaume de Deguilville, môine de Chaalis, and, perhaps, by historical extension, to the Cistercians before him. And this is an intriguing prospect indeed.

---

46. "The Parson's Prologue," 11. 48-51, in *The Complete Works of Chaucer*, p. 229.

JEAN DE CIREY AND THE QUESTION OF AN ABBOT-GENERAL IN THE ORDER OF CITEAUX IN THE FIFTEENTH CENTURY

WILLIAM J. TELESCA

Le Moyne College

THE ORDER OF CITEAUX in the fifteenth century was far removed from the atmosphere that created it. Like all great movements it tried to change with the times while always remaining the same. Jean de Cirey was the last abbot of Cîteaux at the close of the middle ages. His name is more familiar than most of his predecessors of the period. He makes a very good first impression in the records of the Order, and he appears as a dynamic leader. Yet, the more I search into his life, the more perplexed I become. His twenty-five year abbacy was stormy and controversial and produced some of the most interesting developments in the annals of the Order.

Roger De Ganck has written a lengthy article on the notion of the abbot of Cîteaux as abbot-general which was published in the *Analecta Cisterciensia*.[1] The abbot Jean de Cirey has even received special attention, and overall, De Ganck has presented a precise analysis of the powers of the abbot of Cîteaux in relation to the constitutional question of jurisdiction and the role of the General Chapters. It is not my intention to challenge his thesis or any part of it. I shall try instead to offer further insights into the personality of Jean de Cirey himself, to examine the circumstances that prompted his actions, and to look for possible clues to his intentions. While

---

1. R. De Ganck, "Les pouvoirs de l'Abbé de Cîteaux de la Bulle *Parvus Fons* (1265) à la Révolution Française," *Analecta Cisterciensia,* 27 (1971), 3-63.

the statutes of the General Chapters remain the best source of material for this, his own writings are much more emotional, biased, polemical, and therefore interesting.

I have investigated the Order of Cîteaux at the close of the middle ages in reference to other movements and events of European history. Its structural and organizational system, with dependence upon the ideas of Roman primacy, was challenged after the fourteenth century by an atmosphere of doubt, despair, and even rejection of traditional institutions. And if the modern world has finally separated Church and State with advantages for the former, at the end of the middle ages the rising "national" consciousness and the inability to accept the temporal and spiritual orders confounded solutions to emerging problems.

The Order of Cîteaux was the institutionalization of the ascetical ideals of a small group of monks who gave Benedictine spirituality a new slant. So the New Monastery (as it was called) became the proto-order of medieval Christianity. Although Benedictine abbatial autonomy was guaranteed, there was a "bond of love" that united the abbeys in a familial relationship of supervision and concern. The formal instrument for paternal correction, for redress of grievances, for administrative response to problems and change was the annual General Chapter.

The abbot of Cîteaux retained a unique position in this system.[2] He presided over the mother-house of the whole Order and received reverence and respect in the titles reserved for him alone.[3] But according to the constitutional setup of the Order, the "sovereign" body remained the Chapter which delegated and ratified special exercise of power by the abbot of Cîteaux and anyone else. The abbacy of Jean de Cirey is particularly interesting in this context. As I said, he is better known than so many of his predecessors, though his reputation is often controversial. He was energetic and an indefatigable protagonist of the Order's privileges and exemp-

2. *Ibid.*, pp. 5-6.
3. *Ibid.*, pp. 9-12.

tions, but his activity often betrayed ambition and drew criticism. If he did not create the problems that confronted the Order, he could be guilty of manipulating the solutions to his advantage. His vigorous defense of his conduct has come down to us in his own expectedly partial *Defensorium pacis*, written for Pierre de Virey, the abbot of Clairvaux.

Cirey's promotion to the abbacy of Cîteaux was somewhat unusual though not irregular for the time. He was on a special legation with Humbert de Losne, then abbot of Cîteaux, to the Roman Curia. Already abbot of Theuley, he was made abbot of Balerne, and, before the end of 1476, he succeeded Humbert who succumbed to the rigors of the mission. Although he refused Pope Sixtus IV's offer of the abbatial dignity, he was canonically elected by the convent of Cîteaux and accepted the office submissively.[4] The General Chapter, suspended since its decision in 1473 to appeal directly to Rome for redress of grievances, resumed its sessions in 1476 under the presidency of its new abbot of Cîteaux, and its vigorous treatment of business attests to an auspicious beginning for Jean de Cirey. For the next six years, the leadership of the abbot of Cîteaux can be seen in the activity of the Order, but at a glance, there is nothing special that hints at the dramatic irruption of Virey's charges against Cirey treated in the Chapter of 1482.[5] Pierre de Virey had accused the abbot of Cîteaux of mismanagement of the common revenues of the Order, and the charges, published in the soon to be famous *libellus,* had summarily been condemned to burning. The abbot of Clairvaux had publicly confessed his

4. Jean has left a vivid and biased account of these events in the Appendix to *Statuta,* V, 761-65. The death of Humbert de Losne *intra curiam* placed the abbatial office of Cîteaux among the papal reservations, a practice asserted and extended by the papacy in several bulls since the thirteenth century. Cirey's *Defensorium pacis* is MS 11H1 of the Archives Départementales de la Côte d'Or at Dijon. The complete title is *Dyalogus prioris et supprioris super duplici statu prospero scilicet et adverso ordinis cisterciensis contra falsas et scismaticas quorundam anticisterciensium assertiones, seu Defensorium pacis.*

5. *Statuta,* V, 445-46 (1482, 52).

crime and sought forgiveness. What had happened between the two men? A review of the events preceding 1482 sheds some light on this mystery, and Virey himself answered Cirey's indignant defense of his authority in a work that has survived in a copy.[6]

There were grounds for tension between the two abbots. Neither minced his words in his own defense. Cirey mentioned that he exerted himself for Brother Pierre to succeed Humbert of Cîteaux, and that once he was canonically elected, Virey spitefully harassed him and the abbey of Cîteaux for not giving him one vote.[7] This language was even incorporated in the *diffinitio* of the Chapter of 1484.[8] Cirey's authoritorian leadership rankled Virey. No doubt Cirey had certain objectives upon his succession to the abbatial honor of Cîteaux. In 1476 his influence can be detected, retrospectively, in the lengthy statute which established a system of legal advocates to defend the Order's liberties and privileges throughout Europe.[9] But the real evidence of Cirey's determination to guide the Order through its crises is manifested in the unusual Chapter of 1477.

The first of its acts recorded the circumstances under which a handful of abbots, from Longuay, La Ferté, Pontigny, Morimond, Clairmont, Boquen, La Crête, Noirlac, and Conway, "and those named below"[10] met with the abbot of Cîteaux at Dijon to transact business of the Order.[11] Jacques du Breuquet, public notary with apostolic and imperial authority, was also present. This secular cleric was an important figure in the plans of Cirey and became the Order's procurator in Rome, even obtaining the abbey of Ourscamp *in com-*

---

6. MS 129 of the Bibliothèque de Sens, which came from the abbey of Vauluisant.

7. *Statuta,* V, Appendix, 765.

8. *Statuta,* V, 37 (1484, 87): "...Et quasi in vindictam, quia non fuit ultimate electus abbas Cistercii, inhoneste et irreverenter . . . deducere fecit et proponere...."

9. *Statuta,* V, 354-57 (1476, 88).

10. The abbots of Landais, Maizières, and Vaux-en-Ornois also witnessed the document; *Statuta,* V, 359 (1477, 1).

11. *Ibid.*

mendam for his service. It seems that Jean de Cirey raised the question of holding a chapter, and the abbots decided that the wars in France and Burgundy and other perils dictated against any convocation. They implored Cirey "to treat and terminate all the business of the Order according to [his] authority." So for 1477 eight statutes were promulgated and they dealt for the most part with the economic conditions of the Order.

Jean de Cirey was convinced that the problems of the Order derived from its poverty. He felt that the regular procedure of collecting revenues and disbursing them through the Chapter was unwieldy. He presented a program that seemed sensible and promised a more efficient response to the Order's needs. Yet the result was unmistakable. Cirey had given himself a power over the Order's finances quite unlike any that the *Charter of Charity* or subsequent statutes prescribed. The logic of his argument was irrefutable. It was impossible to meet the crises head-on with regular machinery. Cirey pointed to several religious orders that kept a single treasury to preserve their status. To him, the general poverty of the Order was the primary and principal cause of its temporal ruin, and it was due to two things. In the first place, there was the improper method of collecting contributions and keeping accounts, so that scarcely a tenth or twelfth part of the monies ever came into the hands of the Order. Secondly, on those contributions, certain monasteries withheld a portion they claimed for their own needs and only turned over the balance to the Order; this balance did not total more than 300 or 400 florins for the general necessities, the colleges, and the other expenses of the General Chapter.[12] As a result, Cirey pointed out, every year Cîteaux inherited a debt of 200 to 400 francs.

12. The text is very confusing: "...Certa Ordinis monasteria levant et percipiant singulis annis magnum censum seu redditum, quo in primis et ante omnia accepto, remoto et defalcato singulis annis super dictis contributionibus numquam vel raro residuum contributionum ascendit ad 300 vel 400 fl. pro communibus Ordinis necessitatibus, collegiis et expensis Capituli generalis...." *Statuta,* V, 360-61 (1477, 2).

Cirey proposed that a commissioner be appointed for every province of the Order. He would receive the contributions due at Cîteaux according to the regular assessment (*secundum antiquam astallationem*) and submit an account, annually, biennally, or triennally, as distance permitted, for every monastery of his province. The abbot of Cîteaux of course would enter all such information in the Order's accounts for public information. This would permit the Order to deal with its general problems, with the conduct of its business before the Holy See, kings, dukes, and princes, and with the acquisition and custody of its privileges.[13]

The statutes published for 1477 indicate that there was much grumbling about the records submitted by Cîteaux to the Chapters. Cirey was willing to disclose every item to the abbots for audit and defended the expenses presented to the Order by his house. He said he was prepared to answer any objections concerning the Order's debts to the abbey of Cîteaux.[14]

From 1473 to 1478 the General Chapter had convened only once. We can imagine the atmosphere of uncertainty, if not suspicion, at the assembly of abbots in 1478. Cirey met their complaints with assurances that his conduct was rooted in capitular authority. Centralization of judicial and fiscal function in his hands only served to benefit the Order as a whole. Yet, even if we preclude any "constitutional" change in the office of the father-abbot of Cîteaux, Cirey's leadership had become more prominent in the affairs of the Order. Through the 1480s he was the focal point of the Order's activity. Numerous bulls were issued *ad petitionem* by Sixtus IV (1471-1484), and Cirey certainly won the friendship of Innocent VIII (1484-1492).[15] The General Chapters betray Jean de Cirey's concern for the poverty of the Order. And the measures passed in these years reveal the growing influence of Cirey and commensurate irritation of Pierre de Virey

13. *Statuta*, V, 361-62 (1477, 3).
14. *Statuta*, V, 362-69 (1477, 5-7).
15. Carolus de Visch, *Bibliotheca scriptorum sacri ordinis Cisterciensis* (Cologne, 1656), p. 200.

of Clairvaux. Virey was not among the select group representing the Chapter in 1477. This could have annoyed him. Besides, he had a preoccupation of his own with revenues, and under Cirey's direction the acts of the Chapter, purposely or not, seemed always to point at him. For instance, the fathers of the Order who had rents and income from the Order itself were asked to give them up or at least to receive less than the original sums so that the money obtained could be turned to the good of the Order.[16]

Virey came to the General Chapter in 1478 to complain about the derelictions of Clairvaux' debtors, and as was its wont, the Chapter appointed a commission to investigate and obtain reparation.[17] But it also pursued the other issue: it made a specific request of the abbots of Cîteaux, La Ferté, and Clairvaux to give up and remit to the Order the annual rents (*census*) which were allotted to them on the contributions.[18] The General Chapter recorded a second appeal only to the abbot of Clairvaux on the same subject.[19] Apparently, these abbots were deducting for their own use rents which they collected as landlords from tenants on the taxable lands of the Order. But Virey's differences with the Order found another expression. The abbatial office of Morimond was contested in 1476 by Brothers Nicholas Thierry and Antoine de Boredon. Thierry brought the matter to the General Chapter with all the evidence of his canonical election. His proctor protested that Boredon usurped the abbatial dignity by means of royal letters of possession.[20] Virey took part in the controversy with Thierry and against Boredon, who he said was visiting monasteries directly or indirectly subject to Clairvaux. The General Chapter did implore the abbot of Cîteaux not to offer the abbot of Morimond any commission to visit or exact any taxes from the German monasteries.[21] Two years later, the General Chapter declared

16. *Statuta*, V, 362 (1477, 4).
17. *Statuta*, V, 372-74 (1478, 25).
18. *Statuta*, V, 379-80 (1478, 41).
19. *Statuta*, V, 382 (1478, 53).
20. *Statuta*, V, 349-52 (1476, 72-73).
21. *Statuta*, V, 352 (1476, 74).

for Boredon against Thierry[22] and, in 1481, it revoked its *diffinitiones* of 1476 as prejudicial to the abbot Antoine de Boredon.[23]

Meanwhile, Virey engaged in his own dispute with Boredon. A monk of Clairvaux, Bernard Viard, was promoted to the abbacy of Pontefroid near Metz in 1479, by the father abbot of Morimond.[24] In 1480, the General Chapter approved the elevation of Jean de Duaco of Clairvaux to Pontefroid's abbatial office, and Viard was transferred to Larrivour, diocese of Troyes, at the instigation of the abbot of Clairvaux whose reasons were presented to the Chapter.[25] The following year the Chapter asked Boredon to compel Jean de Duaco of Pontefroid to pay the pension of his predecessor. The abbot of Pontefroid, however, challenged the authority of Morimond and claimed direct dependence upon the abbey of Weiler.[26] In 1482, the matter had not been resolved yet, and the abbot of Clairvaux was commissioned with plenary power to investigate the litigation between Morimond and Pontefroid and to terminate it or prepare it for the next Chapter.[27] Virey fell into disfavor after 1482, and the solution seemed anticlimactic. The Chapter approved the promotion of Étienne de Villemaur, ex-prior of Cîteaux, to the abbacy of Pontefroid, effected through the office of the abbot of Morimond.[28]

The relations of Virey with his father-abbot Cirey were already under stress then down to 1482. The abbot of Morimond was in good stead with the Chapter at that date at Virey's expense. Two years earlier, the Chapter ruled that those abbots who received confirmation of their promotions from the abbot of Cîteaux did not need further confirmation by the Chapter itself.[29] Then, in an extraordinary measure,

22. *Statuta,* V, 381 (1478, 50).
23. *Statuta,* V, 428 (1481, 71).
24. *Statuta,* V, 387 (1479, 12).
25. *Statuta,* V, 397 (1480, 9).
26. *Statuta,* V, 415 (1481, 28), 426-27 (1481, 65-66).
27. *Statuta,* V, 439-40 (1482, 39).
28. *Statuta,* V, 453 (1483, 11).
29. *Statuta,* V, 409 (1480, 53).

the Chapter enjoined upon every collector of contributions and subsidies to forward without delay their receipts and records to the abbot of Cîteaux; it appealed to all the fathers of the Order to assist in any way possible and offer whatever they could to him to relieve the enormous debts incurred since the embassy of 1475.[30] Jean de Cirey seemed capable of directing the Chapter to his ends in these years, and Virey must have been terribly frustrated. In fact, the year after Virey's censure before his fellow-abbots, the Chapter declared his promotion of Jean de Spinay to the abbey of Vaucelles improper, then proceeded to examine Spinay's virtues and merits—only to declare him legitimate and indisputable abbot of Vaucelles.[31] Virey's attempts to reverse the decision of the previous year were denied,[32] and worse, the Chapter upheld Jean de Cirey who suspended and revoked, in January 1483, all commissions and authorizations held by Virey.[33]

The position of Jean de Cirey in the Order was strong. He had the confidence of the abbots and the General Chapters and enjoyed an extraordinary preeminence. He accepted his responsibilities energetically and he never shied from the challenge of leadership. The Chapters indicate that he did not hesitate to act on his own in emergencies and that it was his influence that centralized the legal and fiscal machinery to deal with the common problems of the Order. The circumstances contributed to his success. Wars and plague had devastated western Europe for more than a century, and monasteries were always specially vulnerable because of their isolation and economic resources. Everything in the fifteenth century encouraged the trend toward "national" congregations and made the unity of the Order dissolve in the face of sharp political delineations that were always suspicious of foreign jurisdiction. Cirey always emphasized the evil of the commendatory abbot who caused or permitted most of the

30. *Statuta*, V, 409 (1480, 55).
31. *Statuta*, V, 453 (1483, 9).
32. *Statuta*, V, 454-55 (1483, 16).
33. *Statuta*, V, 457 (1483, 17).

ills of the monastic observance because of his selfish concern for gain.

But the most important source of Cirey's strength was the papacy with which he formed an inseparable alliance. The residence at Avignon (1309-1378) and the Schism (1378-1414) had tarnished what had been the most prestigious institution in Europe; but there were no absolute alternatives to Rome before the Reformation, and the monarchies tried to define their powers in respect to traditional papal assertions. Thus the popes could be indispensable allies in the diplomatic and military conflicts of the fifteenth century. Jean de Cirey relied on Sixtus IV and Innocent VIII to achieve his goals, and his friendship with Innocent was common knowledge. The years of the abbot's ascendancy coincide with Innocent's pontificate. He sought papal favors and privileges almost naively, and, at times when the clergy in France were eager to assert their Gallican tendencies, Jean de Cirey often betrayed his ultramontanist loyalty to Rome. In his arguments in defence of his authority contained in the treatise he wrote to answer his critics, he cited the *Charter of Charity* for usual acknowledgments of the mother-house and father-abbot, but he turned to more cogent reasoning. He said that jurisdiction was conferred on the abbot of Cîteaux through the favor of confirmation (*per confirmationis beneficium*) and that *Parvus fons* had reserved that only to the Holy See (c. IV). In his own words, "he receives no part of his jurisdiction from the Order but only from the pope. ...Do we not say that any blessing of the Supreme Pontiff who receives his power immediately from God and in whose hand the treasure of the Church consists is greater than any other?"[34] Cirey raised all the objections to his position (his treatise is called a *Dialogue of the Prior and Subprior*), but his refutations or clarifications are much more effective and based on the *Charter of Charity* and the *Clementina*.

Though 1485 everything went for Cirey and against Virey. The latter was driven to seek justice outside the Order, and, although he appealed to Rome, he pursued the matter in

34. *Defensorium pacis*, I, 31, f. 38-f. 38v.

the Parlement of Paris.[35] This move backfired. The Chapter was very sensitive about its privileged exemption in the forum of justice, and its statutes revealed its relentless exertion to remove the case from Parlement for adjudication before its own abbot-judges.[36] On the question of a public or common treasury, the decision was final. The Chapter explained in great detail the failure of the regular procedures for collecting contributions ("so that scarcely a tenth of them that are imposed are presented to the receiver general") and justified its recourse to special measures under the constant supervision of the abbot of Cîteaux.[37] And to those who failed to cooperate, the Chapter called down the usual penalties and censures of the *Benedictina* (Pope Benedict XII's *Fulgens sicut stella matutina*, especially c. IV) and the statutes, and added privation and deposition from all honors and offices.

Jean de Cirey had things pretty much his way in 1487. The close ties between the abbot and Pope Innocent VIII were evident in acts of the General Chapter. In the first place, the pope issued *Etsi pro cunctorum* in which he rebuked those members of the Order who had taken their cases to secular courts against the statutes; he proceeded to declare his competence over those cases, then remitted them to proper authorities in the Order. But he reserved to himself by exception that case pending between the abbot of Cîtaux and the Order on the one hand and the abbot of Clairvaux on the other.[38] Another bull, *Licet ea*, permitted the union of monasteries that lacked sufficient resources to support singly a "proper number of monks."[39] That would not mean much

35. Virey answered Cirey's work and the *Responsiones* can be found in MS 129 of the Bibliothèque de Sens, a copy from the monastery of Vauluisant. He said that as soon as he learned of the verdict, he appealed to the Holy See; f. 2v.

36. *Statuta*, V, 470-71 (1483, 81), 482-83 (1484, 37); see the detailed treatment of Virey's action in 517-23 (1485, 70-73).

37. *Statuta*, V, 512-14 (1485, 61).

38. Henriquez, *Regula, constitutiones et privilegia ordinis Cisterciensis: Item congregationum monasticarum et militarium quae Cisterciense institutum observant* (Antwerp, 1630), pp. 171-73. In 1485, the Chapter had requested that the pope spare Jean de Cirey the journey since Virey was responsible for the affair; *Statuta*, V, 521 (1485, 71).

39. Henriquez, CXIV, 174-75.

except that Innocent VIII pointed out that the abbot of Cîteaux could take the initiative in such cases when the Chapter was not in session, "since this kind of authority of the Chapter remains with him."[40] The Chapter of 1487 was prefaced by Jean de Cirey's comments on Pope Innocent's exhortation to reform, *Meditatio cordis nostri.*[41] Cirey's summary underlined the points he wanted to emphasize. Referring to three points essential for reform, he mentioned submissive payment of assessments upon each house to the Chapter, with the harsh reminder that no one should impede the collection "directly or indirectly even through the secular court." More interesting still, Cirey certainly wanted to give his interpretation to the phrase cited above before anyone else did. That is, he enjoined all the abbots to come or send proctors to the General Chapters unless they had legitimate excuses or permission "from him who can give it; and for the sake of conscience, see who it is besides the General Chapter and the abbot of Cîteaux in whom alone according to the preceding bull the power of the Order rests if the Chapter is not in session. . . ." In the *Defensorium pacis*, Jean de Cirey thought this idea was worth a chapter, a lengthy one at that.[42] He offered an unusual analogy considering the tensions between the Gallican clergy and the papacy because of the Estates-General of 1484.[43] Cirey wrote:

You have heard quite often that the just and faithful fathers of the Order called the abbot of Cîteaux its monarch and pope. They were certainly not derogating from the highest authority of the Supreme Pontiff in any way, to

40. In *Ex supremae dispositionis*, Pope Sixtus IV had also given the abbot of Cîteaux the right to dispense in matters of abstinence during the Chapter's adjournment; *ibid.*, CIV, 159-61.

41. *Statuta*, V, 567-68 (1487). Canivez prefaces the statutes of 1487 with the letter that Jean de Cirey presented in reference to the bull of Innocent VIII, *Meditatio cordis nostri*. The bull is in J. Paris, *Nomasticon Cisterciense seu antiquiores ordinis Cisterciensis constitutiones* (Paris, 1670), pp. 667-73.

42. *Defensorium pacis*, I, f. 54; c. 46, f. 53v.-f.55v., is entitled *Post generale capitulum, per anni decursum, ipsa ordinis iuridictio communis in solo Cisterciensi patre conservatur et ea plenarie utitur.*

43. The proceedings have been edited in A. Bernier, *Journal des États-généraux de France tenus à Tours en 1484 sous le règne de Charles VIII*, in *Collection des documents inédits sur l'histoire de France* (Paris, 1835).

whose jurisdiction all are subjected as if to the Vicar of
Christ, but in order to show the reverent hierarchy of the
holy Order, they were pointing out and clarifying the
eminent status of the father of Cîteaux under the holy
Roman Church and the Supreme Pontiff, and they [called]
him supreme in the Order, in whom total power of the
Order resides. . . .So without a doubt this general authority
resides from Chapter to Chapter in the father of Cîteaux
alone, supreme head of the Order, its root and font, and he
communicates it when the next Chapter convenes again to
the elected definitors according to their ranks. It cannot be
taken from him or diminished; it is the same during the
General Chapter's session as is conferred by the Supreme
Pontiff in the confirmation of the *Charter of Charity* and
elsewhere both on the abbot of Cîteaux and on the General
Chapter; and, in each case, he is always the head and his
authority is firmly founded in every disposition of the
Order, in sowing, watching, protecting, watering, and giving
increase. And there is no one who can avoid his jurisdiction, as the *Charter of Charity* testifies: it is the mother of
us all, it says, our mother, the church of Cîteaux. . . .[44]

For Cirey, Cîteaux was the mother through generation
itself, the mother in her honor of primacy, the mother in the
care she extended over all houses, the mother in her preeminence, the mother in her authority. Just as the Apostle James
could not act against or derogate from Peter's authority at
Jerusalem, neither could the Chapter lessen the power of the
abbot of Cîteaux when it is transferred to the definitors.
Cirey developed some farfetched legal arguments: the jurisdiction of the Chapter is preserved by the abbot of Cîteaux
upon adjournment and thus can be transmitted to successive
Chapters. "For who would restore it or bring it back or com-
municate it to the definitors, if no one has preserved it" (f.
54v.). And to make a point, Cirey turned to his adversary
Virey and said that even he once boasted that he was a commissioner of the most reverend abbot of Cîteaux who exercised the plenary power of the Order and the General
Chapters (f. 54v.).

44. *Defensorium pacis*, I, f. 54.

Cirey's arguments were polemical, *ad hominem*, and expressive of the literature of the age. They were very blunt and not very convincing. However, the reader can wonder about the real intent of their author. Cirey seemed to act impulsively and often impatiently. His genuine concern for the Order cannot be disputed. Perhaps his leadership was necessary in crisis. Overall, there were just too many circumstances that permitted the abbot of Cîteaux to exercise greater jurisdiction. Cirey himself always blamed the commendatory abbots for the decline of the Order. Poor attendance at the Chapters surely left greater responsibility in the hands of the father-abbot and often, though not always, in the proto-abbots.[45]

Cirey's reliance on papal support and his insistence on obtaining papal bulls of protection, at great cost, made him a staunch defender of the papacy. Naturally he sought and received special powers, from Innocent VIII in particular, on which he put great emphasis in the eyes of the Chapter. Cirey's influence is clearly discernible in the Statute of 1487 that ordered another special subsidy of 5000 ducats. It underscored an almost obsequious dependence on Rome and perpetuated the policies of the abbot of Cîteaux. Not only were moneys necessary to remunerate Jacques de Breuquet, the Order's procurator in the Curia, for his efforts and expenses in the confirmation of Cistercian privileges, but it was pointed out that the Order had never sent its special legation to Rome to congratulate the pope and to commend itself to his protection. This had all become quite necessary to anticipate further privileges and favors from the Holy See.[46]

Frustrated by the conduct of Virey, the Chapter seemed in

45. The Chapter created a special commission under the abbot of Cîteaux in 1487 to examine customs and observances that had arisen, and none of the proto-abbots were named. Besides Virey's "fall," the abbot of Morimond had absconded with the Order's funds; I did not discover why La Ferté and Pontigny were not chosen; *Statuta*, V, 516-17 (1485, 67), 589-91 (1487, 51).

46. *Statuta*, V. 576-79 (1487, 23).

complete accord with Cirey. Not only had Pierre de Virey taken his complaints before the secular courts; now he completed his rebellion by declaring that his daughter-houses belonged to his own Congregation of St. Bernard. The father-abbots condemned this audacity and demanded his submission. In the Chapter, they declared all his actions null. Finally, they insisted upon the unity of the Order which was expressed in the name of Cîteaux and not St. Bernard of Clairvaux. In one instance, the Chapter enjoined the abbot of Eberbach to call upon neighboring abbots, instead of the father-abbot of Clairvaux, for confirmation of his acts; and, in another, it annulled sentences passed against the abbey of Piété-Dieu by the commissioner of Clairvaux.[47]

Before the decade of the eighties had passed, Cirey had done even more to insure his success in the management of the Order's business. When the Chapter of 1488 learned that the commission of the abbot of Balerne to visit the houses of Italy had ended in failure, it decided that Jean de Cirey was extremely suitable to undertake that mission. He could also proceed to Rome to obtain necessary bulls to achieve his ends. And the Chapter added that, though it had no money, it would assume responsibility for whatever debts Cirey and his monastery contracted.[48] But the greatest relief to Cirey and the Order must have come from the decision of the Parlement of Paris to remit the case pending between the abbots of Cîteaux and Clairvaux to the Order. The Chapter immediately set up a judicial committee of eight, the abbots of La Ferté, Pontigny, Morimond, Châlis, La Charité, Elant, Bonport, and Balerne, to settle the dispute with full rights of justice.[49] Cirey's luck continued. He completed a "successful" visitation to Italy and returned with more papal privileges. The Chapter seemed elated over his achievement, and the new documents were read publicly to the definitors and abbot-officers. They were then approved and numbered among the Order's constitutions. The total cost for their

47. For the annulment of Virey's acts, see *Statuta*, V, 611, 613 (1487, 83 and 88).
48. *Statuta*, V, 633-35 (1488, 16).
49. *Statuta*, V, 652-53 (1488, 59).

acquisition was 6000 ducats for which Cirey had obligated the Order to the banks which provided the loans for redemption. The Chapter expressed its satisfaction and ordered that all the expenses of "this fruitful mission" should be paid from the common treasury of the Order.[50]

The most decisive blow was dealt to Cirey's antagonist by Pope Innocent VIII who attempted to end the schism between the two abbots by uniting their monasteries under the abbot of Cîteaux. The bull *Ad sacrum apostolatus* not only gave Cirey juridical administration of Clairvaux, but it also provided him with its abundant wealth.[51] The details of this union are not at all clear. Virey not only survived Cirey by three years (Virey died in 1504), but, in 1496, he resigned his abbey to Pope Alexander VI.[52] His name appeared in the statutes of the Order to the end of the century, and the Chapter was still trying to reconcile the two abbots in 1501.[53]

Virey had a dogged determination. He resisted and ignored the decision of the Order, and he countered in every possible manner his official degradation and humiliation. He complained that Cirey had made it impossible for him to obtain justice in the Order and so he had recourse to the Parlement of Paris.[54] Although he had obtained a favorable decision from Pope Innocent, he claimed that Cirey's procurator Jacques du Breuquet had reversed it.[55] It is important to note that Virey was convinced that Cirey had used the seals of the definitors and the records of accounts to the detriment of the Order, that he had appointed in the name of the Chapter, with abuse, whomever he wanted as proctors since some of the abbots supported him, and that he acted against the regular method of the holy founders.

50. *Statuta*, V, 674-75, 676 (1489, 9 and 13).
51. De Ganck claims this was a great victory for the impoverished Cîteaux; "Les pouvoirs. . .," p. 55.
52. Canivez, "Cîteaux," *Dictionnaire d'histoire et géographie ecclésiastiques*, XII, 864-65; also the *Responses* of Virey, MS 129, f. 253.
53. *Statuta*, V, 250 (1501, 21).
54. *Responses*, MS 129, f. 2v.-f. 3.
55. *Ibid.*, f. 3v.-f. 4,

The immediate cause of the controversy was Cirey's management of the Order's funds. The Chapter had requested the abbots of Cîteaux, Clairvaux, and La Ferté to give up the portions of the general contributions assigned to them. It seems that the kings of France had designated certain lands for the Order's benefits, the rents of which were used to defray abbatial expenses, especially for journey to and residence at the General Chapters. Apparently the Chapter allocated such revenues annually to prescribed beneficiaries, and its action in creating a common treasury concentrated the "power of the purse" in Cirey's hands. Virey complained in 1482 that "among other injustices," the abbot of Cîteaux refused to pay him £300 tournois which were rightfully his annual dues from the Chapter and the whole Order.[56] Furthermore, Cirey influenced the Parlement of Dijon to seize in the king's name the "beautiful, large, and spacious house" and its appurtenances of the abbey of Clairvaux situated at Dijon which were even put up for sale.[57]

For Virey, the actions of Cirey were an abuse of his powers. Aware of Cirey's own assertions, he could not accept them. He conceded to the abbot of Cîteaux only the right of primacy of propagation, not of authority or superiority, and he emphasized the similarity of jurisdiction of all abbots over their immediate filiations. The *Charter of Charity* had accorded no special prerogatives to Cîteaux beyond its immediate dependencies, he argued.[58] In fact, Virey answered his adversary's pretensions quite explicitly: "The general and common jurisdiction and power of the Order and the General Chapter belongs only to the General Chapter to which the abbot of Cîteaux is subject."[59]

In retrospect, Pierre de Virey might appear as the real hero in this rivalry. Perhaps he even understood that Cistercian institutions were being transformed, certainly too often ignored, by an ambitious, and at times even autocratic, abbot

56. *Ibid.,* f. 3; on specific royal benefactors and their grants, see ff. 20-22.
57. *Ibid.,* f. 3v.-f. 4.
58. *Ibid.,* f. 15.
59. *Ibid.,* f. 18-f. 18v.

of Cîteaux. But he could himself descend to the level of personal, spiteful attack. He resented Cirey's role as champion of the Order against the *commenda*, the grant of an abbey to a non-regular "protector" who enjoyed all the benefits of the abbatial office with none of the responsibilities. Cirey had used the pretext of the commendatory menace to achieve most of his ends, the result of which had led to centralization of power in his hands. In Virey's answer to the *Defensorium pacis*, he commented on the chapter entitled "*De gravi commendarum adversitate.*"[60] From his point of view the adversity is certainly evil because the abbots of Cîteaux had had such great "love" for renowned monasteries that

[they] seized and appropriated for themselves contrary to charity and out of a burning avarice the common revenues and possessions of the Order, and [they] want to keep to themselves the common seals of the Order according to the charters of the definitors [and] the letters of those revenues, the records of the statutes and the accounts of the contributions contrary to the proven age-old method of the Order, and whatever they want, they can sign and seal. . . .

And to Cirey's boast that he fought tirelessly in the Roman curia against hardships that even brought about his predecessor's death, Virey replied that his accomplishments were not worth the expenses to the Order. Besides, presiding over his first General Chapter upon his return from Rome, he had to invoke the assistance of the abbot of Clairvaux against the pluralists of the Order itself, the abbots of La Ferté and Pontigny. And although Virey implored his fellow abbots to renounce their commendatory abbeys, so that the Order could concentrate its efforts against the secular abbots of Cistercian houses, Cirey proceeded to convince the Chapter that the regularly elected abbot of Ourscamp, Nicholas Danbenton, should relinquish his office to Jacques du Breuquet, "his, more than the Order's, secular procurator in the Roman

60. *Defensorium pacis*, II, c. 33, f. 126v.-f. 127.

Curia." Virey added that fortunately he prevented this by his action in the Parlement of Paris.[61]

The relentless Virey did not give his adversary any peace. There is no telling what resulted from *Ad sacrum apostolatus*. Clairvaux and its affiliations might have prevented any actual union of the two houses. Perhaps the General Chapter ignored the papal exhortation. When Pope Innocent was succeeded by Pope Alexander VI in 1482, the role of Jean de Cirey in the Order was conspicuously altered. The bulls of Pope Innocent had generously conceded powers to Cirey and gave special dignity to his office. Such favors were not forthcoming from Alexander. Virey reappeared, more active than ever, to challenge the administration of Cirey. For instance, to relieve the debt of Cîteaux, the Chapter had permitted it to annex Cherlieu, in the diocese of Besançon, and apostolic letters had confirmed the action. Virey, however, proceeded to provide Cherlieu with an abbot, Matthew Six, promoted from his own house. Cherlieu was an immediate dependency of Clairvaux and the monks accepted their new abbot. When Cirey protested, a commission was created to examine the situation. In 1499, the Chapter was still giving its attention to the rebel Matthew Six and Cherlieu.[62]

That Virey never lost possession of Clairvaux can be ascertained by his resignation of the abbey into the hands of Pope Alexander in 1496. The pope immediately numbered Clairvaux among his reservations and designated Jean Foucard its abbot. Cirey resisted the papal provision and incurred threats of the most serious penalties from the Curia. His enemies were eager to impugn his integrity by propagating the bulls of Pope Alexander.[63]

61. *Responses,* MS 129, II, c. 33, f. 34v.-f. 35. Virey concluded his argument by quoting Cirey's answer to this, "that he would prefer three secular commendatories in the Order to one abbot who was not pleasing to him or did not condescend to his will" (f. 35). Danbenton was abbot of Ourscamp in 1481 when the Chapter took drastic action against him for his derelictions and offenses against his father-abbot of Cîteaux; *Statuta,* V, 424-26 (1481, 63-64).

62. *Statuta,* V, 107 (1495, 29), 130 (1496, 11), 223 (1499, 67). There are documents defending Virey's action with Cherlieu in MS 129, ff. 183f.

63. *Responses,* MS 129, f. 253-f. 256.

In the end Virey always returned to the question of finances. He claimed as duly his an annual allocation of £300 tournois from the Order's receipts and accused the abbot of Cîteaux of denying him this. Cirey had said, in 1477, that the Order's ruin was its poverty. His efforts on behalf of the Order did not alleviate the problem. Although he administered the common treasury of the Order, he claimed that he never received the quotas that were imposed on the houses. He was forced into deficit spending; he incurred debts and borrowed at interest to pay them. All the while, he insisted that it was the houses' failure to pay their contributions that put him and his Chapter at Cîteaux into such debt. The General Chapter had to accept this. So it took his side in the dispute with Virey. In 1495, in answer to Virey, the father-abbots exonerated Cirey from personal responsibility for debts, arguing that £14,000 tournois were owed to him.[64] Virey had resorted through the secular courts to confiscation of Cîteaux' goods and the Chapter pleaded with him to desist.[65]

Finally, in 1497, the Chapter yielded to Virey and appointed a commission to investigate the charges anew. The outcome was the same. Cirey's honor was upheld; Virey himself was reminded again of the Order's priorities in disbursing funds. As always the Chapter assumed all responsibility for debts incurred by Cirey in the administration of his office. A special proctor was designated to defend the abbot of Cîteaux wherever litigation was still pending.[66] The statute of 1497 even mentioned that Cirey was willing to make amends to Virey for any errors detected in his accounting. In 1499, the Chapter called for a general assembly of all the abbots for 20 November in the College of St Bernard at Paris to bring to an end once and for all the case between the abbots of Cîteaux and Clairvaux. Jean de Cirey was too ill to even attend the Chapter and the abbot of La Ferté was named his vicegerent if necessary.[67] Again, the Chapter identified the

64. *Statuta*, V, 119 (1495, 60).
65. *Statuta*, V, 126 (1495, 126).
66. *Statuta*, V, 170-71 (1495, 20-21).
67. *Statuta*, VI, 198 (1499, 7).

policies of Jean de Cirey as its own and accepted corespon-
sibility for his conduct.[68] In fact, the Chapter reported in
1500 that the thorough examination of the financial records
proved to invalidate the accusation of the abbot of Clairvaux.[69]

Throughout the controversy Jean de Cirey presented his
own vigorous defense. In his last years, old and ailing, he
watched the Chapter come to his aid, and, indeed the Chapter
resumed its direction of the Order as Cirey faded into the
background. He was forced by physical disability to resign his
office in 1501, and he died within the year.

His leadership in very difficult times has earned both praise
and criticism, and it does prompt the question whether he
ever intended to assume the role of an abbot-general. Although DeGanck has shown that the Order never imagined
the abbot of Citeaux in that capacity, I think that the facts at
least admit that changes, some significant, had occurred.
Cirey's friendship with Pope Innocent VIII does deserve some
attention. So many papal bulls issued *ad petitionem* to the
abbot of Cîteaux, offered new and different possibilities to
the exercise of his jurisdiction. And the pope's insistence that
Cirey represented capitular authority in its absence was
quickly asserted by the abbot. In an earlier century the Order
might have resisted more vigorously. The breakdown in the
Cistercian system of monasticism weakened the opposition.
The statutes of the fifteenth century reveal the preoccupa-
tions with poor attendance at the Chapters, with the ineffectiveness of visitation, with poverty and consequent ruin,
and even with flight from the cloister. Cirey himself blamed
much on the commendatory abbots, the non-regular in-
truders who robbed their abbeys of all their material wealth
and did not care for the well-being of the monks. Twice in the
fifteenth century, popes, first Martin V, then Alexander VI,
sanctioned "national" congregations (in Spain and Italy), and
this had drastic consequences for the Order's unity. So it was

68. *Ibid.*
69. *Statuta,* VI, 234 (1500, 17).

that one as ambitious and impatient as Jean de Cirey could not always operate in the proper manner. There is no doubt that he felt his actions were justified and necessary for the good of the Order. And his writings confirm his confidence in his endeavors. True, his treatise is invective, pure diatribe, and his language polemical *tours de force*, and because he did elicit such a bitter protest from Pierre de Virey, we can assume that someone suspected his conduct and motives.

The decline of the Order of Cîteaux and the changes in the European situation challenged the institutions that belonged to another age. Cirey's story might very well epitomize the failure. His attempt to act as the *chef d'ordre*, as an abbot-general, was his response. After him, the idea became more prevalent, and, by the seventeenth century, the proto-abbots and the Chapters were alarmed at the increasing power exercised by the abbot of Cîteaux.[70] Among the writings that appeared is an anonymous tract composed to refute the notion of an abbot-general. This curious document serves as the final proof of my presentation. Entitled *Le vray et ancien regime de l'ordre de Cisteaux*, it reviewed the significant developments that were interpreted favorably for the abbot of Cîteaux' general jurisdiction. Concerned with events of the fifteenth century, its author took time to investigate the abbacy of Jean de Cirey in relation to the papal bulls that broadened his powers.[71] He was satisfied that there were no precedents for an abbot-general in the papal documents, but I shall rest my case instead on his concern that Cirey could be an example to those who supported the idea of an abbot-general in a later century.

70. Louis Lekai, *The White Monks* (Okauchee, Wisconsin, 1953), pp. 87-88. Lekai has dealt with the post-medieval crisis of the Order and the Strict Observance concisely and essentially in *The Rise of the Cistercian Strict Observance in Seventeenth-Century France* (Washington, 1968), especially ch. I, pp. 11-26.

71. The work is MS F85 of the Bibliothèque de l'Arsenal, Paris, and its forty-nine pages examine the powers of the Chapter and the abbot of Cîteaux. It comments on those bulls obtained by Jean de Cirey and the idea of an abbot-general in f. 29v., f. 38v., f. 39v.-f. 40, and f. 46v.

CISTERCIAN FATHERS SERIES

Under the direction of the same Board of Editors as the CISTERCIAN STUDIES SERIES, the CISTERCIAN FATHERS SERIES seeks to make available the works of the Cistercian Fathers in good English translation based on the recently established critical editions. The texts are accompanied by introductions, notes and indices prepared by qualified scholars.

Bernard of Clairvaux

Aelred of Rievaulx

William of Saint Thierry

Guerric of Igny

* available in paper as well as hard cover